LUTON LIBRAR
INFORMATION AND COMMUN
'ON CENTRAL LEND

CW00589233

Sheikh Najib Alamuddin was born in a family in Lebanon. He graduated from sity of Beirut and later studied in Britain at Exeter University. He was already a successful Lebanese businessman when he began the twenty-five-year association with Middle East Airlines, as Chairman and President, that earned him the sobriquet of 'The Flying Sheikh'.

Sheikh Najib's wide-ranging knowledge of the Druzes, and of Lebanese and Arab politics, stems in part from being a Druze, in part from the experience of having held ministerial office in three different Lebanese governments and attending many international conferences on Middle East affairs. He is therefore uniquely placed to write a book on the Druzes, Lebanon and the Arab-Israeli conflict.

TURMOIL

The Druzes, Lebanon and the Arab-Israeli Conflict

NAJIB ALAMUDDIN CBE

Quartet Books

36433642

956.92 ALA

First published by Quartet Books Limited 1993
A member of the Namara Group
27/29 Goodge Street, London W1P 1FD

Copyright © by Najib Alamuddin 1993

All rights reserved. No part of this book may be
reproduced in any form or by any means without
the prior written permission of the Publisher

A Catalogue record for this book is available from the British Library

ISBN 0 7043 7050 6 (Cased)
ISBN 0 7043 0189 X (Paperback)

Typeset by The Electronic Book Factory Ltd, Fife, Scotland
Printed and bound in Great Britain by
Cromwell Press Ltd, Melksham, Wilts.

Acknowledgements

From the moment I decided to write this book, my wife Ida has stood firm in her resolve and encouragement that I should do what I believed to be right and publish what I felt needed saying. She has read and reread the drafts of the text at each stage, and her constructive criticism and insights have been an invaluable influence on the final form the book has taken. To her, as always, go my heartfelt gratitude and deepest love.

The moral support of my children, too, has meant much to me. Having read the manuscript, they all urged me to publish the book.

As we reached the final stages of the writing, my life-long friend Frank O'Shanohun joined forces with my wife Ida in persuading me that I should now go ahead and publish. His help has also been invaluable.

My private secretary, Lilo Weigel, has been unfailing in her enthusiasm and the genuine pleasure she has shown in the book as she has undertaken the successive retypings. She, too, has my grateful thanks.

To David Elliott goes my heartfelt gratitude for his consistent confidence in the book and his invaluable help and advice in monitoring the publishing process.

To Peter Ford I would like to express my sincere thanks and appreciation for having placed his skills as an editor at the service of my text. The book has come to owe a very great deal to his sympathy, care and interest.

Finally, my grateful thanks go to the following for the quotations I have used from the sources indicated: to Dr

Najla M. Abu-Izzedine, for quotations from *The Druzes* (E. J. Brill, Leiden, 1984); to Dr Sami Nasib Makarem for quotations from *The Druze Faith* (Caravan Books, Delmar, New York, 1974); to Jonathan C. Randal, for quotations from *The Tragedy of Lebanon: Christian Warlords, Israeli Adventurers and American Bunglers* (Chatto & Windus, London, 1983; US edn, *Going All the Way: Christian Warlords, Israeli Adventurers and the War in Lebanon*, Viking Press, New York, 1983); to Dr Kamal S. Salibi, for quotations from *A House of Many Mansions* (I. B. Tauris, London, 1988) and *The Modern History of Lebanon* (Weidenfeld & Nicolson, London, 1965); and to Unwin Hyman for a quotation from Bernard H. Springett, *Secret Sects of Syria and Lebanon* (Allen & Unwin, London, 1922).

Contents

Introduction

I am a Druze born in Lebanon before it became an arena of violence for the warring factions of quarrelling man. Lebanon (Libanon) is a Semitic word meaning white, and comes from the fact that the summits of its mountains are covered with snow for most of the year. As a result of its geographic position, it was invaded in history by the Persians, the Greeks, the Romans, the Arabs, the Crusaders, the Tartars, the Ottoman Turks and lastly by the Allies during the First and the Second World Wars. At the time of the Ottoman invasion, early in the sixteenth century, the inhabitants of Lebanon were mostly Druzes. Today the Druzes in Lebanon number about 250,000, thus making up approximately 10 per cent of the Lebanese population. This is, at best, an inspired guess, for successive Lebanese governments have, since the 1930s, permitted no census. The Maronite Christians, who have ruled Lebanon and dominated its politics, would not allow any census after 1932, since they feared losing their majority to the Mohammedan communities, who were more prolific in child production.

The Druzes, though always a minority in recent centuries, have played an important and, at times, a leading role in the political and social life of Lebanon and the Middle East as well as in its economic and cultural affairs. Western historians, explorers, travellers, pilgrims and missionaries have written extensively about them, as have their Oriental counterparts. All that these commentators witnessed and

1

heard about the outstanding fighting ability of the Druzes, their high moral and social standards, their hospitality, their fanatic devotion to independence, their resistance to foreign rule and their fights against Turkish and later French domination, has been accurately and fairly described. Their battles even earlier against the Crusaders and others similarly won the Druzes a reputation for courage and chivalry in which they still today take immense pride. They have a reputation for being among the finest guerrilla fighters of the world.

> The Druze is a born warrior, a fine horseman (he rides armed with a rifle from his childhood), a remarkable marksman and indefatigable walker. His courage is magnificent, a quality common to all Druzes. Their belief in reincarnation, which guarantees for them a better future life if they die for their home and country, endows them with contempt for death. Frequently during the battles we had with them in the Djebel, the Druzes won our admiration, when they bravely stormed our blazing machine guns. They are a proud people, vigorous, courageous, hospitable, hard-working and dedicated.

Thus, in 1937, wrote General Andréa, commander of the French, in his book *La Révolte Druze*. It was a generous compliment, coming, as it did, from a French general whose forces suffered the many humiliating defeats inflicted by Druze warriors at Jabal al-Druze. A tribute in similar spirit was paid by a Maronite Christian chronicler, Ibrahim Bey Aswad, who wrote after the fratricidal wars between the Maronites and the Druzes between 1841 and 1860:

> The Druzes are a militant community brought up on bravery, chivalry, fortitude and immense strength. The community is united and its members are fond of each other and come to each other's assistance. It gives refuge

2

to whoever seeks it and will help whoever asks for help. It strongly resists and rejects oppression and adheres very strongly to its moral code and moral values. The Druzes, in all their battles and wars, have never been the aggressors but always the defenders. In their fighting they observe the noble tradition of respecting women and protecting them and their honour.

Some years earlier, the French traveller, the Comte de Volney, wrote in *Travels through Syria and Egypt* (1787) that the Druzes were:

Daring even to temerity, and sometimes ferocious, they possess, above all, two qualities essential to the excellence of any troops; they strictly obey their leaders, and are endowed with a temperance and vigour of health unknown to most civilized nations. Had they among them a few persons versed in military science, they would readily acquire its principles and become a formidable soldiery. There are no Druzes in the city or on the coast. No people are more precise than they with respect to a point of honour. There is in their manner and discourse a reserve, or, if you will, a politeness which one is astonished to discover among peasants.

'Druses, a people of Syria remarkable for the pertinacity and success with which they have defended their independence against the encroachments of Turkish Supremacy.' So they were described by the *Encyclopaedia Britannica*, ninth edition, 1875. And Colonel C. H. Churchill said of them:

It must be admitted, that the bravery of the Druses is of the very highest order. The valour which they displayed in the Houran [Jabal al-Druze] at the period of the Egyptian conscription in the year 1839, may challenge comparison with the most exalted deeds of heroism on

3

record. Eight hundred Druses not only defeated, but absolutely annihilated upwards of fifteen thousand of Ibrahim Pasha's best [Egyptian] troops.

Colonel Charles Henry Spencer Churchill (1828–77), 60th Rifles, the son of Lord Charles Spencer-Churchill, son of the 5th Duke of Marlborough, was an officer on the British expedition to Syria. He resided in Lebanon for nearly twenty years from 1840 to 1860, and was affectionately called by the Druzes 'Sharshar Bey' when he settled among them in a hamlet north of Beirut. He wore native clothes and opened a school for their children. He befriended them and soon became their confidant. He wrote three volumes, published in 1853 as *Mount Lebanon; a Ten Years Residence, from 1842–1852*. A fourth volume, *The Druzes and the Maronites under the Turkish Rule from 1840 to 1860*, was published in 1862 to form a continuation of his previous three-volume work. His writings describe clearly and vividly the history and society of Lebanon between 1840 and 1860 and have subsequently been accepted by nearly all historians as authoritative reference sources for the history of Lebanon during that period.

Colonel Churchill has left a vivid description of the battle between the Druzes and the army of Ibrahim Pasha, the Egyptian invader of Syria, in 1831:

The Egyptians having conquered Syria resorted to obligatory conscription to strengthen their armed forces. They demanded conscripts from Jabal Al-Druze. In vain did the Druzes plead the hardship resulting from such a request since their population was barely sufficient to cultivate the land. The Egyptian Pasha, governor of Damascus, rudely rejected their demand for exemption in the coarsest language of abuse. He then sent a force of 300 cavalry troops to the Jabal to enforce the conscription demand. They were set upon and wiped

4

out with the exception of their commanding officer who fled to Damascus. The Pasha was furious and dispatched a force of 7,000 infantry soldiers and 500 cavalry under Ibrahim Pasha, the most illustrious Egyptian commander. The Druzes, 800 in number, gathered in Leja, a natural volcanic fortress of impenetrable rocky clusters ideal for ambush and for defence. They fell upon the Egyptian forces and completely overwhelmed them, slaughtering most of them except for a few who managed to flee. Another expedition exceeding the first in numbers was rushed to reinforce Ibrahim Pasha's routed forces. The second expedition did not fare any better than the first.

Seven years later, in 1838, Lady Hester Stanhope wrote, 'The Druze army, I believe, does not at present exceed two thousand five hundred men; but each man of that two thousand five hundred is simply worth twenty.' This indomitable and famous lady traveller occupied a special place in Druze history, as Dr Philip Hitti makes clear in his book, *Lebanon in History*:

Lady Hester Stanhope, the spectacularly eccentric grand-daughter of the Earl of Chatham and private secretary [and neice] of William Pitt, disappointed in love, set out in 1810 on adventurous wanderings in the East. She settled in solitude in a Druze village north of Sidon. She built a castle-like villa with a magnificent garden, dressed like a native, smoked a long pipe, carried a whip and a poinard and surrounded herself with a guard of Albanians and a staff of negro slaves who treated her according to royal protocols. Lady Stanhope studied Arabic, delved into astrology and alchemy and headed caravans to Baalbeck, Palmyra and Jerusalem.

Enraptured with her grace, commanding character and generosity, the Arabs of the Syrian desert proclaimed her 'Queen of Palmyra'.

Over the neighbouring villages, mostly Druzes, she wielded almost absolute authority. When planning his campaign, Ibrahim Pasha sought her neutrality. She had a hand in arousing the Druzes against him. In 1839 Lady Stanhope died, unattended by any Europeans, and was buried on the spot. A visit to her tomb soon became an item in European tourists' itineraries.

I have been prompted to write this book to tell the English-speaking world something about the unique Druze community, whose learned religious teachings and remarkable moral and social codes have remained unchanged since they were inaugurated in the eleventh century, despite fanatic persecution and ruthless oppression. Yet few people have even heard of the Druzes, and fewer still have heard of the Druze secret religion. It appears there are even certain experts and academic researchers on religion who do not know of its existence.

Suppose, for instance, that we turn to two recent publications in the area of comparative religion to discover what we can about the Druzes. The first of these is a Lion Handbook entitled *The World's Religions* (1982), 'a comprehensive, clear and stimulating guide to the world's religions, past and present', its advisory board consisting of eight scholars and theologians of international standing. Secondly there is *An Encyclopaedia of World Faiths – Living Religions* (1990), which likewise claims to be comprehensive. Surely we shall find something here to inform us. The fact is that in both books, intended for students of theology and comparative religion, we search in vain for any entry under 'Druze'. The authors and editors are evidently unaware of the Druze religion and its worship by many thousands of Druzes in Lebanon, Syria, Israel and other parts of the world.

I myself do not claim to be a historian or a theological authority on the Druze religion. As one of the majority of the non-initiated, I have never been privileged nor permitted to read or even to see the Druze religious books. That privilege is reserved to the *Uqqal*, a word which may approximately be translated as the 'class of sages'. Nevertheless I am a Druze, born into a family which played an important role in the Druze community from its origin in the eleventh century. My birthplace was Baaqline, the most important Druze village in Lebanon and the headquarters of Fakhruddin II, the famous Prince of the Druzes. I therefore know my people well, having lived all my life with them. I had intimate knowledge of them professionally, as head of Middle East Airlines, where a number of them were employed, and officially as a minister sectarianly representing them in the Lebanese government on three different occasions. This experience equips me to write about them now, together with the fact that I have read most of the books written on the Druzes by Western historians, explorers, pilgrims, travellers and missionaries. I have, moreover, read as many books by Arab historians and scholars as I could obtain, and most importantly, I have studied closely the books written on the Druzes and their faith by the most capable of Druze scholars.

Books written by Druze historians and scholars are, of course, accurate, and present the true facts, but nearly all of them are scholarly works of reference, not easily accessible to the general public. Some were written in English, but most were written in Arabic. Western and Oriental historians have for their part, as briefly indicated, been unanimous in praising the Druzes for their chivalry, hospitality, moral and social codes and outstanding fighting ability. But they have also, by contrast, tended to be highly inaccurate in their considerations of Druze racial origin, or even downright offensive when writing about the Druze religion.

It is the secret, or hermetic, nature of the Druze religion that has been a source of tantalization and frustration to outsiders, and even if I were privy to its inner secrets, I would not be permitted to write about them. I have never myself been privileged to see the religious books. I well remember how, the first time I arrived in New York, an immigration officer, for reasons of his own, asked about my religion. 'Druze,' I replied.

'Jews,' he stated.

'No, no, Druze,' I repeated.

'What sort of religion is this?' he asked.

'It is a secret religion,' I replied.

He looked at me sternly, thinking I was making fun of him, and said: 'Come, come, now. There are no secret religions. Tell me something about it.'

'Friend,' I replied, 'it is so secret that I know nothing about it myself.'

Fortunately his superior arrived at this moment to find out what kept us so long at the head of a queue that steadily grew longer. My passport was quickly stamped, and I was glad to move out of the immigration hall into the land of opportunity without having to give further explanation.

My aim here is to do my best to present a true account of the religion as it is known to me and as I have learned about it from reading the accounts of Druze scholars. I shall describe those moral and social codes that are generated by it and which are strictly followed by the Druze community. Even more importantly, I shall expose the fictions and myths that have been written about it by biased, misinformed or, at times, ill-intentioned non-Druze writers.

But why should I write specifically for the English-speaking public? Because, for one thing, there has been a special relationship between the British and the Druzes which goes back a long way, to 1860. If, with time, this special relationship seems to have been forgotten by the British, it has never been by the Druzes. My hope is therefore to bring it to life again, for ever since childhood I heard of the Druze gratitude to the British when they came to our aid after the civil war of 1860. The Maronite Christians, in losing this war, suffered heavy casualties, though it was they who were the real perpetrators, as is confirmed by the Christian historian, Dr Kamal Salibi, in *A House of Many Mansions* (1988), where he writes: 'The planned Maronite revolts in the Druze territory were aborted within a few weeks in 1860 by a series of ghastly bloodsheds.'

Having lost the 1860 war, which they themselves planned against the Druzes, the Maronites, together with the French, who supported them, demanded that 4,600 Druze leaders be executed for what they called the crime of the massacre. Among these 4,600 was my own grandfather. The British intervened and the Druze chiefs were saved with two exceptions: one was executed and the other died in prison. Apart from this, the French military forces which landed in Lebanon to help the Maronites continued to massacre many Druzes and loot their property as they marched against them in the Druze mountains. These killings and lootings were also stopped by British intervention, and the memory of those acts of justice live on in Druze consciousness.

Besides being termed *Muwahhideen* (Unitarians) for believing in one God, the Druzes are also known as *Beni Ma'ruf* – those who never forget a favour done them nor ever forget the donor. The Druzes became eternally grateful to the British, and aside from proclaiming their love and affection for them at all times, helped them whenever they were asked. Thus they harassed and successfully fought the Turks during the First World War in Hauran (Syria), east of Damascus. They succeeded in defeating the five Turkish battalions stationed in Hauran, but later paid dearly in lives and property to the Turkish government. Their valiant action prompted Canon Joseph T. Parfit to write the following tribute in *Among the Druzes of Lebanon and Beshan (Hauran)* (1917):

When the time of deliverance comes to Syria, it will be our paramount duty to render substantial aid, at the earliest possible moment, to those faithful friends of

Britain. We must endeavour to discharge our debt to the Druzes for the risks they have run and the sacrifices they have made on our behalf, and for their staunch adherence to the Allies' cause in our desperate time of need.

In 1880, long before Canon Parfit's tribute, Lawrence Oliphant expressed similar feelings towards the Druzes in *The Land of Gilead*:

The day may come when it may be well to remember that we have a warlike people in Syria absolutely devoted to us, and only longing to prove that devotion in acts. No doubt they believe that they would derive ultimate advantage from the cordial co-operation with England. All alliances are, in fact, based on this anticipation; but there are degrees of loyalty and degrees of fighting capacity, and England may look far before she would find a recruiting-ground which could furnish so brave and loyal a contingent as the country of the Druzes. So firmly are they penetrated with the closeness of their relations to England, that I was surprised to find how many knew a little English, that language being the only foreign tongue they ever learn.

In addition to the gratitude that the Druzes felt for the rescue of their 4,600 leaders, they had made many friends among the British who chose to settle in Lebanon and live among them. The British established among the Druzes such a good record for integrity and high business principles that the term *kalimah Inklizieh*, 'English word', came for the Druzes to stand for honest and honourable dealing. In particular, the Druzes had many friends among the British and American missionaries, who had been treated very badly by the Maronite Christians. In *The Druzes and the Maronites under the Turkish Rule*, Colonel Churchill documents some of the practices used against the missionaries during 'the latter part of the administration of the old Emir Bashir', Lebanon's ruler at the time, when the dominating influence of the Maronite patriarch and his clergy diligently worked on the emir to secure his stern prohibition of 'anything to do with religious toleration'. The influence of the British came to be especially feared: they were depicted by propaganda as 'freemasons and infidels' who stood outside the pale of the true Church. Even to hold a conversation with an Englishman or an American could mean excommunication for a Maronite Christian, while the emir decreed the putting out of the eyes of any who went to gaze at the British Fleet when it arrived off the Lebanese coast in 1840.

All those British who had a high regard for the Druzes could only have shared with them their dismay and disillusionment on discovering how their own country, under the infamous Sykes-Picot Agreement of 1916, had delivered the Druzes of Lebanon and Syria to the French; who had less than sixty years before demanded the execution of all their leaders and murdered hundreds while looting and destroying their homes. The Druzes were baffled and disappointed by this unexpected let-down by the British, whom they saw as their friends. The sense of injury ran deep, especially since the French had always hated the Druzes for their affection and loyalty to the British. The French then took advantage of the Mandate given to them under the terms of the Sykes-Picot Agreement to harass the Druzes and treat them badly, until finally driven out by the British in 1943, as representatives of Vichy France.

In this way the British indirectly helped to redress the wrong done the Druzes under Sykes-Picot, though in more recent years, during the present and intermittently continuing war in Lebanon, they have distanced themselves from the Druzes and their fight for survival. The French, by contrast, have sprung to the assistance of their friends, the Maronite

Christians, at every conceivable opportunity. In 1983, a group of Druzes living in England founded the British Druze Society, a charitable organization with the objective of soliciting donations to help needy Druzes everywhere, and especially in Lebanon. Ten years after its foundation, in 1992, the society had still received no British donations, nearly all its funds having been donated by the Druze community in England.

The Druzes nevertheless remain loyal to the British and continue to hold them in marked affection. They acknowledge with gratitude the humane attitude shown by the British government towards the Lebanese in general during the Lebanese war. Few other governments, if any, except for the British, granted the Lebanese, including many Druzes, compassionate visas with a permit to work, renewable so long as war continued to ravage Lebanon; though this assistance has since been halted, after Lebanon was thrown into further confusion by a fresh wave of political intrigue and sectarian dissent.

At this point an anecdote may help to lighten the dark clouds of historical irony. Some time before my active involvement in the airline business, my wife and I were travelling from England to the United States on board the *Queen Elizabeth*. Shortly after we took to sea, the steward came to our cabin to offer assistance. He must have read the title of 'Sheikh' on the passenger list, because a look of bewilderment came over his face when he opened the door to find not the flowing robes, the olive skin, nor even the hooked nose he expected. He asked my wife, who was reading one of Agatha Christie's novels, whether she needed assistance. She declined his offer in faultless English, having taken her elementary and secondary studies at a Scottish school and her medical training at the American University. He then turned to me and, in slow and clear English, asked whether I needed any help myself. I replied, 'No,' with thanks, since I always prefer to do my own unpacking. As he backed out of the cabin, I heard him tell the maid waiting outside, with a sneer in his voice: 'He is nothing but a bloody Englishman.'

This compliment from the steward was one I had worked hard to earn. I did my post-graduate education in Britain and was the first Arab to receive a British Council scholarship. Subsequently I established the most friendly and successful business relations with Britain and secured hundreds of millions of pounds sterling in export trade between the United Kingdom and Lebanon and the Arab world. I was honoured, as a result, by being awarded in 1976 the CBE (Commander of the British Empire), to which I may add the privilege of having made many British friends. I have also been a frequent and regular visitor to London, and today consider London my second home after Lebanon. It is therefore natural for me to wish to acquaint as many of the British public as possible with a community which has, for more than 130 years, harboured a sentiment of affection, gratitude and loyalty towards Britain and the British.

From the viewpoint of English-speaking Americans, the story is quite different. Apart from having been able to help and show friendship towards the persecuted missionaries, the Druzes never had an opportunity to be of any particular service to the United States. Nevertheless I personally have had many ties and friendships with Americans. To begin with, I graduated from the American University in Beirut, which was founded in 1866 by American missionaries as the Syrian Protestant College. Its sole objective was to give spiritual guidance and genuine educational help to the people of Lebanon and the Middle East, and many hundreds of Druzes owe their college and university education to this institution.

An uncle of mine was, indeed, the first Druze to graduate in medicine from the Syrian Protestant College. His sons followed, as in turn did their sons and daughters, who graduated from the same institution after it became the

13

American University of Beirut. My wife and I did the same, as did our children.

Those missionaries who founded the Syrian Protestant College, later the American University of Beirut, and all the dedicated American teachers they recruited from the United States, taught their students, among other important matters, that justice is the sacred right of every human being; that democracy as practised in the United States guarantees this sacred right; that all human beings are equal in the eyes of God and hence should enjoy equal opportunities; that a shoeblack has the opportunity and right to become the President of the United States if he has it in him to qualify for the task. Their teachings were, in other words, the basic principles of social justice and human rights.

It is melancholy to record how we have seen, in more recent times, human rights being interpreted not only in political terms but also blatantly manipulated and exploited. The attitude of the world today is very different from the honest and principled Christian teachings of the early American missionaries of the Syrian Protestant College. Unfortunately a change set in as the sources of dedicated missionaries for the university dried up. Different types of Americans began to replace the missionaries: personalities not religiously dedicated but more attracted by the salaries and a desire to see the world. Later, after the creation of Israel, the American University became politicized. The change was marked when a president was appointed to the university who had, during the Second World War, occupied a very senior position in the US Intelligence Services. The impact of this change was naturally resented by nearly all the Arab students. They continued even so to flock to the university, for lack of better institutions in the Middle East.

Meanwhile the Druzes continued to believe in and admire the principles of American democracy, social justice and the respect for human rights they implied. Having consistently been in a minority in the countries in which they lived, they had needed to fight for equal rights, and on most occasions valiantly achieved them. They aspired to and fought to be given equal opportunities, and strongly believed themselves equal to any other community in the eyes of God. Many even thought that they enjoyed a favoured status with the Almighty. It was therefore natural for the Druzes to love and admire the Americans for the principles they preached. Many a sincere and lasting friendship was formed between the American missionaries and the Druzes, and the missionaries were always welcomed as honoured guests in Druze homes.

The attitude of the US government towards the Druzes changed dramatically when the Druze leader, the late Kamal Jumblatt, formed in 1949 his Progressive Socialist Party, whose members were, in the main, Druzes. These were not actually so much progressive socialists as 'Jumblattis', who would have followed Kamal Jumblatt in whatever political creed he chose to lead them. Unfortunately, the Americans have a habit of confusing evolutionary socialism with communism, and Kamal Jumblatt and his Druzes were branded dangerous leftists. Jumblatt also committed the unforgivable crime, in the eyes of the American government, of supporting the Palestinians in their desperate struggle to regain the land and homes taken from them by Israel. During the war which subsequently raged for over sixteen years in Lebanon, the Americans therefore showed no sympathy for the Druzes in their most recent fight for survival.

Kamal Jumblatt was treacherously assassinated in 1977. The huge Druze crowds attending his funeral, including a vast majority of the religious *Uqqals*, promptly elected his son Walid as leader by clamorous ovation. Since Walid is an American University graduate, widely known to be highly intelligent and courageous, and a moderate in his politicial views, it was then naturally expected that the American attitude towards both him and the Druzes would change from hostility to one of sympathetic support. It was too much to hope for. Walid, quite apart from the absolute loyalty given him by the Jumblatti Druzes, also inherited the leadership of his father's Progressive Socialist Party; and progressive socialism remained and remains taboo in the eyes of the Americans.

In 1983–4, President Reagan committed a powerful United States armada to the eastern Mediterranean. It consisted of thirty warships, including two aircraft carriers with 300 fighter bomber aircraft, the battleship *New Jersey*, with its immense guns, supported by a sprinkling of warships from Nato countries, and was stationed in Lebanese waters bordering on the capital Beirut. This massive naval force was designed as a deterrent against the possible use of advanced Russian missiles, planted during the war, together with their Russian technicians, in Lebanon and Syria, and capable of striking at the heart of Israel. The missiles were never used and the US Navy thus achieved its initial purpose. The Russian missiles were dismantled and, together with their technicians, found their way discreetly back to the Soviet Union. But before the US Navy left Lebanese waters, it acquiesced in a request from the Maronite President of Lebanon and shelled Druze villages, destroying many and damaging others. The anger of the Druzes at this wanton and futile destruction of their homes will take a long time to fade. Nor was American hostility towards the Druzes confined to the destruction of villages, but was extended to exerting pressure on many Arab governments to prevent aid of any kind reaching the Druzes, thus forcing them to turn to the Soviet Union for help.

The Druzes never were communistic. Their religion forbade them to be so. They are better known as the *Muwah-hideen* (Unitarians), whose faith is based on the strict, uncompromising belief in the unity of God. They are, however, socialists at heart, having been, for centuries, dominated by feudal lords, and feudalism and feudal attitudes foment and hasten the growth of socialism. The long-endured social injustice and the fact that the movement had at its head

16

a feudal lord who was a socialist whom they respected and loved, led many Druzes, all of whom were Jumblattis, to hasten to embrace the progressive socialism of Kamal Jumblatt. However, no one who truly understood the situation could ever accuse them of communism.

Fostering just such an understanding with American readers is also one of my main aims in writing this account as a graduate of the American University in Beirut – twice president of its Alumni Association, a member for life of its Board of Trustees and someone who has numerous American friends. It should make interesting reading for the large Druze community in the United States, especially for the younger generation, but my hope is that many Americans, including executives of the US Administration, may be drawn towards discovering the truth about the Druzes and become better acquainted with their history and their legitimate place and role in Lebanon and in Middle Eastern affairs.

Part One
The Druze Peoples in History

1. Misapprehensions about the Druzes

All that has been written by historians, travellers and missionaries about the fighting ability of the Druzes, their courage, valour and exceptional moral and social codes, has tended to be accurate and to imply a general acclaim and respect. But when it came to their racial origin, certain of these writers, mainly Western, have been far from accurate, and have sometimes wandered into the realms of pure fantasy. Some have even promulgated distortions of the truth which can only be maliciously inspired.

The French poet and historian, Lamartine, claimed the Druzes to be the remnants of the Samaritans. On the other hand, Mrs Worsley, sister of the famous Bishop Gray of Cape Town, who left her comfortable home in London to establish herself as a missionary at Ayn Anoub, a Druze village near Beirut, thought they were Hittites. This latter theory was shared by Professor Felix von Luschen, the famous anthropologist of the University of Berlin, who bracketed them with other sects in the area as the modern representatives of the Hittite tribes. Elsewhere they have been described as the remnant of Israel who fled the wrath of Moses.

Philip Hitti asserted in *The Origin of the Druze History and Religion* that he remembered hearing Druzes in Lebanon claiming their origin to be Japanese. Hitti was a Maronite Christian, born in Lebanon and educated at the Syrian Protestant College, where he taught before going to the

21

United States to become an American citizen and professor of Middle East history at Princeton University. According to Professor Hitti, Miss Gertrude Bell also observed that the 'Druzes believe that the Japanese belong to their own race', while he claimed as well to remember, on more than one occasion, prominent contemporaneous Druzes claiming common descent for their people with the British. To this I can only respond that the Alamuddins adopted the Divine Call at its proclamation in 1017, have been proud to be Druzes ever since and have lived consistently in the Druze communities of Lebanon and Syria. Not once was it said in our or any other Druze family, and we knew them all, that the origin of the Druzes was Japanese, British or anything other than Arab. Professor Hitti should have known better than to publicize such distortions, and one cannot dismiss the suspicion that he had a malicious motive.

Another bizarre belief, held by certain French scholars, was that the Druzes are the descendants of a Crusader colony which owed its origin to Comte de Dreux, who, after the fall of Acre, led his Crusading regiment into the hills of Lebanon. A similar line was taken by the English traveller Henry Maundrell, who wrote of his travels in 1697 in *A Journey from Aleppo to Jerusalem* that the Druzes are: 'A people supposed to have descended from some dispersed remainders of those Christian armies, that engaged in the Crusades, for the recovery of the Holy Land: who afterwards, being totally routed, and despairing of a return to their native country again, betook themselves to the mountains hereabouts; in which their descendants have continued ever since.' It is a theory that seems to have been accepted by a number of other English travellers, though more discriminating writers were quick to detect the absurdity of the hypothesis, for the Druzes were in Lebanon long before the Crusades. Indeed, they were on record as having fought fiercely against the Crusaders.

The list of more outlandish theories continues with the

22

linking of the name 'Druze' with 'Druids', and many
Masonic lodges have claimed relationship with the Druzes,
whose 'ancestors were none other than the original subjects
of King Hiram of Tyre, the builders of Solomon's temple'.
The Rev. Hasket Smith published a detailed paper in January
1891 in an attempt to prove this arcane theory.

The *Encyclopaedia Britannica*, ninth edition (1875), recorded of the Druzes:

> Though they speak Arabic with a correctness that
> would do credit to the people of Mecca, and their feudal
> artistocracy refer to their Arab descent with feelings of
> pride, it is generally agreed that whatever may be true
> of certain families the main body of the people does not
> belong to the Semitic family. Mr Cyril Graham regards
> them as an Indo-Teutonic race, and describes them as 'fair
> haired, of light complexion, and well made, and often as
> tall as northern Europeans'.
> They do not, however, for a moment believe that all
> real Druzes are confined to Syria. China, for example,
> is a land of which they have some dim knowledge; it
> figures vague and vast in their untutored minds. They
> have heard that there are beliefs common to them and
> the Chinese; this is sufficient to create the conviction
> that the Chinese are really Druzes too, and that, when
> the proper time comes, that mighty empire will pour
> forth its millions in the cause of El-Hakim.

The Chinese legend was actually taken seriously by this
edition of the *Encyclopaedia Britannica*, for it goes on to
state authoritatively: 'Their own tradition vaguely connects
them with China, where they firmly believe that to this day
there exist numerous adherents of their creed, and whence
they expect the advent of their deliverer.' By the time it
came to its eleventh edition (1910–11), the *Encyclopaedia
Britannica* was stating more diffidently: 'There is, of course,

23

information from non-Druze sources, though these sources are not always accurate. Muslim and Christian accounts of historical events, as well as comments and assessments on Druze religion and customs, should be treated with reserve and caution.'

Professor Felix von Luschen stated that he had during his anthropological researches measured the skulls of fifty-nine adult male Druzes, and not one single specimen was that of an Arab. In contradiction to this, Dr Kappers, a Dutch anthropologist, invited by the American University of Beirut to work in its laboratories, found from measuring the skulls of many Druzes that they resembled those of the Arabs, and especially those of Arabs inhabiting Yemen. Likewise, travellers such as Niebuhr and scholars such as von Oppenheim have classified the Druzes as Arab, a conclusion in which nearly all Arab historians concur. Here the general consensus has been that the Druzes are descendants of twelve Arab tribes which migrated to Syria from the Arab peninsula with or preceding the advent of Islam. However, the statement of the British explorers David Hogarth and Gertrude Bell, that the Druzes are a mixture of stocks in which the Arab largely predominates, grafted on to an original mountain population of Aramaic blood, seems to come closest to the truth.

Nevertheless, in the face of this common-sense view, and in addition to saddling the Druzes with Japanese and British kinship, Professor Philip Hitti challenged their genuine Arab racial origin in *The Origin of the Druze History and Religion* when he stated:

Evidently the Druze claim of Arab descent is the result of their application of the principle of dissimulation (*taqiyyah*) to their racial problem, they being a small minority amidst an Arab majority which has always been in the ascendancy. According to this principle, one is not only ethically justified but is under obligation, when the exigencies of the case require, to conceal the reality of his religion, or race, and feign other religious or racial relationships.

Dr Hitti, eminent historian as he was, committed a grave error in challenging the Arab racial origin of the Druzes and in accusing them of claiming Arab origin because of *taqiyyah*, for when the Druzes first came into being during the eleventh century, the Arabs were no longer in ascendancy. Syria (including Lebanon), where nearly all the Druzes lived, was by that time ruled by non-Arab dynasties, Kurds, Turks, Circassians and Ottomans. They thus could have reaped no advantage by claiming, under *taqiyyah*, that they were Arabs. On the contrary, any claim to be of Arab origin would have been looked upon unfavourably by their non-Arab rulers.

Taqiyyah is the doctrine that authorized all the Shi'a secret sects, including the Druzes, and justified those sects in concealing, whenever necessary, their religious beliefs for the sake of saving themselves from persecution. The Druzes did indeed practise *taqiyyah* to safeguard the secrets of their religion, but never to claim a racial origin to which they did not belong.

These criticisms of Professor Hitti's book are serious, but it may also be said that he gives a good account of the historical and social background of the Druzes, with a useful summary of what various Western historians and travellers have written about them and a brief résumé of their folklore. His comments on the Druze religion are of interest:

A study of Druzism is especially valuable and interesting not only because its adherents, unlike the adherents of the other sects, have shown remarkable vitality and thrust themselves repeatedly upon the attention of the world – as in the case of the current events in Syria – but because of its historic connection with Christianity

25

and Oriental Christian sects. In its rise and development from Moslem soil, Druzism held close relationship to Christianity and became heir to a number of Zoroastrian and Judaeo-Christian sects, as well as to a body of Hellenistic and Persian philosophies. Many of those sects and schools of thought have since disappeared, but Druzism is still with us; and, through its medium, their ideas have survived to the present day. The religious and philosophical concepts of many Shi'ite Moslem, and a few semi-Christian, sects have been preserved to us through Druzism, though the original sects and their votaries have long become extinct.

He then states further: 'The Druzes consider all former religions, including Christianity, Judaism and Islam as fore-runners and varied types of Druzism, which supersedes and excels them all.'

As we have seen, the confusion and muddle of ideas on the racial origin of the Druzes seem bad enough, but these are of small significance compared with the farrago of false statements about the Druze religion made by virtually all non-Druze historians, explorers, travellers, pilgrims and missionaries. The Druze religion is shrouded in mystery and muffled by the strictest secrecy; and secrecy breeds suspicion. Such writers therefore fantasized, invented and imagined all kinds of theory, which ranged between the scurrilous and the malevolent, and were totally untrue. Most based their writings on prejudiced hearsay from non-Druze communities (mainly Christian), living on the plains by the eastern Mediterranean seashore, who feared and hated the Druzes because of their warlike character, their notable courage and their love of freedom and independence.

Such people in fact had little social contact with the Druzes, for the mountains where the Druzes lived were extremely rugged and mostly inaccessible. And since the Druzes had ardently and most successfully guarded the secrecy of their religion from both them and others, it is by no means surprising that their enemies in the non-Druze communities should seize on the erroneous conclusion that so much secrecy and caution must indicate a cover for sinister religious principles and diabolic practices. It surely gave these informants much pleasure to string along innocent and credulous travellers, explorers and missionaries, by selling or telling them sensational libels on the Druze religion, trumped up for the occasion.

Many of these writers never visited the Druzes, nor even the Middle East where the Druze communities were located. Silvestre de Sacy, who took two volumes of over 500 pages each to write his *Exposé de la religion des Druzes*, considered by many Westerners to be the ultimate authority on the Druze religion, had never visited the Druzes or even set foot in the countries where they lived. In the introduction of his first volume, he says that he based his writings on the translated texts of four volumes 'of the *Book of Testimonies* to the mysteries of the unity (Druze religion)' that were to be found in the Bibliothèque du Roi in Paris. There follows a strange and extremely odd story about the origin of these four folio volumes, three of which, Silvestre de Sacy says,

> were discovered in the house of Nasr-eddin, the Chief of the *Uqqals* in Baclin [Baaqline], and presented on 15 July 1700 to King Louis XIV by Nasrallah Ben Gilda, a Syrian doctor. The fourth volume was found in the library of M. Piques, doctor at the Sorbonne. The four volumes were translated, in 1701, into French by M. Patis de la Croix, Royal Professor of Arabic, on the order of Secretary of State, Monsieur de Montchartrain.

How the fourth volume reached the library of M. Piques is never explained. The question therefore arises of how the Syrian doctor (most probably a Christian) succeeded in

27

reaching, in the year 1700, Baaqline, the seventeenth-century headquarters of Emir Fakhruddin, the Prince of the Druzes and the heart of the Druze community. And how he then found a copy of the *Book of Testimonies*, available for easy acquisition, in the house of the Chief of the *Uqqals*, the most religious members of the Druze sect.

The initiated among the Druzes are few and live truly monastic lives, which they spend working, praying, doing good and walking humbly in the Faith. They distance themselves from the weaknesses of the flesh and are called the *Uqqal* (the Wise). The uninitiated make up the majority of the Druzes and are known as the *Juhhal* (the Ignorant). They are not allowed to read or even to see the books, which have been strictly guarded for centuries and are secured in secret hideouts. These volumes were, and still are, the preserve of the *Uqqal*, and are kept hidden from all others with the utmost strictness. Any one of the religious *Uqqals* would readily part with his life before parting with any of the Druze religious books.

It was my mother, who belonged to the *Uqqals*, who kept the books in our family. I, as a non-initiate, was not supposed even to glimpse them. No matter how much I tried – and very hard I did try – I could never find them. My mother, the kindest of souls, who would never normally refuse me a wish, could on no account be persuaded to show them to me, despite my imploring on several occasions. It was an unforgivable sin for an uninitiated to set eyes on the books, and a crime punishable by death should he be caught reading them. Many lost their lives in attempting to acquire Druze religious documents, and the rest were too frightened even to contemplate such a highly dangerous venture. Yet here we are asked to believe that Nasrallah Ben Gilda, a Syrian doctor, found in the year 1700 three volumes of the Druze religion in the house of a religious Druze pontiff and walked away with them unnoticed and unharmed.

We may say for certain that several books purported

to be related to the Druze religion are deposited in the Bibliothèque du Roi in Paris. But are they authentic? And who is to confirm their authenticity even if they are? Only a Druze *Uqqal* could pronounce on this with authority, and it would be utterly impossible to persuade one to do so. There is no one else who could ever possess the required knowledge.

Silvestre de Sacy spent long years of toil in producing his *Exposé de la religion des Druzes*, and he sincerely believed his *exposé* had truly unveiled the secrets of Druze belief. He is to be admired for his tenacity and appreciated for his creation of such a painstaking analysis of what he took to be the Druze religion. But his claim to the authenticity of his research material has been strongly challenged, not only by Druze scholars but also by many Western historians and chroniclers. As Bernard H. Springett wrote in *Secret Sects of Syria and Lebanon* (1922):

> There are missionaries in Syria who boast of having in their possession a few copies. The volumes alleged to be the correct expositions from these secret books (such as the translation by Patis de la Croix in 1701, from the works presented by Nasr-Allah to the King of France), are nothing more than a 'compilation of secrets' known, more or less, to every inhabitant of the Southern ranges of Lebanon and Anti-Lebanus. The *Exposé de la religion des Druses*, in two volumes, by Silvestre de Sacy is another network of hypotheses.

Madame H. P. Blavatsky, who in 1875 founded the Theosophical Society in the United States, gave her opinion on Silvestre de Sacy's sources in an article in the *Theosophist*:

> The work presented by Nasr-Allah to the French king as a portion of the Druse scriptures, and translated by Patis de la Croix in 1701, is pronounced a forgery. Not

29

one of the copies now in the possession of the Bodleian, Vienna, or Vatican Libraries is genuine; and, besides, each of them is a copy from the other. Great was always the curiosity of the travellers, and greater yet the efforts of the indomitable and ever-prying missionary, to penetrate behind the veil of Druse worship, but all have resulted in failure.

A hundred or so manuscripts, presumed to relate to the Druze religion, found their way into Western libraries following extensive looting during military disturbances in the Druze region, especially at the time of the Egyptian invasion by Ibrahim Pasha in 1831–8 and the French military intervention after the civil war of 1860. But not one of the Druze *Uqqals*, who alone are qualified to do so, has ever confirmed the authenticity of these manuscripts. On the contrary, many have denounced them as no more than unimportant letters exchanged by the *Uqqals*.

In recent years, a number of highly qualified Druze scholars have written enlightening books on the Druzes, their origin and their religion. Presumably they must have had access to the Druze religious books, but understandably, none of them openly admits to the fact, though some have implied they did. One Druze scholar who wrote a book stating that the time had come to divulge what had hitherto been secret, was attacked, badly beaten by a group of *Uqqals* and left for dead. Fortunately for him, advanced medical care saved his life.

The most malicious fabrication concerning the Druze religion to be adopted by Western writers and enjoy wide-spread circulation was that they worshipped the 'Golden Calf'. As W. B. Seabroke told the story in *Adventures in Arabia* (1928):

Though French officials back in Damascus had tried to dissuade us from visiting the Mountain of the Druses, it was a missionary who had given us the really exciting warnings.

We had listened with scandalized faces as we drank his tea – hoping meanwhile in our unregenerate hearts that the half of what he told us might be true.

'They hold secret and abominable rites in the worship of a golden calf,' he said. 'They believe in black magic. They practise awful cruelties on women. They bury corpses in the walls of their houses.'

As confirmatory evidence, he had taken down a copy of old Silvestre de Sacy's book and read:

'It is a secret cult, rendered to the head of a bull or a calf, rudely made, of gold, silver, or bronze, which they keep in a box hidden from all eyes, and open for the veneration of the initiates.'

Silvestre de Sacy never said any such thing. In fact he wrote exactly the contrary and denounced all those who claimed that Druzes worship the Golden Calf. He was adamant in asserting that the Druze religion condemns idolatry. It therefore seems strange that a missionary should volunteer to relate such a false accusation, but stranger still was the hope expressed by Mr Seabroke that, in his 'unregenerate heart', he hoped half the calumny the missionary told him might be true.

Silvestre de Sacy's actual views on the Golden Calf fabrication were strongly re-emphasized by the Earl of Carnarvon in *Recollections of the Druzes of the Lebanon* (1860):

Of the lowest and most degrading form of idolatry, or feticheworship, which teaches man to bow down to an image of his own workmanship, there would not appear to be many indications in the Druse faith. The image of a calf has been said to be the object of such a worship; but no real proof has ever been adduced in confirmation. Travellers, to whose writings elegance of style has given

31

an unfortunate currency, have accepted with credulity, and asserted with hardihood, stories which they have been either indifferent or unable to verify. To take but two out of many instances, Marshall Marmont, in speaking of the Druses, says, 'ils adorent une petite statue qui représente un veau': and M. de Lamartine, in alluding to their religion, adds, 'ils adorent le veau: c'est le seul fait constaté'. Lamartine travelled in 1832–33, and Marmont in 1834; but the real nature of the Druse calf had been hinted at long before, and more particularly explained at least fifteen years previously by M. de Sacy: and had either of these writers taken the trouble either to inquire of others, or to refer to the works of their learned countryman, then in print and accessible, they would probably have been less positive in their statements.

Since the Druzes are Unitarians (*Muwahhideen*), a fact attested to by most historians, Western, Arab and Oriental – Christian, Moslem and Jewish – their religion is based on a strict, uncompromising belief in the unity of God. Worshipping idols would by definition be a stark violation of the Unitarian doctrine. Had the Druzes worshipped the Golden Calf, then surely examples of calf idols should have been visible in their homes and religious meeting places. But nobody ever yet saw one, for the simple reason that they do not exist.

It seems that some religious documents were looted by Egyptian and French military forces when they invaded the Druze land. How much more attractive and profitable a golden calf would have been as booty, but no golden calf was ever found to loot. None of those writers who claimed that the Druzes worshipped the Golden Calf ever admitted to having seen one. Had the Druzes worshipped the Golden Calf, then they might have been expected to follow the Indian Hindu example by considering cows and calves as sacred, never to be used or slaughtered. On the contrary, the Druzes use oxen and cows extensively and exclusively to plough their fields and gardens, and they enjoy eating beef and veal.

As for accusations against the Druzes of conducting secret and abominable rites, of believing in black magic, of practising awful cruelties on women, of incest, of burying their corpses in the walls of their houses and of many other slandrous tales, these were just one type of the stories that the most ardent and bigotted of the missionaries loved to hear and to circulate widely. They hated the Druzes for their stubborn refusal to be converted to Christianity and retaliated vindictively by spreading ugly villifications. Fortunately for the perpetrators of such stories, they could not be read by the Druzes at the time, being written in foreign languages unknown to them. As soon as an educated younger generation of Druzes was able to read them, the authors had long since died, or had returned to their distant homelands, and so escaped the wrath of those they libelled.

Nevertheless, certain of these stories, untrue as they were, make highly entertaining reading and show how the imagination of such writers is drawn towards sensationalism and the fanciful, even when they purport to be writing fact. This may be illustrated by just two of many anecdotes written for the sake of mendacious sensationalism. The first, indirectly complimentary to the Druzes and their religion, which tells of a person who was proud to claim initiation into the Druze faith and to the rank of the *Uqqals*, is referred to by Bernard H. Springett in *Secret Sects of Syria and Lebanon*: 'So far as is known, only one Western initiate has ever been received into full brotherhood with the Druzes. This was the late Professor A. L. Rawson, of New York, a well known artist and traveller, who passed many years in the East, four times visiting Palestine.'

It transpired that Professor Rawson mistakingly thought

that Madame Blavatsky, the founder of the Theosophical Society, had also been initiated into the mystic and secret sect of the Druzes. Under this misapprehension, he sent her a detailed account of his 'initiation ceremony' into the ranks of the Druze *Uqqals*. His letter, dated 6 June 1877, appeared in *Isis Unveiled*, Vol. II:

> ... Your note, asking me to give you an account of my initiation into a secret Order among the people commonly known as Druses, in Mount Lebanon, was received this morning. I took, as you are fully aware, an obligation at that time to conceal within my own memory the greater part of the 'mysteries' with the most interesting part of the 'instructions'; so that what is left may not be of any service to the public. Such information as I can rightfully give, you are welcome to have and use as you may have occasion.

By a 'special dispensation', Professor Rawson claimed, he had been granted a probation period of just one month, rather than a year, during which he was '"shadowed" by a priest, who served as my cook, guide, interpreter, and general servant, that he might be able to testify to the fact of my having strictly conformed to the rules of diet, ablutions and other matters'. This mysterious personage, the priest, had also instructed him in the 'text of the ritual', which they practised reciting together from time to time, 'in dialogue or song, as it may have been'. On a Thursday, if they found themselves close by a Druze village, they would join the inhabitants in an 'open' meeting, at which 'men and women assembled for instruction and worship, and to expose generally their religious practices'.

> I was never present at a 'Friday close' meeting before my initiation, nor do I believe anyone else, man or

woman, ever was, except by collusion with a priest, and that is not probable, for a false priest forfeits his life. The practical jokers among them sometimes 'fool' a too curious 'Frank' by a sham initiation, especially if such a one is suspected of having some connection with the missionaries at Beirut or elsewhere.

The professor said he had been unable to find any truly bad features in the system, such as idolatry, though he claimed to have detected 'relics of what was once a grand form of Nature worship . . . contracted under despotism into a secret Order, hidden from the light of day, and exposed only in the smoky glare of a few burning lamps, in some damp cave or chapel underground'.

The initiates, he noted, included men and women, while the ceremonies were 'of so peculiar a nature that both sexes are required to assist in the ritual and "work"'. The places he termed the 'prayer-house' and the 'vision chamber' were simply furnished and had just one strip of carpet, but there were 'rich decorations and valuable pieces of ancient furniture, the work of Arab silversmiths five or six centuries ago, inscribed and dated' in an unnamed, underground location he calls the 'Gray Hall'. The initiation ceremony itself was marked by a day of continual fast, 'from daylight to sunset in winter, or six o'clock in summer', and consisted entirely of a set of tests and temptations designed to stretch the endurance of candidates to its mental and physical limits. These challenges to the 'neophyte's self-control' included:

. . . choice pieces of cooked meat, savoury soup, pilau, and other appetizing dishes, with sherbet, coffee, wine and water . . . set, as if accidentally, in his way, and he is left alone for a time with the tempting things. To a hungry and fainting soul the trial is severe. But a more difficult ordeal is when the seven priestesses retire, all but one, the youngest and prettiest, and the door is closed and barred on the outside, after warning the candidate that he will be left to his 'reflections' for half an hour. Wearied by the long-continued ceremonial, weak with hunger, parched with thirst, and a sweet reaction coming after the tremendous strain to keep his animal nature in subjection, this moment of privacy is brimful of peril. The beautiful young vestal, timidly approaching and with glances which lend a double magnetic allurement to her words, begs him in low tones to 'bless her'. Woe to him if he does! A hundred eyes see him from secret peepholes, and only to the ignorant neophyte is there the appearance of concealment and opportunity.

Seldom did any young man or woman succeed in '"winning" all the prizes', stated the professor, 'since Nature will some-times exert itself in spite of the most stubborn will, and the neophyte fail of passing some of the tests'. In that event, there was another year's extension on the probation period before the trial was repeated. Evidently the professor himself came through his ordeal with flying colours.

The main consequence of undergoing this 'initiation' seemed, he found, 'to be a kind of mental illusion or sleep-walking, in which the neophyte saw, or thought he saw, the images of people who were known to be absent, and in some cases thousands of miles away'.

I thought (or perhaps it was my mind at work) I saw friends and relatives that I knew at the time were in New York State, while I was then in Lebanon. How these results were produced I cannot say. They appeared in a dark room, when the 'guide' was talking, the 'company' singing in the 'chamber', and near the close of the day, when I was tired out with fasting, walking, talking, singing, robing, unrobing, seeing a great many people in various conditions as to dress and undress, and with great mental strain in resisting certain physical manifestations that result from the appetites when they overcome the will, and in paying close attention to the passing scenes, hoping to remember them – so that I may have been unfit to judge any new and surprising phenomena . . .

He was aware of the uses to which a magic lantern and other apparatus could be put in such circumstances, and had somehow managed to examine the room to satisfy himself that there was nothing mechanical behind these 'visions' that he saw that evening, and which recurred. He was convinced that the voice of his 'guide and instructor' was solely responsible for these phenomena.

On several occasions afterward, when at a great distance from the 'chamber', the same or similar visions were produced, as, for instance, in Hornstein's Hotel at Jerusalem. A daughter-in-law of a well-known Jewish merchant is an initiated 'sister' and can produce the visions almost at will on anyone who will live strictly according to the rules of the Order for a few weeks, more or less, according to their nature, as gross or refined, etc.

Professor Rawson felt confident in saying that the extremely peculiar nature of the initiation ceremony made it impossible to even think of reproducing it in a printed version. This, in his view, made the true secrets of the Druzes even more secure than those of the Freemasons, for they were 'acted and not spoken, and require several initiated persons to assist in the work'. In conclusion, he hardly felt it necessary to acquaint Madame Blavatsky with the way certain Druze notions perpetuated ancient Greek beliefs – such as 'the idea that a man has two souls' – since she had probably become familiar with them during her own passage 'through the "upper" and "lower" chamber'.

> If I am mistaken in supposing you an 'initiate', please excuse me. I am aware that the closest friends often conceal that 'sacred secret' from each other; and even husband and wife may live – as I was informed in Dayr-el-Kamar was the fact in one family there – for twenty years together and yet neither knew anything of the initiation of the other. You, undoubtedly, have good reasons for keeping your own counsel.

The most fundamental fact to be recorded and emphasized about the Druze Faith is that, in 1043, twenty-six years after Al-Hakim bi-Amrillah decreed the Divine Call, an end to it was announced once it had fulfilled its purpose. At that point the door was officially and permanently closed. After that date, no newcomer was ever permitted to join the Druze Faith. Thenceforward, to be a Druze one had to be born a Druze.

> The door is shut; no one can enter it, and no one can pass out. No one but the offspring and blood of Druzes are eligible for admission to their mystic rites. It is a matter of sheer impossibility to convert a Druze to any other religion, and it is an equal impossibility to be initiated into Drusedom.

Thus writes Mr Springett in *Secret Sects of Syria and Lebanon*. Yet the same Mr Springett contradicts himself in his own pages when he states that, so far as is known, only one Western initiate has ever been received into full Druze brotherhood, assuring us that the late Professor A.L. Rawson of New York was converted into the Druze Faith over 800 years after conversion was officially and permanently terminated. And not only was he converted into the Druze Faith, but was further initiated into the rank of the Druze *Uqqals* by a ceremony he describes in detail, albeit that it is either entirely imaginary or a fraud. He also hints at one other outsider besides himself who was converted and further initiated into the ranks of the *Uqqals*: 'the daughter-in-law of a well known Jewish merchant in Jerusalem' – another unlikely tale, needless to say.

According to Professor Rawson, the 'special dispensation' he was allowed of only one month to prepare for initiation involved his being 'shadowed' by a Druze priest to teach him all he needed to know before joining the ranks of the *Uqqals*. He also mentions Druze priestesses in his account of the ceremony. The fact of the matter is that no Druze who yet lived ever heard of a Druze priest or a Druze priestess, and those who would dare to call any Druze *Uqqal* a priest may expect to find their lives seriously at risk. In other words, the whole ceremony, 'Gray Hall' and all the other details constitute a sensational fiction of which the best to be said is that it makes interesting reading. The manifestations it produces seem to relate most closely to the expectations of credulous clients attending the séances of fraudulent mediums in Victorian London and New York.

It is hard to believe that Professor Rawson fabricated this elaborate farrago of untruths exclusively out of his own head. The only possible explanation is that he was taken for a ride by an ingenious trickster of the Levant, who sold him a sham initiation, conceived and arranged at an exorbitant price, exclusively for his benefit. It seems extraordinary that the professor was so gullible as to fall into this trap, especially when he himself states his scepticism of trickery in general and his awareness of such sham initiations in particular.

In the Druze religion there are no ceremonies, no formalities and no prescribed tests for initiation. All that a Druze *Juhhal* has to do to be accepted among the *Uqqals* is to remain free of a criminal record, to be of good behaviour in his family and within the community, to be willing and ready to abandon every vice. He must neither smoke nor drink wine or spirits; he must be content to wear plain and simple clothes, renouncing every thought of splendour and luxury, to distance himself from the weaknesses of the flesh and regularly attend the prayer meetings where the basic elements of the Druze religion will ultimately be revealed to him. He must show his sincerity in his request to join the rank of *Uqqals* by demonstrating, in demeanour and life-style, a devotion to the observed habits and principles of the *Uqqals* and by being prepared to live a truly monastic life, which he is willing to spend working, praying, performing good works and 'walking humbly in the Faith'.

For our second and final anecdote we go back to 1697, when Maundrell referred in *A Journey from Aleppo to Jerusalem* to the Prince of the Druzes:

> Their present prince is Achmet [Ahmed], grandson to Faccardine [Fakhruddin], an old man, and one who keeps up the custom of his ancestors, of turning day into night: a hereditary practice in his family, proceeding from a traditional perswasion amongst them, that princes can never sleep securely but by day, when men's actions and designs are best observed by their guards, and if need be, most easily prevented; but that in the night it concerns them to be always vigilant, lest the darkness, aided by their sleeping, should give traitors both opportunity and encouragement to assault their persons, and by a dagger or pistol, to make them continue their sleep longer than they intended when they lay down.

None of the books written about the Druzes, their customs, habits and traditions, contains any reference to Druze princes who slept through the day and stayed awake through the night as a security precaution, nor do the elders ever speak of such a bat-like practice. It takes a fertile imagination to tell, and a gullible Western traveller to believe, such a story. The Druzes pride themselves on their bravery, and it is impossible to accept that their princes or sheikhs, who lead them in battle, would ever manifest such cowardice as to stay awake at nights for fear of assassins.

2. The Origin of the Druzes

To know the Druzes, their origin and their religion, we must go back to the earliest days of Islam, when the followers of the Prophet Mohammed split into the two great sects of Sunnis and Shi'ites. The dispute was over the succession to the Prophet and on the true interpretation of the Qur'an. The Sunnis believed the caliph ought to be elected. The Shi'ites believed he should be a relative of the Prophet and should be hereditary from father to son. The Sunnis adhered to the literal meaning of the Qur'an. The Shi'ites tried to search for possible hidden meanings beyond the merely literal.

The Shi'ites wanted Ali, the first cousin of the Prophet and the husband of Fatimah, his daughter, to succeed Mohammed as caliph. In this they were overruled, and Abou Bakr, followed by Omar and afterwards by Othman, was elected first in the succession of caliphs. Eventually Ali was elected as fourth caliph, but after five years he was assassinated, whereupon his followers chose his son Hassan to succeed him. It is said that Hassan then abdicated in favour of Muawiyeh, his father's rival, at the time the governor of Syria, on the understanding that Hassan would, at Muawiyeh's death, succeed him to the caliphate. In the event, the agreement was completely ignored by Muawiyeh's son, Yazid, who took over the caliphate for himself. He further raised an army to fight against Hussein, Ali's son by Fatima, elected caliph by the followers of his father after the sudden death of his brother Hassan. A terrible battle was then fought between the opposing factions in Kerbala in Mesopotamia. Hussein and his brother Abbas were killed, and the Shi'ites have never forgiven or forgotten the slaying of Hussein. The event put the final and permanent touch to the split between Sunnis and Shi'ites in Islam, and is commemorated annually with grieving and sorrow by Shi'ites all over the world. They consider his death to be an atoning sacrifice for the sins of all faithful believers.

The Shi'ites refused to accept other caliphs, recognizing only Ali and eleven others as the divine successors to the Prophet Mohammed. They gave them the name of imams rather than caliphs, and the imams were considered the sole interpreters of the Qur'an and to be endowed with divine insight. Most illustrious of the imams was the sixth, Jaafar, but now there occurred a split among his followers in turn. A majority wanted his second son, Musa, to succeed him as imam, while others favoured his elder son, Ismail. The latter group thus became known in history as the Ismailis. Their beliefs differed from the prevailing doctrines of Islam, and so they were forced, for some time, to go underground, to operate secretly and not to divulge their beliefs to outsiders, but only to fellow believers. The Druzes trace their religion to the Ismailis.

The Shi'ites are today a majority of the population of Iraq and Iran. They also exist in large numbers in Lebanon, the eastern part of Saudi Arabia, the Arabian Gulf states, Afghanistan, East Africa, Russia and Upper Yemen among other parts of the world. In recent years, the Shi'ites have dominated international public opinion through the Iraq-Iran war, the war of liberation of Kuwait and their repeated attacks in Lebanon on the Israeli army and its sponsored ally, the South Lebanese army.

The Druze religion came into being in the eleventh century, during the reign of the sixth caliph of the Fatimid dynasty, Al-Hakim bi-Amrillah ('Ruler by God's command'), as a direct result of his influence.

Al-Hakim bi-Amrillah came to power in A.D. 996, at the age of eleven, after the death of his father. On Thursday, 30 May 1017, at the age of thirty-two, he announced the Unitarian doctrine, the Divine Call (the Druze Faith), by issuing a decree inviting the people to choose freely and openly to practise their belief. He encouraged them to have the courage to distinguish between truth and falsehood so as to live in compliance with God's will. The Druze scholar and historian, Dr Sami Nassib Makarem, sets out the following English translation of Al-Hakim's decree in his book *The Druze Faith*:

> Remove ye the causes of fear and estrangement from
> yourselves. Do away with the corruption of delusion
> and conformity. Be ye certain that the Prince of Believers
> hath given unto you free will, and hath spared you the
> trouble of disguising and concealing your true beliefs,
> so that when ye work ye may keep your deeds pure
> for God. He hath done thus so that when ye relinquish
> your previous beliefs and doctrines ye shall not indeed
> lean on such causes of impediments and pretensions. By
> conveying to you the reality of his intention, the Prince
> of Believers hath spared you any excuse for doing so.
> He hath urged you to declare your belief openly. Ye are
> now safe from any hand which may bringeth harm unto
> you. Ye now may find rest in his assurance ye shall not
> be wronged.
>
> Let those who are present convey this message unto
> the absent, so that it may be known by both the
> distinguished and the common people. It shall thus
> become a rule to mankind; and divine wisdom shall
> prevail for all the days to come.

The Caliph Al-Hakim was proclaimed the manifestation of Divinity, and Hamzah ibn Ali was appointed leader of this new Unitarian movement, the Divine Call. According to Dr

Philip Hitti, Hamzah went so far as to 'declare Al-Hakim the Messiah'. His argument in defence of deification was a clever one, comments Dr Hitti: 'If ye Christians and Jews believe that God spoke to Moses through a dry tree and, on another occasion, through a mountain . . ., is it then improper to believe that our Lord (Al-Hakim) is a more worthy means through whom God manifests to the world his power and behind whom he conceals himself?'

But before proceeding further, we must see how the Druzes acquired their name. After the Divine Call was announced by Al-Hakim and Hamzah proclaimed imam, *da'is*, or missionaries, were appointed to spread its message. Among them was one named Nashtakin Ad-Darazi, who believed that he, rather than Hamzah, should have been appointed imam. Jealousy and ambition led him to propagate the Divine Call in such a way as to win to his side as many adherents as possible. In this he swerved from the true doctrines of the Divine Call and resorted to such unscrupulous methods as have been used by politicians in every age, including bribery, intimidation, threats and promises of permissive practices. He even counterfeited coinage for bribing people, but he drew large crowds, especially in Syria and Lebanon, and did untold damage to the Divine Call, imposing a very serious setback on the movement. He even attempted to overthrow Hamzah by force, and Hamzah and his aides were rescued by Al-Hakim himself in the resulting battle. As Druze historians have remarked, Ad-Darazi was cursed by the Druzes as Satan. Yet the irony remains that the name of this man, repudiated and spurned, cursed and reviled by the *Muwahhideen*, came to be affixed to the movement.

Puzzled by this paradox of a religious sect bearing the name of a man it reviles, various historians have indulged in elaborate research projects. They have discovered that Darazi never went to Syria and Lebanon, where the Druze Faith was mainly adopted and the Druzes acquired their name, but was eventually beheaded in Cairo. He may have sent *da'is* to those other countries, but was never there himself. Had his followers adopted his name, they ought surely to have been called Daraziehs rather than Druzes. These sceptical historians have gone even further to conclude that 'Druze' must in fact derive from *durus*, which in Arabic means 'teachings'; originating from the verb *darasa*, which means 'to study'. It is a theory to which many Western historians subscribe, but Druze historians do not accept it and the Druzes believe that they were indeed named after the man they curse, hate, revile and call Satan. The incongruous mystery has been in existence long enough to continue for ever.

The Druzes differed from Moslems in the interpretation of some of the basic doctrines of Islam. For example:

Fasting: fasting in Islam means that, during the month of Ramadan, a Moslem abstains, from dawn to sunset, from all bodily pleasures, food and drink, and devotes his time to prayer. The Druzes believe that it is more important to abstain from doing harm to others, from lying, stealing and all kinds of wickedness which affect not only the individual but others around him.

Hajj: the Druzes reject the obligation to visit Mecca and insist that the meaning of *Hajj* is the direct communication with God when the soul of man travels to God; that this can be done without visiting Mecca.

Prayer: the Druzes believe that prayers are a personal religious practice, and that since God is everywhere, you pray to him wherever you are and as many times as it pleases you; there is no need to pray a fixed number of times a day. As for turning towards Mecca when you pray, this is rejected by the Druzes, for God is everywhere and not confined to Mecca.

These deviations from the interpretation of some of the doctrines of Islam were before long to provoke strong suspicions that the Druzes were not true believers, and they would, in A.D. 1021, set the machinery of persecution in motion for a seven-year campaign of terror such as few communities can ever have had the misfortune to endure. The account that follows of the rule of the Caliph Al-Hakim bi-Amrillah and the troubled times that succeeded his reign is deeply indebted to the work of Dr Najla M. Abu-Izzedine. Many of the quotations used are from her book, *The Druzes* (1984).

When Al-Hakim inherited the throne of the Fatimid Empire, it was the richest and largest area of the Moslem world, mainly comprising most of North Africa and Egypt. During his reign he also brought parts of Mesopotamia, the Hijaz and a number of Mediterranean islands under his firm control. In addition he fought successfully the Greek campaign against Syria and finally concluded a ten-year truce that confirmed his absolute supremacy over that country too.

But though he inherited a rich empire, he also inherited many problems. These included rivalry in the army, the struggle to snatch power from the boy caliph, hatred between Moslems and non-Moslems, the threat to the Fatimids from the Christian Byzantine empire, enemies of Islam, widespread corruption in the wake of his father's great tolerance and, most important of all, the failure of the caliphs who preceded him to fulfil the *Ismaili Da'wa* (mission) to establish a state of social equality and permanent peace.

The Ismailis had a grand vision to unite all mankind, including Moslem and non-Moslem peoples, in one universal empire of true believers, to be governed by a single divinely guided spiritual ruler who would flood the world with equality and justice. They sent their *da'is* to preach this ideal among the people, but failed to achieve results. Such a unification of all people into one faith could never have been achieved. Equality and justice, the ideals loved by the masses, remained an unattainable dream.

Undaunted by such problems, Al-Hakim proceeded to search for the right solutions to them. From the start he was convinced that capital punishment and fear were the most effective deterrents against serious crime. His exaction of penalty was resolute and ruthless. Corruption he eradicated by execution, and most of the culprits were high-ranking officials. Ambitious rivals for power he eliminated. The rivalry within the army he allowed to remain, but kept it balanced and under control. And to fulfil the Ismailis' grand vision, he embarked on a programme of training for the *da'is*. Two special buildings were constructed in Cairo for this purpose, built and endowed out of Al-Hakim's personal wealth, and equipped with every facility. A great number of books on relevant subjects and all materials necessary for writing, copying and studying were provided.

The new centre was named Dar al-Hikma and Dar al-Ilm (the House of Wisdom and the House of Science), and Al-Hakim presented Dar al-Ilm with his own splendid collection of invaluable books. Scientists and men of learning were commissioned as teachers and lecturers, and the two foundations soon developed into an institution where not only Moslem theology was instructed, but also mathematics, logic, philosophy, history, languages and medicine. Students from all over the Moslem world flocked to study and specialize in an atmosphere of Ismaili teaching and preaching. Al-Hakim himself would frequently visit the centre, joining debates and granting bonuses to encourage outstanding capabilities.

Once he was satisfied that the *da'is* were adequately trained, he sent them to spread the *da'wa* through all parts of the Fatimid Empire. They achieved a degree of success, though it still fell short of Al-Hakim's ambition. It must then have dawned on him that if he were to unite all the people of his empire in a state of social equality and permanent peace, they should have one religion, which of course must be the Ismaili religion. To this end he set out to convert the Christians and Jews to what he saw as the true faith. From this his persecution of them followed, along with the destruction of their shrines. Only after he was convinced of the impossibility of such a task did he allow the rebuilding of churches and synagogues and return to their worshippers the freedom to follow and practise their own beliefs. Having failed to unite all his subjects into one faith, he turned to concentrating his efforts on creating a world of equality and justice within the Fatimid Empire.

He embarked on an extensive programme of reform to achieve justice, economic prosperity and social justice for all. He reformed the judicial system to guarantee a fair trial and justice for any accused. He doubled the salaries and other benefits and privileges of judges to prevent material needs from influencing their judgement, and ordered them to observe absolute honesty and to distance themselves from accepting gifts or favours. He then maintained a close personal surveillance to ensure that his orders were strictly obeyed. Any infringement evoked immediate mortal punishment, as in the case of one qadi (judge) who was a trustee of 'Amwal al-Yatama' (monies of the orphans), executed after being found guilty of embezzling 20,000 dinars from this fund, which comprised the money and property of orphans entrusted to its trustees by deceased parents. He provided justice to a degree his subjects had never before known. They slept soundly in their homes, secure in the possession of their properties. Many chroniclers describe Al-Hakim as the champion of justice. There survive some contemporary Hebrew writings that sincerely praise his unparalleled justice.

Most of the state land he distributed among his subjects. He confiscated most of the properties of the members of his family and donated these to the state treasury. He announced that his door was open to anyone who had a complaint of any kind, and that he himself would look

49

into any such complaints, whether they were addressed to his court or to him personally in the street. He created a special department to deal with the properties and monies confiscated from those executed or punished under his rule – assets which were redistributed among the poor and needy.

He regulated the market: verified weights and measures, combated dishonesty in the manufacture and sale of commodities, checked prices and punished hoarding. Units of weights and measures were standardized to protect the people from the greed of shopkeepers and merchants. He issued a decree fixing the prices of bread, meat and most other vital commodities. During the years of a low Nile or other adversities affecting agriculture, landowners were exempted from tax. He also ordered that water courses and conduits should be kept constantly cleared and that new ones should be built. In combatting profiteering, he used a drastic method.

In 398/1008 the Nile was low, food was scarce, and the people appealed to Hakim for help. The Caliph stood outside the palace gate and announced that he was riding out to Rashida mosque, on the outskirts of the city; by the time he returned all the stored up grains should be placed on the street outside the hoarders' houses; whoever failed to bring out his store would pay with his life. When he returned at the end of the day, there was no one in Cairo and Misr (the old city) but had brought out his stock on the road, 'and the people's eyes were filled and their appetites satisfied'. Hakim ordered the grain merchants to supply the quantity needed each day at the price he fixed which allowed them a reasonable profit, failing which he would seal up their stocks until the new harvest came in. They obeyed; the price fell and the distress was relieved.

He saw to it that schoolmasters did not punish their pupils severely, and that owners of animals of burden were humane in their treatment. He issued laws to combat immorality. Brothels and houses of ill-repute were closed. The sale of slave and singing girls was prohibited. The drinking, sale and manufacture of wine were forbidden. In 1015 he freed all his slaves, male and female, and gave them the liberty to dispose of their possessions as they wished.

An incident illustrates the kindly side of his nature. A poor man, having stolen a silver lamp from the Old Mosque, was brought before the Qadi who brought him before the Caliph. Al-Hakim said to the man: 'woe to you for stealing the silver of the mosque!' The man answered: 'I have stolen what belongs to God my Lord. I am poor and my daughters are hungry. The silver is better spent on them than hanging in the mosque.' Tears rose to the Caliph's eyes. He ordered the Qadi to find suitable husbands for the young maidens and endow them with 3,000 dinars for their trousseau. And the lamp was restored to the mosque.

At intervals he gave lands and other properties to common people, to an extent where, by the end of his reign, little was left of the state domain.

Al-Hakim would frequently ride out with one or two of his servants to the desert. On the night of 27 February 1021, he rode out with one servant, but as he went, he ordered the servant to return to the palace. Al-Hakim did not return, and after an extensive search the ass he had ridden was found, but never a trace of the caliph. 'He himself went alone into the inner parts of the desert and never returned, nor is it known to this day where he retired.' So wrote a chronicler thirty years after the event.

Before he disappeared, Al-Hakim had summoned his son

and heir, the Fatimid Prince Ali, and exacted a solemn promise from him that he would 'protect his followers, the Druzes, and not maltreat them'.

> It was said Al-Hakim had made the prince take forty oaths to that effect. But as soon as Ali was officially proclaimed Caliph, he went back on his forty oaths and claimed they had expired, at the rate of one a day, forty days after Al-Hakim's disappearance. He was therefore free to inflict on the Druzes any persecution he wished, and this he promptly ordered.

As Ali unleashed his bloodbath, thousands upon thousands were massacred, burnt alive, drowned at sea, crucified and subjected to the cruellest tortures. Infants were slain in their mothers' arms and men were 'slaughtered and had their heads impaled on warriors' spears or suspended from the necks of their wives and daughters. Others were dragged by their feet through the streets.'

> From Antioch to Alexandria the Druzes thus suffered their seven-year nightmare of horror and terror in the Caliph's determination to annihilate them. Secrecy therefore became essential for survival, and the Druze religion was forced underground; and so it has remained until the present day. Where a secret has been kept closely guarded for over eight hundred years, it becomes a self-perpetuating, integral part of the life of the community which shares it.

The door to the Divine Call was as a consequence closed in the year 1043. No new aspirants to the Druze Faith were accepted thereafter because the Druzes were afraid that the new Caliph Ali might plant among them informers who could expose them to his ruthless persecution.

Yet there is really nothing to hide. It is a religion chiselled out of Islam, based on the strict, uncompromising belief in the unity of God and on a direct communion between the individual and the Almighty. There are no intermediaries. Prayer meeting-places are simple structures, indistinguishable from the houses around them. There are no calls or reminders for prayers, no bells or muezzins, and attendance is absolutely voluntary. The religion is not taught in schools. The secret religious books and studies are the preserve of those who [are] initiated into the religion and are kept secret from all others.

Shortly after Al-Hakim's disappearance, a document appeared suspended on mosques and hence known as the 'Suspended Proclamation'. It forms an important text in the Druzes' religious teachings and consists of a complete account of Al-Hakim's tireless efforts for reform, the difficulties he encountered and the disillusionment that led to his departure. Once again, varous historians have found in his disappearance the occasion for advancing strange and bizarre theories. Some have claimed that he was murdered by the collusion of his sister, Sitt Al-Mulk, whom he had accused of immoral behaviour. Another chronicler made an absurd assertion that 'it was the handiwork of the Druzes themselves to create yet another disappeared imam who would reinforce their *da'wa* or religious call'. As for the Christian historians, Bar Hebraeus and Al-Antaki, they maintained that 'Al-Hakim, whose mother was a Christian from a patriarchal Orthodox family, disappeared in order to become a Christian monk after Christ appeared to him in a vision chastising him for having persecuted Christians'.

The Druzes revere and respect the seven prophets they inherited from the Ismailis. At the head of the list comes Adam, and then follow Noah, Abraham, Moses, Jesus, Mohammad and Mohammad ibn Ismail. But the divine hero in their history is, of course, Al-Hakim bi-Amrillah, a figure greatly maligned by nearly all Western historians, who have claimed he was insane. Most of those making such claims never set foot in Egypt, but copied from or were influenced by the Arab Christian chroniclers, who never forgave Al-Hakim for burning down the church of the Holy Sepulchre in Jerusalem, the holiest shrine of Christendom, and for the persecution of Christians during the early part of his reign. They may have been additionally influenced by the works of Arab chroniclers employed to write adversely on him by the Abbasides of Baghdad, who were set on destroying their rival Fatimids out of jealousy for their spectacular achievements.

On the other hand, many Arab chroniclers, some of whom were contemporary with Al-Hakim and his reign, faithfully recorded his outstanding personal qualities. Among the most significant of these was 'his almost monastic simplicity'.

> His clothes were simple, made chiefly of wool, and he
> chose to ride an ass rather than a horse. He discarded
> the diamond turban and wore a plain white scarf.
> He disliked ceremonies and feasts and these were
> banned in his palace. He prohibited his subjects from
> prostrating themselves before him or from kissing
> the ground or his hand when they saw him. His
> food was simple. He would frequently pause in the
> streets of his capital to exchange greetings or answer
> questions from his poorer subjects. The life of frivolity
> seems to have been against his principles and singers
> and dancers were not welcomed in his palace. His
> internal policy and personal behaviour indicate that
> he was deeply religious. He did not build palaces but
> built mosques, more than any other Moslem caliph.
> He was a pleasant man with a sense of humour. He
> often exchanged jokes with those he spoke to in the
> streets . . .

It was true that 'Law and justice reigned triumphant under him. And . . . no great man was quite sure of his life', but his kindness to his people belied the depiction of a tyrant projected by hostile commentators. Historians are meanwhile agreed on his generosity. His donations to charity and his gifts to the poor and needy were so great as to cause concern to the controller of his and the empire's finances. When the official conveyed to Al-Hakim his concern, the reply he received was: 'Wealth belongs to God, the people are God's servants, and we are God's trustees on earth. Give out to the people their due and withhold it not.' The Druze religious teachings consider such actions of Al-Hakim to represent miraculous qualities and therefore confirm that at least some of the Ismaili *da'is* interpreted them as such. The *da'is* believed in Al-Hakim's divine guidance and superhuman qualities, so crediting his actions with a divine inspiration that renders them unquestionable.

Jewish historians and chroniclers have also spoken well of Al-Hakim. They praised him and his rule and recommended that Moslem and Christian writings on him should be treated with caution. An Egyptian scroll of 1012 mentions Al-Hakim as 'the protector of the Jews', who are said to have 'assembled in the Great Synagogue of Fustat to thank God that the Caliph had saved them from a rioting mob'.

In addition to his divine attributes, believed in by the Druzes, who offer him worship, Al-Hakim bi-Amrillah proved by his achievements, dedication and application of justice that he was one of the greatest of all caliphs, if not the greatest. He was a fine sovereign who, faithful to the Ismaili doctrines, sought reform and justice and attempted to unite all the people of his empire in a state of social equality and permanent peace. These facts again give the lie to those Western and Arab historians who have tried to present Al-Hakim as mentally unstable for their own prejudiced reasons.

Dr Najla Abu-Izzedine writes in *The Druzes*: 'Recently

uncovered manuscripts reveal that Al-Hakim departed east to Sijistan in eastern Iran on the border of India . . .' Be that as it may, the believers of the Druze Faith remain convinced that he went away of his own free will, to return, when the time is right, as saviour and redeemer.

3. The Character of the Druze Faith

We have seen that the Druzes believe in the divinity of Al-Hakim bi-Amrillah and his Divine Call with all its teachings. Although the religious books are kept secret and are available only to the *Uqqals*, the Divine Call and its doctrines inspired and established for its followers well-founded codes of ethics, moral and social behaviour which every Druze adheres to faithfully and respects. For the majority of the Druzes, the *Juhhals*, abiding by these codes is the only religion they know. The *Uqqals* alone have the honour of understanding the philosphy of the Divine Call and the privilege of interpreting its teachings. The Druzes are thus united by their moral and social codes, which were widely taught under the Divine Call.

The Earl of Carnarvon in 1860 wrote in *Recollections of the Druses of the Lebanon*:

> There is nothing which surprised me more than the
> self-possession, the delicate appreciation of wishes
> and feelings, the social ease, and to a great extent the
> refinement which distinguished the conversation and
> manner of those amongst the Druze chiefs whom I then
> met, and on which no drawing-room of London or Paris
> could have conferred an additional polish. Both then and
> subsequently I have seen many Orientals but in none have
> I recognized the same remarkable combination of social
> qualities.

The Druze community is known to possess the highest codes of ethical, moral and social behaviour, and it is truthfulness which heads the list. The Druzes strongly believe in absolute truthfulness by professing the truth, acting according to the truth and living for the truth. 'Tell the truth and fear nothing but your sin' runs a Druze maxim. They never break their word. Observance of the truth may be relaxed, however, when outsiders inquire about the Druze religion or if telling the truth could bring harm on the community. In both these circumstances, white lies are permissible.

Gentleness and humility are also qualities of the Druzes, except when the community is in danger; then they spring to its defence like tigers. Old and young alike, they will then swiftly close ranks and emerge as a formidable fighting force to confront any who attempt to threaten their survival, their rights, their land and their well-being as a community. This ability has often been demonstrated throughout history. To help one another is a sacred duty. The Unitarians are brothers and sisters, and fraternal love guarantees the obligation of mutual assistance in every possible way, materially and in combat. Their primordial duty in any case of personal conflict is to give support and to make peace. A man is obliged to come to the aid of a fighter who is his closest relative. He is under an obligation, however, to try to make peace if he is equally related to the two fighters. For example, if my brother and I fight, my first cousin should try to make peace between us; if my brother and my cousin fight, I must fight alongside my brother; if my cousin fights another cousin, my brother and I must try to make peace between them; and if my cousin fights an outsider, my brother and I must fight alongside him.

Because of their unfailing support for one another, there have never been, during their long history, any beggars among the Druzes. During the First World War, when famine hit all of Lebanon, the Druzes were spared because of the assistance they received from their Jabal al-Druze brothers. Despite the horrors of the recent war in Lebanon and the collapse of the country's economy, there was still not a single beggar to be found in the Druze community.

The original command to the Druzes was that they should renounce all other beliefs which they may have held before the Divine Call and adhere only to the Unitarian faith. As we have seen, the call to the Faith was ended very early in Druze history, and the door to enter the religion was sealed for all time. Since then a Druze is born and never converted from another faith. Likewise, he will not himself accept a conversion. Missionaries have exerted years in strenuous but futile attempts to persuade Druzes to change their religion.

A British Anglican mission moved to Baaqline, the village of my birth in Lebanon, and there built a prestigious and prominent compound with many substantial buildings, the first to have tiled roofs in the village. They set out to help the needy under the efficient leadership of Miss Louisa Kitchen, head of the mission. After a couple of years of dedicated mission work and appreciable help and assistance to the local population, Miss Kitchen succeeded in convincing Abou Qasim, the mission's gardener, that he should convert to Christianity. There was jubilation in the mission, and at its headquarters in England, as hopes soared that the Druzes, following Abou Qasim's example, might at last be brought to see the light. Things went well for Abou Qasim, who had a large family and much need for his newly increased salary and privileges. However, no other Druze followed in his footsteps, and as time went on, old age took its toll of Abou Qasim. He fell ill and sent for Miss Kitchen, who hurried to his bedside. He told her how much he enjoyed being a Christian and thanked her profusely for all she had done for him. But he had one last request before he passed on. 'Anything you wish, dear Abou Qasim,' replied Miss Kitchen. After a long sigh, Abou Qasim uttered his death-bed wish: 'I was honoured and dearly loved being a Christian, but I want to die a Druze.'

There were many enthusiastic attempts by missionaries to convert Druzes, but all were in vain. A similar experience to that of Miss Kitchen befell another British lady missionary who started a girls' school in a Druze village near Beirut. She made it a condition of entry for girls who wished to attend that they should be converted to Christianity. Many girls were anxious to be educated, and accepted the conversion with their fingers crossed behind their backs. The mock conversion was then renounced the moment they left school, and all, without exception, lived out their lives as Druzes.

The most tempting offer ever made to a Druze to convert to Christianity was that extended by the Spanish monarch, Philip III, to Fakhruddin II, the Prince of the Druzes, when he travelled to Italy to solicit assistance against the Ottoman Turks. King Philip warmly invited Fakhruddin to Madrid, promising him a government superior to that of Lebanon on condition that he became a Christian. Fakhruddin tactfully rejected the offer, saying that he came to Europe to seek military assistance, not a new government or a new religion. It was Philip III, incidentally, who was responsible for expelling the Moriscos (Christians of Moorish ancestry) from Spain.

To accept and resign one's self to God's will, in prosperity or adversity, is a foremost tenet among the teachings of the Druze religion. It is for this reason that the Druzes are fatalists. They strongly believe that what is written is written, and that, at birth, a Druze's age on this earth is recorded in the book of destiny. Nothing in the world can prolong or shorten their days. 'He who is destined for ten will never die at nine.' 'Every bullet has an address, and will find it no matter what you do.' These are universally popular sayings among the Druzes. Their belief in an age fixed at birth goes some way to explain their extraordinary courage and lion-hearted bravery in battle. Incredible feats of daring and heroism abound in Druze legend. Their fatalism is fundamentally based on their belief that 'whatever comes is ordained by God'.

The Druzes' religious teachings also command them:

To keep themselves apart, clear and distinct from those who are unable to see the right path and are therefore in error; to dissociate themselves from selfishness.

To recognize the Unity of God in all ages, times and epochs, and to be in union with Him as much as is humanly possible.

To be content with God's will and his works whatever these may be. Suffering and pain are therefore to be endured patiently and accepted as coming from God as means of purification. By doing so, man enters the 'Kingdom of God wherein there is real life, true happiness and absolute goodness'.

Intoxicants of all kinds are prohibited. The drinking of wines and other alcoholic liquor as well as the smoking of hasheesh (marijuana) are forbidden. The Druze religious teachings speak of intoxicants as the concentration of all evil. Usury is not allowed. Monopoly is a sin, especially that of foodstuffs.

The Druzes strongly believe in reincarnation, technically known as metempsychosis. All souls were, according to Druze belief, created at the same moment in time. Upon death, a soul is instantly reborn in another human body. The body serves on this earth as a temporary home for the soul, all souls being created with an equal capacity for good and evil: free to choose between right and wrong and responsible for the consequences of their choice. The soul experiences in its successive reincarnations all conditions of life, such as fortune and misfortune, riches and poverty, health and illness. Souls are thus granted repeated opportunities to redeem themselves and face an equitable sentence on the Day of Judgement. This must be the case, the Druzes believe, for otherwise there would be no divine justice among mankind.

Reincarnation, however, produced a dilemma for those who advocated it: how to explain the excess of deaths over births in the Druze community. The solution was ingenious: surplus Druzes, whose souls were unable to find a habitat in the community, were reborn in China; that country being chosen because, at the time, it was so far away that verification would have been impossible. It is common in Druze funerals to hear the mourning chant: 'Niyyal ahl al-sean sa'at wasltak,' which translates as, 'Happy are the people of China at the hour of your arrival.'

Reincarnation, of course, is not a belief exclusive to the Druzes and their religion. Searchers, scientists and thinkers all over the world, throughout the ages, have believed that an explanation was necessary to give meaning in life where death is not the end nor birth the beginning. In the Old Testament, ancient Jews believed in rebirth, and there were great sages in Israel who believed in the transmigration of souls. The ancient Egyptians believed in life after death and constructed boats for their pharaohs to 'sail on' in them. The very same belief surfaces in early Christianity, Mohammedanism, Masonry and Theosophy, and is fundamental to the Hindu and Buddhist doctrines of the East.

The Druzes firmly believe in universal brotherhood and in keeping faith with all those who live in their midst, whatever their religious beliefs, provided they offer no insult and do not threaten the welfare and independence of the community; or are not involved in any case of blood vengeance.

From its very inception in 1017, the Druze Faith demanded the abolition of slavery and polygamy – courageous and revolutionary measures at a time when both institutions were an accepted part of life. It was many centuries later before the West abolished slavery by law. Concubinage and temporary marriage, or *Muta'h*, were likewise forbidden, *Muta'h* being the right given to a man to marry a woman on a temporary basis for a period of a month or more, usually practised when a man was on a visit away from home. Once his visit was over and he wished to return to his permanent residence, he then divorced the woman. This social device supposedly served as a deterrent to prostitution, and was practised alongside permanent marriage at the outset of Islam. It continued during the rule of Abou Bakr, the first caliph, who succeeded the Prophet Mohammed, but was prohibited by Omar, the second caliph, though the Shi'ites, unlike the Druzes, continued to consider it a legitimate practice.

The Druzes respect their women and treat them with the utmost courtesy. From the beginning, the Druze religion preached equality between the sexes. It rejected the traditionally entrenched belief that woman was inferior to man and established women's right to share privileges as well as responsibilities equally with men. Druze women, in the past, attended councils of war, were consulted and had their opinions respected. They were chosen to head delegations of men on important missions. When, in 1034–5, a dissident movement arose within the followers of the Faith in the far regions of Wadi et-Taym, in the Anti-Lebanon mountains, Baheddin Al-Muqtana, the chief aide to Hamzah ibn Ali, the proclaimed Imam of the Druze Movement, chose a young woman, Sitt Sarah, to head an all-male delegation to proceed from Cairo to quell the dissidence in that turbulent and hostile place. It was a most delicate and dangerous mission. A previous male messenger, one of Hamzah's close aides, had been assassinated upon arrival.

Sarah's mission was a success because the dissidents were captivated by her wisdom, knowledge and sincerity. What was most remarkable, apart from her leadership as a woman in charge of what was, in those times, definitely a man's job, was the fact that the delegation she headed included her father, the brother of Baheddin Al-Muqtana. He did not mind serving under his daughter and was unconcerned that his brother had not entrusted him with this important mission. Both reactions were an early example of the Druze belief in the equality of men and women. It is hard to find a more dramatic example of disciplined acceptance of women's leadership and authority. Sitt Sarah was the earliest of many women to earn their place in the gallery of fame in Druze history. The principle of equality applies as much in the community as it does within the family. There have been wives who, after the deaths of their feudal husbands, ruled and governed efficiently, with benevolence and justice.

Colonel Churchill noted in *Mount Lebanon* how 'the status and position given to females, amongst the Druses, are peculiary characteristic of that people', and contrasted it with the attitudes he observed among both the Mohammedan and Christian Arabs, who were alike in viewing the 'intellectual pretensions' of women 'with supreme contempt ... the duties of the harem, and superior excellence in household arrangements' being 'the highest meed of praise to which they can ever aspire'. Mohammedan women seemed 'little better than slaves'.

> The Druses, on the contrary, by the very nature of their religious proceedings, invite and acquiesce in the influence of female superiority. In the Druse Holowés [*Khalwis*], the male and female Ockals [*Uqqals*], though, as a matter of form, divided by a screen, imbibe together the truths imparted by the reading of their sacred books, together sympathize in all the emotions which they call forth ...
>
> Indeed there are some Druse ladies now in Mount Lebanon, whose wisdom, tact and discrimination, are so highly prized by the immediate relations amongst the Sheikhs, and they too, some of the most influential leaders of the Druses, that no project would be considered complete, unless it had been submitted to their judgement and approval.

Druze women possessed 'great physical, as well as moral courage', in the words of Colonel Churchill, and were capable of animating their husbands into action on the field of battle, or even of shaming them by their own tenacity and valour.

> During the last civil war of 1845, when the village of Betater was threatened by an overwhelming body of Christians, the Druses contemplated abandoning the place, and one of the principal Sheikhs proposed to give the signal for retreat. 'Do you call yourselves men!' exclaimed the wife of Sheikh Kassim Abdel Melik. 'Give me a tarboosh and sword, and I'll lead out the clan!' The voice of the heroine prevailed, and the Druses went forth to battle, and conquered.

As a rule, the women join the ranks of the *Uqqals* soon after marriage. Most of the men join once age catches up with them and they realize the time has come to renounce the pleasures and passions of life and accept they should spend their time in the work of prayer, doing good and following the teachings. This gives the elders a position of prestige in both the family and the community. The Druzes revere their elders and treat them with the utmost respect. Old age for them implies wisdom and experience. Children seek advice from grandmothers and grandfathers, and then abide by it. They accept that their elders will know what is best for the younger generations.

The Divine Call was addressed to men and women alike. In fact, women accepted it more quickly and enthusiastically than men. Their reputed piety, chastity, modesty and sobriety greatly helped to promote their rapid admittance to the ranks of *Uqqals*, and the number of *Juhhals* among them has been small indeed by comparison with the men. From the start, the Druze religion called upon women to learn how to read and write so they might comprehend fully the religious teachings and join the ranks of the *Uqqals*.

A nineteenth-century Lebanese scholar noted: 'Few are the Druze women who cannot read and write.' Colonel Churchill observed in 1853 that 'reading and writing became common, even amongst Druze females'. Puget de Saint Pierre, writing his *Histoire des Druzes, peuple du Liban* in the middle of the eighteenth century, stated that, 'Druze women were better instructed in religion than men. It is they who are charged with teaching other women the content and meaning of their sacred books.' He might have added that it is they who are also charged with teaching their children the most basically important moral and social codes of their religion.

Hence it is in their homes that Druze children learn from their mothers and grandmothers the difference between right and wrong, and it is there, in their early years, that their character is shaped for life. It was my mother who taught us, her children, our religion, our faith in God and in ourselves, and the standards of behaviour we were expected to adopt towards our fellow human beings.

The Druze religion has allowed divorce under certain conditions, and the woman, equally with the man, has a right to ask for a divorce. In practice, however, divorce has, contrary to the Druze religious teachings, been the husband's prerogative. When the Imam Hamzah instructed that equality between men and women should be established, he issued the following instructions to regulate that equality:

When a Unitarian takes to himself a Unitarian sister as a wife he shall treat her as his equal and share with her all that he possesses. If separation becomes necessary and it is the wife who wishes to leave her husband, although it is known, to trustworthy people, that he is fulfilling his obligations towards her, then he is entitled to half what she owns. If he fails in his obligations and she chooses to leave him, he has no right to anything that belongs to her. Should the husband decide on the dissolution of the marriage through no fault of the wife, she is entitled to half of all his possessions.

Possessions were later defined as including silver and gold, clothes, house and furniture, livestock, orchards, vineyards, shops, commerce, books and papers.

A bride is, by Druze tradition, chosen by the groom's mother and the groom vetted by the bride's parents. Yet it is forbidden to marry a Druze woman against her will, and seldom has any bride been coerced by her parents into accepting a groom she does not wish for. The young woman herself has always had the final word. Nevertheless the intended couple will not have had the slightest chance of meeting or even of seeing each other. They will have needed to rely on their parents' choice and on what they hear about one another's virtues and faults from the community. In the case of my own father, his mother chose his bride, but my father was a rebel and stubbornly insisted on at least being allowed to see his future partner. In the end a compromise was reached. The bride-to-be was invited, with her mother and aunts, to visit my grandmother. My father was then secretly allowed to glimpse his future bride through a keyhole. Despite this novel process of bride selection by peep-hole, the marriage lasted sixty-six years in an atmosphere of happiness and exemplary family life.

Nearly all the parentally prearranged marriages of my father's generation and earlier were successful, secure and happy. Druze girls were taught early in life how to be good housewives, to believe in marriage as a holy institution, to live in peace with their husbands and to live for their children and the family life in which they chose to be partners. Yet times change, and such a style of marriage is no longer acceptable today, except among the religious *Uqqals*. Others are free to make their own choice of partners, to court, to flirt and even dance with them. I recently heard that a disco has been built in Baaqline, in the heart of the Druze country. My father would turn in his grave at the news; my grandfather would perform somersaults.

The present generation thus make their own choice, and also their own mistakes. Divorce has become more frequent, whereas it was very rare among earlier generations. There was never a divorce in my own family, which traces its history back to before the eleventh century, until lately among the younger generation of Alamuddins.

Charity is enjoined on the Druzes. It is the suggested responsibility of a person of means that he should, when he makes his will, leave one twelfth of all he possesses to the poor, the needy and the pious. However, this requirement is voluntary and it is left to each to act according to his own discretion and conscience.

Compassion is also enjoined when slaughtering animals, so as to cause a minimum of suffering. The same applies to birds. 'Know that birds are communities, like yourselves. They are secure in their nests, protected by God,' is a proverbial Druze belief. This injunction is, alas, shamelessly violated by members of all religions in the Lebanon of today, where birds of every kind are shot mercilessly for sport. It is impossible to forget or forgive the way storks overflying Lebanon were senselessly slaughtered during the war, shot down with rifles and machine guns. It was no consolation or justification that the Lebanese were also at that time ruthlessly gunning down one another, so why, in their opinion, should the storks be spared?

Giving hospitality and aid to those who ask for it is second nature and earns a blessing. To the Druzes, the most blessed food is that around which many hands gather. A Druze will sacrifice his only sheep or his last chicken to feed a guest. To refuse help to whoever seeks it is a dark shame, not only for the one who refuses but also for all his family. The French traveller Volney often witnessed the lowliest of peasants giving their last morsel of bread to hungry travellers, their only answer to the accusation of imprudence being, 'God is great and liberal, and all men are brothers.' 'It would be easy to illustrate by many a striking incident the fidelity with which they keep inviolate the pledge tacitly given to the guest who has eaten their bread and salt.'

'In Druze land,' wrote General Charles Andréa in *La Révolte Druze*, 'hospitality is sacred.' No Druze, whatever his social level, would refuse to admit to his house even 'his most mortal enemy if he comes seeking food and refuge'. A malefactor or dangerous criminal would receive the same privilege, and any attempt by the authorities to enter the house to arrest such a person represented 'a blow to the honour of the head of the family'. Colonel Churchill had made similar observations almost a century before when he said that the Druze sheikhs invariably received strangers of every description with the utmost hospitality.

> Should persons in distress arrive, or wandering minstrels, as is often the case, a collection of money is made for them. Each Sheikh is taxed according to his known means, and the Kahwaji, or coffee maker, goes round and collects the respective contributions . . . As an asylum for fugitives, or persons seeking concealment, the abode of a Druse Sheikh is inviolable. Nothing can induce him to give up the individual to whom he has extended his shelter and protection, or to give the slightest intimation as to his locality . . .

These customs were observed by all Druzes, not just the sheikhs, though the sheikhs claimed a priority in honouring such obligations. The visitor to a Druze village where no feudal sheikh lived would find the inhabitants vying with one another over the honour of being his host. As a result there was never, in the past, any reason for hotels to be built on Druze land, though in this respect too times have changed.

A few years ago a hotel was built in Baaqline, the heart of Druze land. Others will no doubt follow, so long as there is a period of lasting tranquillity in the region to allow it.

At this point it may be helpful to explain what it signifies to be a Druze sheikh. It is simply the hereditary title of a male member of a noble Druze family. He is thus the head of a clan, and not to be confused with the more recent phenomenon of the so-called 'oil sheikhs'. There is less than a score of Druze families whose male members may claim this honoured title. High-ranking *Uqqals* and Moslem religious leaders are also called sheikhs, but in their case it is a religious denomination which has no feudal standing and is not hereditary.

Self-discipline holds a prominent position in the Druze code of ethics, self being defined as man's worst enemy when it embodies pride, envy, hatred, anger, fears and desires. Such passions, if allowed free play, enslave the individual and bring about his perdition. To control and rule them rather than be controlled and ruled by them requires the most arduous of struggles. It takes the strictest training and strenuous self-discipline to help one to gain mastery over the rebel self, but that is the surest path for man to find God.

One of the most deeply rooted aspects of Druze traditional behaviour is their extreme sensitivity and their dauntlessness in the exaction of revenge. Blood feuds are a stern reality. The duty of the avenger of blood is a sacred obligation. Should the occasion fail soon to present itself for the fulfilment of revenge, they will wait with patience for the opportunity, and when it is found the waiting will in no way have diminished the heat of their desire for vengeance. Some might contest the propriety of including such an obligation among the commanded social behaviours, but for a majority of Druzes the failure to honour it brings shame not only on the individual directly concerned but also on his whole family. It needs to be strongly emphasized, however, that Druzes mainly seek revenge for murder. They will take to this trail only after the authorities responsible for law and order have shown themselves unable or unwilling to apprehend and punish the murderer.

Druze folklore and legend abound in grim and daring stories of retribution. Two from recent times deserve special mention, the first of which concerns a group of young men, from a prominent Druze family, who emigrated in 1904 to Buenos Aires in the Argentine. Shortly after their arrival some of them left the capital for the countryside in a quest for work and trade. There they were set upon by a gang of bandits, and two of their number were killed.

The news reached their family in Lebanon, who, in accordance with Druze tradition, declined to hold a funeral service for the dead until their murder had been avenged. The brother of one of those killed, and Mohammad, his young cousin, who was of giant physique and famous for his fighting ability, assembled their travel papers and departed for Buenos Aires, where, upon arrival, they were given the fullest details of the ambush. They then began to formulate their plan, which started with learning the language. When they were ready, they contacted the Argentinian authorities and obtained approval to mount a raid against the culprit gang. Finally, accompanied by other family members from Buenos Aires and volunteers from other Druzes in the country, they launched a successful attack on the bandits, killing four, wounding others and dispersing the rest.

The story of this mission of vengeance spread widely among the Lebanese community in the Argentine and among the Argentinians themselves. Mohammad, as leader of the Druze raid, was asked to call on the chief of police of Buenos Aires, who offered him a job in the force. The offer was thankfully declined. Since he had fulfilled his mission, Mohammad only wanted to return to Lebanon. The chief then asked whether, as a special favour, he might consider performing one further mission, to capture or kill a notorious *bandido* named Juán Córdoba, who had given the police force much trouble.

There was a generous reward for his capture, dead or alive, and so Mohammad accepted the assignment, attracted by the challenge, the substantial reward and the desire to return the favour of having been allowed to avenge his cousin's murder. At the head of a force of Argentinian police, Mohammad then engaged the bandits' headquarters in a ferocious six-hour battle. The *bandido* Juán he slew himself in a fierce, hand-to-hand knife battle, and most of the gang also died in the engagement. The reward was promptly honoured by the government and Mohammad presented with the personal effects of the *bandido* Juán. These included, among other mementoes, a magnificent broad gun-belt studded with silver coins and silver ornaments. Mohammad ever after proudly cherished the belt as a valued trophy. It was hung, for all to see, on a special peg in his sitting room, only leaving its prominent position when he presented it as a gift to Sultan Pasha Al-Attrash, the hero-leader of the Druze revolt against the French in 1925. Even today, a blown-up photograph of Mohammad dressed in the garb of the *bandido* Juán Córdoba continues to hang on the wall of his family home in his Lebanese village.

The second saga of revenge also occurred in Latin America, this time in Brazil, and concerned the former Syrian President, Adib Shishakli, who came to power in 1949 by ousting and killing his predecessor through a *coup d'état* engineered by agents of the CIA. He ruled until 1954, when he, in turn, was ousted by another American-inspired *coup* and fled the country for Brazil, that haven of political refugees guilty of crimes against humanity. During his years in power, Shishakli had launched a vicious campaign against the Druzes in Syria, jailing many and murdering others. He had ordered the Syrian army to invade Jabal al-Druze, where it destroyed villages and killed many innocent people. This campaign of persecution was precipitated not by any act of the Druzes against the Syrian government or other fault, but purely by Shishakli's vindictive hatred of them.

The Druzes never forgot or forgave Shishakli for his treachery. They helped first with toppling him from power and then, according to their tradition, began to plot how they would exact a full revenge. They trailed him for ten years after he absconded, until, in 1964, he was assassinated by a young Druze who travelled to Brazil especially for the purpose.

The deep-rooted influence of their moral and social codes places the Druze peoples among the most, if not *the* most, ethical, moral, well-behaved and courteous of the Lebanese, Syrian and Palestinian communities. Those same codes have united the Druzes into a close-knit solid community, and though they are a minority, they command the highest respect and play a most important role in the affairs of the countries where they represent a significant part of the population. Of course, there are rotten apples in every barrel. There have been Druzes over the years who have failed to abide by the codes of ethical, moral and social behaviours prescribed by their religion. The Druzes have had their share, though a small one, of the misfits to be found in any society.

All the aforementioned codes of behaviour are still strictly adhered to and respected by the *Uqqals* (females and males) and by most of the *Juhhals*. But today it is also true that some of the younger generation, contaminated by the disruptive backwash of modern civilization and influenced by the evils of the war in Lebanon, are failing to adhere to or have respect for all the strict traditional standards so faithfully practised by their parents and grandparents. Those few Druzes who took advantage to appropriate what was not theirs during the civil war in Lebanon, have sought to justify their actions as a right to the spoils of war. Yet their actions, whatever their justification, remain stark violations of the codes of ethics uncompromisingly respected by the Druzes since the Divine Call was first proclaimed. Fortunately those who have compromised their

73

own people's standards to this extent are so far a small minority, but the longer that chaos continues its reign in Lebanon, the larger their numbers will sadly grow to be.

4. The Ottoman Empire and the Reign of Fakhruddin II

The headquarters of the Druze Faith may have been in Cairo, but its doctrines were to thrive in Mount Lebanon and the Anti-Lebanon range, in northern and south-western Syria, in and around Damascus and in northern Palestine. Thus were the Druzes in Lebanon from the very beginning. And for seven hundred years Lebanon was known as the 'Mountain of the Druzes'. Lebanon and Palestine were, at the time, part of Syria, and the Arab tribes who responded to the Divine Call and became Druzes spread all across Syria in more areas than they occupy today.

The Tanukhs, or Buhturs, were the first powerful feudal Druze tribe to leave north Syria early in the eleventh century to settle in the Lebanese mountains east of Beirut. They were ordered to do so by the caliph, to defend the coast and protect communications. The Ma'anids were, in the twelfth century, the second feudal tribe to leave Syria for Lebanon after their defeat in the north by the Crusaders. They followed in the footsteps of the Tanukhs, with whom they were related through marriage, their orders being to assist the Tanukhs in protecting the coastal plains. The Tanukhs welcomed them as honoured guests and kinsmen, and legend tells how, one clear sunny day, the Tanukhi host took the elder of the Ma'anids up to the highest mountain east of Beirut, which overlooked not only the coastal plains but also a large and mostly uninhabited stretch of hills and valleys to the east. The host said to his guest, '*Shoof,*' which in Arabic means, 'Look.' The Ma'anid elder liked what he saw and gratefully accepted the proposal that he should move with his clans to settle in that land, thereafter called the Shouf. There the Ma'anids prospered and grew in strength until they equalled and eventually surpassed the Tanukhs in Druze supremacy. They became emirs of the Shouf and ruled as feudal lords over that important part of Lebanon, which was, and continues to be, the heart of Druze land.

At the time of the Ottomans, Lebanon was, as it is still, divided into fiefdoms ruled by political feudal lords of all the indigenous religious sects, Druzes, Christians, Shi'ites and Sunni Moslems. The one distinction between the political feudal lords then and those of the present is that the Ottomans appointed the feudal lords, whereas the feudalism of today has become hereditary and self-appointed, even though its roots in most cases go back to the feudalism of Ottoman times.

The Ottomans were so named after the Turkish Sultan Othman (1288–1320), who founded the Ottoman Empire, which comprised most of the countries of the Middle East. Every subject of the conquered countries was considered to be an Ottoman, but the Turks alone held power and ruled the empire from Istanbul. The Ottoman Empire was to last for six and a half centuries, until replaced in 1919, much reduced in size by Atatürk's democratic movement, to what is now known as the republic of Turkey.

The Ottomans commissioned the feudal lords of Lebanon to levy and collect taxes on their behalf. This task the feudal lords performed efficiently and excessively, exploiting the people they ruled and passing very little of what they collected on to the Ottoman treasury. The greater portion went to line their own pockets. Similarly, most of the political feudal lords of Lebanon today exploit the people in their fiefdoms. The manner and style of exploitation may differ from Ottoman times, but the spirit remains the same.

In the early sixteenth century, the most powerful of the Druze feudal lords was Fakhruddin I, appointed by the Ottoman Sultan Selim to be King of the Mountains (Sultan el-Barr) for having given support to the sultanate in its struggle with the Circassians and their ultimate defeat in 1516. The Sultan had also been greatly impressed by Fakhruddin's eloquent and courageous speech when he and other feudal lords of Lebanon travelled to Damascus, the seat of the Ottoman governor, to congratulate Sultan Selim on his magnificent victory in crushing the Circassians. Sultan Selim was one of the very few Turkish monarchs to speak Arabic well.

Fakhruddin's power and prestige soared to majestic heights after his appointment, and he was soon acknowledged as the supreme chief of Lebanon's feudal lords. He gathered most of them about him, and they all looked to him for leadership. One of his greatest achievements was to befriend the Christian feudal lords and the Christians, and make them feel an important part of the Lebanese family. He appointed Kiwan Ibn Ne'meh, a Maronite Christian whose mother was from the Gemayel family of Bikfaya in Lebanon, to be his ambassador to Damascus.*

The Maronite Christians of Lebanon derive their name from their patron saint, Saint Maron, who lived near Antioch in Syria and died about the year A.D. 410. Persecuted by the Jacobites, his followers found a safe refuge in Mount Lebanon. The newcomers were amalgamated with the Mardaites, whom the Byzantines had used as recruits against the invading Arab Moslems. Under their patriarch, John Maron, who died in A.D. 707, the community developed a degree of autonomy in northern Lebanon. As an offshoot of the early Syrian Church, the Maronites still use

---

* In the twentieth century, Sheikh Pierre Gemayel was the founder of the Phalangists, the militia of Maronite Christians, and, with his sons Bashir and Amin, played an important role in the Lebanese war.

Syriac in their rituals, though they are Arabic-speaking. It is a fact well-attested to that they rendered at the time of the Crusades a significant service to the Franks by acting as guides and fighting on their side. They were drawn close to Rome, but union with Rome was not effected until the eighteenth century.

The career of Fakhruddin I ended when he was invited by the Ottoman Turkish governor to visit him in Damascus and was treacherously assassinated on arrival. No reason was ever given for this act, but it was suspected that Fakhruddin's friendship with the Christians of Lebanon had aroused the governor's fanatic Islamic wrath.

Fakhruddin I was succeeded by his son Qurqomaz, whose name in Turkish means 'He who is not afraid'. Qurqomaz married Sitt Nassab, a Tanukhi Druze princess, who begot him two sons, Fakhruddin and Yunis. Sitt Nassab was a very capable and wise lady, a perfect wife and a caring mother. George Sandys, the English traveller who visited Lebanon in 1610, wrote of her eldest son, the great Druze prince Fakhruddin II, in *A Relation of a Journey* (1621) that 'he never commenced battle, nor executed any notable design without the consent of his mother Al-Sitt (Lady) Nasibah (Nassab)'.

Qurqomaz followed his father's policies of befriending the Christians and rallying them to be equal partners in the affairs of Lebanon. Many Christians were welcomed to enlist in his army, others were employed in his administration, and Christian peasants were encouraged to work as tenants on Druze agricultural estates. One of his wisest decisions, as was later proved, was his appointment of a Maronite Christian, Kiwan Ibn Ne'meh, his father's former ambassador to Damascus, to be general manager of his affairs.

Things were going well for Qurqomaz, and for the Druzes and Christians of his fiefdom, but fate moves in the strangest way. In 1584, a convoy *en route* for Constantinople, carrying taxes levied by the Turks in Egypt and Palestine together with other treasures destined for the Sultan Murad III, whose passions were gold and women, was ambushed and looted in the north of Lebanon. The Ma'anids and their Druzes were promptly accused by their enemy, Youssef Sayfa, the Turkoman feudal lord of Tripoli in north Lebanon, of being perpetrators of the ambush. In fact, it was Sayfa himself who attacked and looted the treasure-bearing caravan.

The Sultan dispatched Ibrahim Pasha, the Ottoman governor of Egypt, at the head of a considerable military force to retrieve the looted treasure, punish the culprits and teach a lesson to Qurqomaz and his Druzes, who, in the opinion of Murad, were now thoroughly above themselves. Sultan Murad's lessons were invariably taught in terms of murder, blood and treachery. As soon as he succeeded his father Sultan Selim II, he had inaugurated his reign by murdering his five younger brothers. (It is also said that when Murad III died, his son Mehmet III emulated and outdid his father's bloodthirsty style, and celebrated his accession by strangling his nineteen brothers.)

Ibrahim Pasha arrived with prodigious military trumpetings designed to strike terror into every heart. He at once sent ultimatums to the feudal lords of Lebanon, and to Qurqomaz in particular, ordering them to hand over the looted treasure and the culprits, and demanding that they pay the total expenses of his expedition. Once again, Qurqomaz was probably singled out because of his and his father's friendly policy towards the Christians, a tendency regarded as distinctly unottoman.

Most of the Lebanese feudal lords took fright and attended Ibrahim Pasha to assure him of their obedience and loyalty, but Qurqomaz, seeing his friends and allies deserting him and anticipating treachery from the pasha, fled with his wife Sitt Nassab and the rest of his family, Kiwan Ibn Ne'meh and a few of his most trusted aides, to a secret and inaccessible cave in the south of Lebanon. This refuge was chiselled out of the middle of a vast solid rock, inside which it stretched for over fifteen metres, with a number of interconnecting cave rooms leading off from the central passage. The face of the rock was a sheer cliff 350 metres high, with the cave's entrance 150 metres above the base of the rock and 200 metres from its top. It was accessible only through a very narrow path like a goat track, and entrance could only be effected by wooden ladders, lowered from the cave and withdrawn once their use was over. The cave could therefore be defended against the most determined onslaught.

It was not in Qurqomaz's character, nor in that of the Druzes, to flee any fight, no matter what the odds against them. The desertion of his allies was not a factor responsible for his action, nor was his mistrust of Ibrahim Pasha. He believed, however, that the anger and vindictiveness of the Ottoman Turks were directed at him personally, and at his family, rather than at the Druze community as a whole. He sincerely thought that, by removing himself and his family from the scene, he would ensure that the Ottomans left the Druze community in peace. In this he was grossly mistaken, as were 600 Druze *Uqqals*, invited by Ibrahim Pasha to meet him as a delegation so they might discuss and settle the ambush question peaceably.

The delegation accepted and paid their respects to Ibrahim Pasha, hoping to convince him that the Druzes could have played no part in an ambush at a location in north Lebanon more than five days' march from Druze land. The pasha received them cordially and invited them to dinner, then ordered their cold-blooded assassination in their sleep. Proud of this ruthless act, he decapitated their 600 corpses and sent the heads to Hafez Pasha, the Ottoman governor in Damascus, who, in appreciation, gave his daughter in marriage to Ibrahim Pasha and was pleased to acknowledge him as a son-in-law. As a great majority of historians record, Hafez Pasha was the most unprincipled, corrupt and bloodthirsty of all the governors the Turks ever sent to Syria.

Following the hideous slaughter of the *Uqqals*, Ibrahim Pasha proceeded to destroy Druze villages and massacre thousands of innocent Druzes. He also sent a large force to besiege the cave where Qurqomaz and his family were in refuge. Although the cave was a secure fortress, it had one vulnerable feature. The spring supplying it was located a little distance from the cave, and its waters needed to be brought in by a secret tunnel. The location of both spring and tunnel was known only to a very few of Qurqomaz's intimate group, but one among them betrayed him and managed, by a prearranged signal, to communicate the secret to the besieging force. They lost no time in polluting the water by slaughtering animals and throwing them into the spring. Despite every effort to purify the water, the pollution remained and Qurqomaz fell ill and died. The siege was then lifted only by the intervention of Sitt Nassab Tanukhi's family, through a payment of gold, that universal language of communication so effective with the Ottoman Turks at the time. Qurqomaz's family and his entourage were thus enabled to leave the cave for safety, but Sitt Nassab had every reason to mistrust the Ottoman Turks and to fear for her two sons' lives. Her elder son, Fakhruddin, was then only twelve years old.

Taking the advice of her Tanukhi brother, Prince Saif el-Deen, she decided to entrust the two boys to the Maronite Christian, Kiwan Ibn Ne'meh, her late husband's loyal friend and general manager. He, in turn, took them to the Al-Khazins, Maronite Christian feudal lords, who brought them up for six years, shielded from the threat of the Ottoman Turks' vindictiveness.

The story of the two boys being brought up by Al-Khazins has been challenged by a number of Druze historians as a propaganda invention recorded by Maronite Christian chroniclers. Others have claimed it to be only partly true, and that the Ma'anid boys were given refuge for a very short time before being returned to their Tanukhi uncles, who thereupon brought them up. Yet, in the light of Fakhruddin's subsequent actions after he acceded to power – he appointed the Al-Khazin sheikh as his prime minister and chief adviser, elevated the Al-Khazins to the highest rank of feudal sheikhs and showed generous tolerance towards the Christians – one is inclined to give credence to the story of the Ma'anid boys being taken into refuge by Al-Khazins for at least a period after the death of their father.

As the future Fakhruddin II grew, he came to be driven by three dominant passions: friendship towards the Christians; a desire to exact vengeance on Youssef Sayfa, the Turkoman feudal lord of northern Lebanon, for his false accusation against his father and the Druzes; and a deep-rooted hatred of the Ottoman Turks for having caused the deaths of his father, his grandfather, the 600 Druze *Uqqals* and the thousands of other innocent Druzes ruthlessly slaughtered.

As soon as he was eighteen, his uncle's family, the Tanukhs, turned over to him the rule of the Druze Shouf, the land they had managed to retain for him by making payments of gold and presenting lavish gifts to successive Ottoman Turkish governors sent to rule over Syria and Lebanon. Significantly, the appointments of all such governors were for short periods only, after which they were replaced by others from Istanbul. Doubtless this was to offer the chance to as many Turkish politicians' relatives and favourites as possible to make their fortunes quickly (a practice not infrequently turned to later by various colonial powers). In less than thirty years, it was said, the Ottoman Turks changed governors in Syria thirty-two times.

When the feudal power over the land of the Shouf was handed to Fakhruddin by right of inheritance, it marked the commencement of his reign as Fakhruddin II. In no time, the force of his three passions, combined with an unrestricted ambition and outstanding qualities of courage, determination and tact, a ruthless love for discipline and a brilliant personality, he succeeded in establishing a state that was virtually independent of the rule of the Ottoman Turks. His ultimate ambition was to free all Lebanon and Syria from their grip, and he managed, as a first step, to gain for the two countries an autonomous status. This he achieved by showering the Turkish governors and persons in authority with lavish gifts of gold and other treasure while paying Istanbul more in taxes than the Ottomans had ever before obtained from any other source.

Islam is a highly tolerant and compassionate religion, and Christians under Islam have on the whole been well treated in the record of history. An exception to this occurs with the treatment of the Christians of Lebanon under the Islamic Ottoman rule of the Turks, during which they were humiliated, persecuted and maltreated. Not long ago, a young Druze woman, studying for her PhD in Islamic architecture, visited Tripoli, a Moslem town in the north of Lebanon, where examples of Islamic architecture still abound. While walking down a well-preserved street of the Islamic period, she noticed it had two raised side-walks running parallel with the central section, which was sunk very much lower. This must, she remarked, be to channel flood water when it rained. 'No,' her guide corrected her, 'it is the part of the street which Christians were obliged to use.' In other words, they were intended to feel at all times that they were a very inferior breed. They were not even allowed to bury their dead in Tripoli. Even to the present day, Christians do not have a cemetery in the city, but must use one in a neighbouring Christian village.

In this context, the rule of Fakhruddin II represented a period of peace and freedom for the Lebanese Christian community. Following through with the policy laid down by Fakhruddin I and Qurqomaz, his grandfather and father, he put a decisive end to their persecution and annulled all practices of discrimination against them. He permitted them to build churches, toll their bells and practise their religious rites openly. They were allowed to ride horses, to wear white turbans, baggy trousers and silver-studded belts. They were also free to possess and carry silver-inlaid and decorated rifles. He enlisted many in his army and employed others in his administration. As we have already seen, his first act was to appoint the Maronite Al-Khazin Christian feudal sheikh, who had given refuge to him and his brother and brought them up as his own, as his prime minister and chief adviser, which posts the sheikh held for thirty-five years. He elevated the Al-Khazins to the highest rank of feudal sheikhs, and also retained the loyal Maronite Christian, Kiwan ibn Ne'meh, his father's general affairs manager, in the same post on his own staff.

Such was the radical change he brought about in attitudes towards the Christians that Pope Paul V dispatched to him a letter, dated 16 January 1609, in which he thanked him for his protection of the Christians and assured him of his friendship. With the letter the Pope sent gifts by the brother of the Maronite patriarch in Lebanon, who, stated the letter, 'will express to you our desire to help you against the Turks in order to liberate the Holy Land'.

Fakhruddin even allowed the Catholic missions, mostly French, to descend on Lebanon, to build their missions, convents and monasteries on land he freely donated. He gave them the freedom to practise their religious activities, which in retrospect was one of his few grave errors of judgement, for it was they who were to be mainly responsible for creating the religious fanaticism that sparked dissension between the Maronites and the Druzes and led to the fighting in 1841 and 1845, and to the bloodbath of 1860; and which has continued to inflame fanatical religious hatreds to the present time.

Freedom was similarly extended to the Jews to build their synagogues and practise their religious rites freely without restriction or hindrance. Fakhruddin went so far as to appoint a Jew, Abraham Nacmias, as his private treasurer.

As for Youssef Sayfa, who had falsely accused his father and the Druzes of the ambush of the treasure, the young ruler began to work for his destruction. There followed a long saga of battles, despite intermarriage relations, and Fakhruddin systematically annexed important areas of Youssef Sayfa's fiefdom. It took time for him to defeat his enemy completely, for the latter was a favourite of the Turkish governors in Damascus, who extended him every support. The Ottoman Turks had realized that the feudal system, as it then existed in Lebanon, contained all the elements for dissension and discord inherent in feudal ambitions for power and supremacy. This they were able to utilize to advantage and thus maintain power and control in Lebanon with a minimal military presence. Yet the domain of Fakhruddin II grew, until it extended, at one time, almost as far as Anatolia in the north, while in the east it included Palmyra in Syria, and in the south reached to Sinai.

Naturally enough this expansion of territory and spectacular growth of power, together with the ruler's religious tolerance of the Christians, were greatly resented by the Ottoman Turks, despite his generous gifts and strenuous efforts to keep their minds at ease. There was no shortage either of jealous Lebanese Moslem feudal lords to intrigue against him and pass on to the Ottomans accusations concerning his reckless policy of allowing freedom to the Christians, which they claimed represented a threat both to the Ottoman Empire and to Islam. The Turks, though resentful of Fakhruddin's expansion of power, paid little serious heed until, in 1613, he joined forces with Ali Pasha Djenboulad, the Kurdish Druze feudal lord of Aleppo, in open revolt. The two rebel leaders then marched on Damascus together and forced its surrender.

It so happened that, in 1611, Fakhruddin II had sent, as his envoy to the Grand Duke Ferdinand I of Tuscany and the Vatican, a Maronite bishop to negotiate a possible alliance against the Turks. The mission had been successful and the duke signed a commercial treaty with Fakhruddin, to which was appended a secret treaty of mutual military aid. As a result, when word of the victory over the Turks at Damascus spread to Europe, it prompted Ferdinand I to contact both leaders to offer aid in their fight against the Turks and to solicit their assistance for his scheme to liberate Jerusalem and the Holy Land. A former cardinal before his ascension to power, the duke was zealously motivated to achieve this sacred ambition.

In Istanbul, news of the surrender of Damascus and the agreement with the Grand Duke of Tuscany enraged the Imperial authority and it decided it could no longer ignore such an arrogant challenge to its power. An army of over 50,000 of its best fighting troops promptly marched on Aleppo and Damascus to quell the rebellion and re-establish authority over Syria and Lebanon. Advancing on Ali Pasha Djenboulad, they crushed his army outside Aleppo in a fierce battle. Ali Pasha himself withdrew his forces into the fortress of Aleppo, where he secured the commander of his army, his closest aides and his family, with provisions and ammunition to last at least three months, before proceeding to Persia to seek help.

With Ali Pasha out of the way, the commander of the Turkish forces proposed to the pasha's commander and a number of his aides that they should surrender the fortress in return for a substantial reward. Their greed made traitors of them and they accepted. The Turks at once slaughtered most of those inside the fortress and sold the members of Ali Pasha's family into slavery at public auction. The traitors then went to the Turkish commander to claim their promised reward, only to be addressed as follows, 'You dogs who betrayed your master and benefactor of yesterday will surely betray your master of today. This is why your heads will be cut off.' And so they were, and thus they became a well-deserved example to all treacherous opportunists.

When he learned of Ali Pasha's disastrous defeat, Fakhruddin acted swiftly to appease the victorious Turks. Knowing the most effective argument to be the use of gold, he sent his youngest son with Kiwan ibn Ne'meh to Aleppo, bearing 3,000 gold pieces. The precious metal exerted its usual charm and the danger was for the moment averted.

Fakhruddin felt sure this respite was temporary and a formidable Turkish military force would march against him before long. Anxious to avoid the defeat and humiliation suffered by his ally, he worked out a plan of action. He had established three impregnable fortresses in three well-chosen strategic locations in his domain, and these he stocked with enough provisions and ammunition to stand off any siege lasting at least three years. Each fortress had its own water supply from springs within its defences. One of the fortresses, that of Niha, known as 'Chekif Tiron', was in fact built around the very cave in which his father took refuge from the Turks some years before.

These three fortresses he then handed over to one of his sons and two of his closest aides respectively. Each commander was instructed to resist to the bitter end. Should he, Fakhruddin, be captured by the Turks, and should the Turks propose to exchange his freedom and life for the surrender of a fortress, then no such proposal was to be agreed to and fighting must continue to the last man alive. With the organization of all this complete, he handed the rule of Druze lands over to his brother and, on 25 October 1614, sailed with his company of sixty in three galleons, two French and one Flemish, headed for the court of the Medicis in Florence, there hoping to consolidate the promised alliance against the Turks. With him he took several members of his immediate family and a few of his trusted aides, led by Kiwan Ibn Ne'meh. The voyage was a long one of fifty days as a consequence of storms and rough seas.

Ferdinand I, with whom Fakhruddin signed the original treaties, had in the meantime died, but the delegation from

Lebanon was warmly and courteously received by his son, the new Grand Duke of Tuscany, Cosmo II. A palace was placed at their disposal, complete with servants, carriages and horses. A generous monetary allocation was also offered to take care of expenses. Invitations arrived from all over Italy, and Fakhruddin accepted every one to give himself and his party the opportunity to study Italy, the Italians and European progressive achievements and compare them with those of Lebanon. He took a keen interest in museums and homes for foundlings, and was astounded to learn that banks paid interest on deposits, such a practice being prohibited in Moslem countries. He was intrigued and amused to see men and women joining together in dancing, and was surprised to find sheep with no fat tails. In particular, he was charmed and dazzled by Florentine architecture, which he was in due course to import into Lebanon, where many old houses today still display the mellow beauty of that influence.

But Fakhruddin II had been right to assume that the breathing space won by his gold would be short-lived in Lebanon. As soon as he heard of Fakhruddin's departure for Europe, Hafez Pasha, at the head of an army 50,000 strong, marched on south Lebanon, his aim being the capture of two at least of Fakhruddin's three fortresses. He laid siege to the first he reached, but after eighty-four days of desperate but vain assaults, abandoned the attempt and marched on the Shouf, the headquarters of the Ma'anids.

Here Sitt Nassab, Fakhruddin's mother, came out to meet him at the head of a delegation of thirty notables, but most importantly with sacks of gold pieces and a promise of more to follow. Impressed by the gold, that paramount language, Hafez Pasha agreed to withdraw from the Shouf and to lift the sieges on all the fortresses. Nevertheless he insisted on holding Sitt Nassab as a revered and respected hostage in Damascus.

It was nothing strange to Hafez Pasha's character, but all too typical, that within the year he violated his own undertaking and marched on Fakhruddin's domain. This time he was badly defeated before he even reached the Shouf, and sent a cry for help to Istanbul, which quickly dispatched a large military force led by three Turkish pashas. Their fate against the Druzes was no more happy than Hafez's, and the enraged Turks brought up yet more reinforcements. Now Hafez, assisted by the toadying Youssef Sayfa and his men, and other Lebanese feudal lords jealous of Fakhruddin, marched on the Shouf and burnt the Ma'ani palaces and the houses of their followers, killing, looting and indulging in every form of atrocity. These outrages he then followed up by inflicting the same sufferings on the Ma'anids' kinsmen, the Tanukhs.

Meanwhile the Ma'anids Druzes had regrouped in a secluded Shouf valley, where, as Hafez marched against them at the head of a force of more than 20,000, they fell upon him with only 1,200 fighters and, with typical tenacity and supreme fighting skill, utterly routed his troops. Hafez fled with the remnant of his army towards Damascus, leaving behind large numbers of dead and wounded.

Smarting beneath this humiliating defeat, Hafez gathered together what was left of his forces and again requested reinforcements. He plotted to lay siege to and attack the two Ma'ani fortresses which lay alongside his route back to Damascus, but his plans of vengeance were still in the early stages when word came from Istanbul that his pasha protector had been strangled in his bed on orders of the Sultan. Devastated and demoralized, Hafez abandoned the planned fresh offensive and beat a hasty retreat to Damascus, from where he was quickly recalled to Istanbul.

He was replaced in Damascus by a governor whose strategy of government followed a completely different style. The new governor at once released Sitt Nassab and assured her of his friendship towards the Ma'anids. He also, it is said, sent messages to Fakhruddin in Italy, inviting him to return and resume his rule over the Druze lands. Simultaneously he resorted to the tested and tried policy of divide and rule, inciting feudal lords and party factions in Lebanon to fight between themselves rather than turn against the Turks. In this success came to him easily and civil strife between the various factions raged for two years, with the Turks as satisfied spectators, enjoying the spectacle of the devastation of Lebanon at the hands of its own inhabitants.*

Matters reached a climax on one single day in 1617, when four bloody battles took place between the feudal lords, leaving many mansions and villages destroyed and hundreds dead and wounded. The Ma'anids and the Tanukhs, however, emerged victorious from this latest bout of feuding and consolidated their power over Lebanon as a whole.

In the meantime, in Tuscany, Fakhruddin II was discovering, as he pursued the main objective of his visit, that the Grand Duke Cosmo was beginning to prove evasive. It seemed he did not share the zeal of his late father to liberate Jerusalem and the Holy Land, nor was he enthusiastic about dispatching troops to fight in those distant territories. To give him his due, he did send emissaries to consult the other European powers who might hold views on the subject. France meanwhile, being on especially friendly terms with Turkey, offered to mediate to settle Fakhruddin's problems with Istanbul. On this basis, King Louis XIII invited Fakhruddin to visit Paris. The Lebanese leader thanked the king cordially for his kind invitation and excused himself from accepting the offer of mediation.

Spain showed a keen interest, and the Spanish king, Philip III, sent by way of Duke Cosmo a warm invitation for Fakhruddin to visit Madrid, promising, in addition to the required assistance, the gift of 'a government superior to

---

* The Lebanese of today have fallen into the self-same trap, as they have pursued, for almost two decades, an insane war of destruction to fulfil the interests of outsiders.

that of Lebanon on condition of his becoming a Christian'. Fakhruddin duly expressed his thanks and gratitude to the Spanish monarch for this generous gesture, but stressed he was in Europe to seek military assistance, not a new government or a new religion.

The Vatican itself, of course, remained anxious to join in any effort to liberate Jerusalem and the Holy Land. To the Pope, too, Fakhruddin therefore sent a message of grateful thanks. He expressed his appreciation of His Holiness's interest in Lebanon and its affairs, but also courteously reminded the Pope that he, Fakhruddin II, 'protected the Christians' and that the Maronites of Lebanon 'were very dear to him'.

Nearly five years had passed since Fakhruddin's arrival in Italy. During that time he had become steadily more convinced that it would be impossible to obtain aid from the Europeans for his struggle against the Turks. He suspected that he had been paraded as an Oriental curiosity and that his refusal to convert to Christianity was a turning-point in his relations with his hosts. The atmosphere had cooled considerably and courteous hospitality been replaced by an aloofness bordering on hostility. The Grand Duke Cosmo cut his monetary allocation and Fakhruddin had to sell some of his wife's jewellery to meet daily expenses. When, in retrospect, he commented on this episode, in a letter to his people, Fakhruddin wisely observed: 'For a weak party to negotiate with a strong one is a variety of begging. I therefore advise you to depend upon yourselves, above everything else, if you desire to achieve a secure independence with a respectable position among nations.'

By now he was tired of it all and wanted only to return to Lebanon. A ship had arrived with letters from his mother, Sitt Nassab, asking him to return, and from the Turkish governor of Damascus, awarding him again the government of Lebanon. He therefore sought an audience with the grand duke, and told him that his ageing mother had written to ask him to return to his homeland and he was anxious to comply with her request. 'Then we will not detain you,' said the duke curtly.

Happy with this permission so instantly obtained, Fakhruddin sent his family and the rest of the party ahead to board at Leghorn (Livorno) the ship that was to take them to Lebanon. But when he later arrived at the port to rejoin them, he was told by the harbourmaster that he must once again obtain the permission of the grand duke. Back he went to Florence, where the duke now told him that he opposed his departure. Had he not, during his long stay in Italy, acquired knowledge and information that could be invaluable to the Turks should they seek to invade Italy? Fakhruddin was deeply shocked by this insult to his integrity, and even more so when the grand duke then advised him to go to Istanbul. He told the Duke Cosmo, 'If I had wanted to go to Istanbul, I should not have come hither.' He felt disgusted by this transparently shabby trick to discover whether he had thoughts of travelling to the Ottoman capital to betray the Italians.

The look of indignation and dismay on Fakhruddin's face at this insulting insinuation from the host who welcomed him so warmly when he first arrived in Italy must have been only too clear to the grand duke. After a further interval of just a few days, Fakhruddin was told that Duke Cosmo opposed his departure from Italy no longer and he was free to join his family and followers on shipboard, bound for Lebanon.

Yet Fakhruddin remained wary and suspicious of Duke Cosmo's intentions, and boarded the ship with a large barrel of gunpowder. He let it be known that, at the slightest attempt to hinder his departure, he would fire the gunpowder and blow up the ship, its crew, himself and his family and followers rather than set foot again on Italian shores. The ship then sailed without a hitch, to bring Fakhruddin and his group back to their homeland in the spring of 1620.

The weather was so stormy that spring that the ship was only able to anchor in the port of Acre, but within a short time all the feudal lords of Lebanon had arrived to congratulate Fakhruddin on completing his journey safely and welcome him back. His journey from Acre to Sidon then became a triumphal march to re-establish him in his palace there.

Once he was settled down again, Fakhruddin II undertook an objective review of his European experience. He had been badly let down and a signed treaty had gone unhonoured. But though he was greatly disappointed, he was not discouraged. Far more was he convinced that, if he was to succeed in liberating Lebanon from Ottoman Turkish rule, he must do it himself with the help of the Lebanese and no one else. He had meanwhile gained much useful experience in Europe, but even more important than that was realizing who his friends were, on whom he could count at home, and who his enemies were, who would readily betray him.

His plans to consolidate his power after his return, together with whispers leaked by the Europeans to the Turkish government about his efforts to solicit aid against them, reawakened anger and fury in Istanbul. Fakhruddin II therefore perceived his position as highly precarious, and once more resorted to gold, the true 'Turkish delight' and the strongest tool of persuasion. He sent the colossal sum of 200,000 gold pieces to Istanbul and requested confirmation of his power over Syria and Lebanon. The gold did the trick and an Imperial *Faraman* (decree) was promptly issued, appointing Fakhruddin governor supreme of the entire region from Aleppo to Jerusalem. He was addressed in the decree as 'Sultan el-Barr', 'King of the Mountains', the same title given by the Ottomans to his grandfather, Fakhruddin I. The decree invested Fakhruddin II with unrestricted powers to levy and raise taxes, repair roads, construct fortresses and outposts and take any action he considered necessary.

This important title to power was resented intensely by the local Turkish governor, the Pasha of Damascus, who declared he would not abide by it and would resist any attempt by Fakhruddin II to exercise his rule over the domain granted him by Istanbul. He gathered a large military force and proceeded to demonstrate his defiance of the decree. Fakhruddin at once assembled a counter-force of 12,000 fighting men and went to meet the pasha in a battle that went decisively in his favour. The governor himself fell into the hands of Fakhruddin's warriors and was carried off a prisoner. As his scattered troops turned to beat a hasty retreat to Damascus, Fakhruddin ordered a cessation to the fighting and asked them to remain. The Pasha was then brought before Fakhruddin in his shame and humiliation, and was astonished to be offered every courtesy and respect, as if the Druze monarch still considered him governor. The release of all prisoners was then ordered and Fakhruddin's warriors escorted the governor on the first leg of his journey back to Damascus. Thus pacified, and bearing with him Fakhruddin's gifts of twelve pure Arabian horses and a purse of 30,000 gold pieces, the pasha acquiesced in all the powers given Fakhruddin by Istanbul.

The feudal lords and other rival factions in Syria and Lebanon were as stunned by Fakhruddin's daring victory over the Pasha of Damascus as they had been by the unexpected and unprecedented conferment of immense powers by the decree from Istanbul. They ceased their quarrels and rallied about Fakhruddin, seeking his favours and hoping for a share in his power. The result was five years of undisturbed peace. Fakhruddin proceeded to take back lost territories and to annexe new ones, carrying out his plans with military skill and diplomatic astuteness. He eliminated his old enemies, starting with Youssef Sayfa, who was crushed with his family and his followers, though the lives of women and children were spared. Also spared was the life of his son-in-law, the son of Youssef Sayfa, to whom Fakhruddin had given his daughter in marriage at a time of an attempted reconciliation, forced on him by the Ottoman Turks. He then continued his drive for retribution by liquidating all others who had betrayed him or the Ma'ani family during his absence in Europe.

Secure in his position as undisputed chief and ruler of Mount Lebanon, Sidon and Galilee, Fakhruddin II began to devote time to modernizing his domain, especially Lebanon, and to leading it into the path to progress. Architects and irrigation engineers were imported from Tuscany, as were agricultural experts to introduce the Lebanese farmers to improved agricultural methods and up-to-date agricultural implements and bring in cattle to improve local breeds. In return, Fakhruddin exported horses to Tuscany, and meanwhile the Italian architects helped to beautify and fortify Beirut and to introduce an Italianate style in architecture to Lebanon and the Lebanese. European merchants were encouraged to settle, attracted by specific privileges, including protection from pirates.

As Fakhruddin ruled over his extended domain with fairness, firmness and wisdom, so all the communities came to prosper, especially the Christians. This was the period when European Catholic missionaries were welcomed and permitted to build their convents and their monasteries on freely granted land. The Shouf also received from north Lebanon considerable numbers of Christians who became the founders of the Maronite villages to be found in Druze land even till today.

Fakhruddin welcomed them and extended to them assistance and courteous treatment. More churches, monasteries and convents were built on land freely given by the ruler. For the first time, Druzes and Maronites came into close contact and lived peaceably and amicably alongside each other. Fakhruddin's chief counsellor was a Maronite, and another commanded his army, while at times up to 20,000 Maronites were enlisted in his forces.

As time went on, more and more Europeans came to the shores of Syria and Lebanon and freely practised profitable trade with the inhabitants. All of this, however, especially the favoured treatment of the Christians of Lebanon and the successful expansion of his power, created hostages of fortune for Fakhruddin. Certain lords, fired by jealousies encouraged by the Turkish pashas in Damascus, intrigued to enrage the Ottoman Turks and earn Fakhruddin the angry displeasure of the Sultan Murad IV. Murad was the most powerful of the Ottoman monarchs, the conqueror of Baghdad, whose two most potent passions were, according to many historians, gold and the shedding of blood. It is estimated that he had 25,000 people executed during five years, a large number of whom he killed by his own hands.

In 1632 Murad IV instructed his military commanders to put an end to this adventurous upstart in Lebanon, and a formidable land force, supported by the most power-ful Ottoman fleet, was ordered to proceed to Syria and Lebanon to finish the career of Fakhruddin II once and for all. The land forces engaged the Ma'ani forces, led by Fakhruddin's son Ali, in the plains mid-way between Damascus and Beirut, and Ali was killed in the battle. His death greatly saddened his father, for he had been not only his favourite son but his right hand on which he greatly depended. Fakhruddin became deeply depressed and determined to prevent further loss of life in a struggle he believed to be futile. He knew, this time, that his forces could never withstand the powerful Turkish land forces and their mighty navy. He also believed that it was he whom the Turks sought to destroy, rather than his own or the other Druze communities in the domain over which he ruled. Therefore, to save his people's lives and the destruction of their properties, he allowed himself to be captured by the Turks, together with his three surviving sons, the youngest still being yet a child.

Father and sons were sent as prisoners to Istanbul to await the Sultan's pleasure, and again Fakhruddin made offerings. He took with him mules loaded with gold and other valuables. The accounts of historians vary as to the number of loads, and while some say it was two mule loads, others raise the number to fourteen. Regardless of amounts, the gold calmed even the fierce heart of Murad IV. The Sultan, pleased with the gifts, listened to Fakhruddin's explanations and forgave him on condition that he did not return to Lebanon, but stayed on in Istanbul. Thus, for two years, Fakhruddin and his sons lived quietly and in peace. Not so Fakhruddin's enemies, who continued to foment intrigue and at last convinced the Sultan that Fakhruddin had committed an unforgivable crime against the Ottoman Empire and Islam. They claimed that not only did he love the Christians, but that he was a secret convert to Christianity itself. A forged document, leaked to the Ottomans, falsely stated how, in 1633, he was baptized by his Capuchin physician.

As a result, on 13 April 1635, Fakhruddin II and two of his sons were executed by strangling, Turkish style, with bow-strings in a public square. His third son was spared. Fakhruddin's head was then spiked on a spear and paraded through the streets as the head of a renegade who had dared to defy Islam and the Turks. Such was the Sultan's pleasure. To justify inflicting these cruel deaths, the Ottomans then spread the fabrication that a crucifix had been discovered on Fakhruddin's person at the time of his execution.

Historians have been unanimous in their tributes to Fakhruddin II and all that he achieved for Lebanon. In his assessment of him, Colonel Churchill wrote, in *The Druzes and the Maronites under the Turkish Rule*:

Thus perished this famous Arab Emir, whose ambitious
activity, energy, and talents, might, under better
auspices, have been made subservient to the welfare of
his countrymen. For his mind was grand and capacious,
his disposition mild and tolerant, and his general
character calculated to elicit the love and confidence
of the people. During the short space of time he
was in possession of plenary power, his measures
were framed for the promotion and advancement of
the public interests, and evinced a zeal and taste for
improvement, almost amounting to patriotism. His
inflexible sense of justice, tempered and fostered no
doubt by the exigencies of his political position, rather
than instigated by principles of religious toleration, left
him entirely free from even the slightest tinge of bigotry
and fanaticism; and all sects, but more especially the
Christians, found security and protection under his
government.

The Lebanese sectarian communities, who rarely harmonize
on anything, agreed without exception that Fakhruddin II
was the greatest of all their rulers. Whereupon each tried
to claim him for its own. The Moslems claimed he was a
Moslem, the Christians that he was a Christian. The Druzes
alone knew for certain that he was one of themselves: a great
Druze leader in whom they could for all time continue to
take immense pride.

The outstanding feature of Fakhruddin's reign had been
religious tolerance, especially towards the Christians. To
them he had granted the right freely to exercise their faith
and privileges hitherto reserved for Moslems. But he himself
stood above sectarian religions. He was a Lebanese who lived
and died for Lebanon, and for its unity. Today that unfortunate war-torn country badly needs another Fakhruddin II
to show the insanely destructive Lebanese by example how
their survival depends on their unity as one Lebanese family,

and that the question of who wields power in Lebanon is unimportant beside that of how that power is used to serve the interests of all the Lebanese, and not merely those of one or another religious sect alone.

5. The Ma'anid Succession and the Two Bashirs

Lebanon lost its autonomy with the death of Fakhruddin II, and all who governed after him did so under dominant Turkish rule. It was a rule exercised with malice and retribution in mind, for the Ottomans continued to smart over the memory of Fakhruddin's victorious independence and could never forgive him for having sought Christian European aid. The Druzes especially were hated by the Ottomans for their unceasing struggle for independence and the frequent defeats they inflicted in battle, which represented humiliations for the Turks. During the Ottoman rule of Syria and Lebanon, the Druzes are said to have waged fourteen battles against them, winning eleven and losing only three. The factor to irk the Ottomans most was that while the Druzes represented the most powerful community in Lebanon, so that the Turks could not avoid continuing to appoint them as rulers, they were also, by definition, the group from which there was most to fear.

Several Ma'anid Druze princes therefore succeeded Fakhruddin II, all appointed by the Ottomans. The first of these was Ali Alamuddin, the Alamuddins being the Druze standard bearers, whose name in Arabic means 'The Flag of Religion'. Prince Ali, then his sons, ruled the Mountain of the Druzes from 1633 to 1667. Other Ma'anids were next appointed to take over from the Alamuddins, until, in 1697, the Ma'anid male lines became extinct and the Lebanese feudal lords were instructed by the Ottoman Turks to meet and elect a successor. The man they chose was Bashir Shihab I, a notable Sunni Moslem and a kinsman of the Ma'anids by marriage. The Ottomans, however, withheld approval and insisted the succession must go to twelve-year-old Haydar Shihab, grandson of Ahmad Ma'an and a distant relative of Bashir. In this they were insisting on the principle of hereditary descent, and it came about that a compromise was reached whereby Bashir I would rule as regent till Haydar came of age.

It would be a mistake to think of this election of an emir of Lebanon by the feudal lords as a liberal democratic practice sponsored by the Ottoman Turks. Far from it: such a practice was primarily designed to provoke jealousy and dissension among the Druze feudal lords and to fire individual aspirations to be selected ruler of Lebanon. By provoking the Druzes into fighting between themselves, the Turks could thus cleverly exploit to the full their policy of divide and rule.

The Druzes and the other communities in Syria and Lebanon had for quite some time been split into two feuding clans – the Qaysites and the Yamanites. These divisions were a legacy of two early Arabian parties, the Qaysites being emigrants from north Arabia, and the Yamanites earlier emigrants from southern Arabia. The Ottoman Turks had naturally encouraged the split, especially among the Druzes, the most warlike of the communities, for it was far easier to control and rule two parties than it was a motley collection of unruly feudal lords; and while they were in power, the Shihabs followed the same tactic.

Bashir Shihab I's rule (1697–1707) in fact turned out to be relatively peaceful, but his ward, Haydar, when he came of age and assumed power, soon fell foul of the Ottomans. The governing Turkish pasha took the decision to appoint Yousef Alamuddin as Emir of Lebanon to replace Haydar, and Yousef ejected Haydar from his headquarters at Dayr al-Qamar and assumed power in his place. His rule, however, was short-lived, for the Alamuddins were Yamanis, and the Druze Qaysis, who supported the Shihabs, were furious at Haydar's defeat. They gathered their forces and attacked the Yamanis at Ayn Dara, a village east of Beirut, defeating them and wiping out the Alamuddins, together with their closest supporters.

According to some historians, the Alamuddins were exterminated in the Ayn Dara massacre. Others have claimed that one or more younger boys escaped and eventually kept the Alamuddin line going, hence the family's existence today. These claims may be substantiated in the light of the Druze rule of war, which decreed that only males between the ages of seven and seventy were to be killed in battle, the inference being that there must have been Alamuddin males under the age of seven who escaped. Whatever the truth may be, the princely title proved to be expensive to keep up after the Alamuddin's assets were plundered by the victors in the battle of Ayn Dara, and a wise ancestor changed it to the more modest sheikh.

The Qaysi massacre of the Yamani Druze leaders drove their followers out of Lebanon to settle in what later became Jabal al-Druze in Syria. It was a migration that greatly weakened the Druzes in Lebanon by losing them their dominant position. In the meantime, Haydar Shihab was restored to power and took advantage of the Qaysi victory at Ayn Dara to reform the Lebanese feudal system at the expense of the defeated Yamanis. Their fiefdoms and property were redistributed among the Qaysi feudal families, while the Maronite Christian feudal families received an increased share of the Yamani lands and of feudal power, the aim being to create a balance of power between them and the Druzes.

The Maronites, owing allegiance to the powerful Jumblatt feudal lords, were happy and contented with Haydar's reshuffle of the Lebanese feudal system. For one thing, there was the sizeable loot they received as their portion of Yamani land and property. For another, there was the privileged and influential position they gained with Haydar Shihab, the Emir of Lebanon. Working to their advantage above all was the suppression, for the time being, of the dissensions among the Druzes, leaving the Qaysi Druzes under the Jumblatt leadership as the only strong Druze party in Lebanon. Little did the Qaysis realize the price they and the rest of the Druzes would have to pay in the future for the Yamani defeat and Haydar's reshuffle of feudal power.

Under Haydar Shihab (1711–32) and his son Milhim (1732–54), Lebanon enjoyed a further period of political and peaceful stability, during which the influence of the Christian Maronites grew. They prospered in trade and in silk production. They became rich and started money-lending businesses which were the precusors of modern banking. They made loans to the Druze feudal lords, who never believed in the need for work and indulged in lavish expenditures; and then, unable to repay the loans, parted with their lands to the Maronite money-lenders. Money, as we know, breeds money, and generates power and even more power. The Maronites went from strength to strength to the extent where Emir Milhim Shihab, the Sunni Moslem, anxious for their political support, baptized his two sons and converted them to Maronite Christianity. Thus began the reign in Lebanon of the Christian Shihabs, which was to last all the way through to the year 1842.

The consequence of that initial act has been assessed by Dr Kamal Salibi, a Christian, in *The Modern History of Lebanon*:

The conversion of Emir Mulhim's sons to Christianity in 1756, and the succession of the Maronite Yusuf Shihab in 1770 finally set the seal to the Druze decline. But although the Maronites were now recognizably the dominant group, the Druzes remained a powerful force with which the Shihabs had to reckon. The Maronite

Shihabs, in fact, were so concerned about keeping Druze goodwill that they refrained from publicly admitting their Christianity, and for a long time continued to profess Druzism.

It is difficult to estimate how soon the Druzes became aware of their own loss of power. For a long time they continued to regard the Maronites as allies, and apparently remained without suspicion of Christian political ambitions. Maronites were allowed to settle freely in the Druze villages; so were the Greek Orthodox and Greek Catholic immigrants from inner Syria, who arrived in Lebanon to swell the country's Christian population. But Druze hospitality was not always received with good grace by the Christians. Visiting Lebanon during the reign of Emir Yusuf (1770–88), Volney was struck by the Druze religious tolerance 'which contrasts sharply with the zeal of the Moslems and Christians'. Druzes and Christians live together at peace, he says; 'but the Christians often display an indiscreet and annoying zeal which might cause this peace to be disturbed'.

As it was, the peace between the Druzes and the Christians in Lebanon remained undisturbed for many years. Throughout this time, the prevailing issues in the internal politics of the country were the unceasing struggle for power among rival Shihabs and the conflict between the Yazbaki and Janbalati Druzes.

The Druzes lost their control over Lebanon with dignity and grace and showed no rancour. They remained, however, a political power to be reckoned with and continued to live in perfect harmony alongside the Christians as valued neighbours and good friends. Any disagreement in Lebanon at that time was taken up on party lines and never had a sectarian religious basis.

When Milhim retired in 1754, he nominated his brother

Mansour to replace him. This angered his other brother, Ahmed, and a rift between the brothers now split the Lebanese feudal lords between two new sets of allegiances: the powerful Qaysi Jumblatts, who supported Mansour, and the equally strong Yazbakis, whose leader was Sheikh Abdal-Salam Yazbak, chief of the Druze Imad family. It was thus that the Qaysi–Yamani clan rivalry was replaced by that between the Jumblattis and Yazbakis, to which Druzes and Christians in Lebanon both continued to belong until the nineteenth century, when the Christians renounced their membership of the clans and it became exclusive to the Druzes down to the present time.

The Jumblattis, led by the Jumblatt family, and the Yazbakis, led by the Arslans, are the two families which have shared equal power and authority in the Druze community until the time of the present war in Lebanon, when the Jumblattis took the unquestioned absolute lead. The rift between the two clans has been consistently utilized in the cause of 'divide and rule', originally encouraged and spurred on by the Turks, but then also by the French and finally by the successive Lebanese governments since independence in 1943. These internal political differences notwithstanding, the Druzes never ceased to show their ability quickly to close ranks and emerge as a formidable fighting force to confront any who threaten their rights or land, or their well-being and survival as a community.

But, in the perspective of history, the quarrel between the two Shihab brothers was to bring about their downfall. Mansour relinquished power in 1763 to his nephew Yousef, the son of Milhim, who reigned from 1770 to 1788. It was Yousef's bad luck to have to deal with Ahmad Al-Jazzar, the governor appointed by the Ottoman Turks, whose career, according to Professor Philip Hitti's account in *Lebanon in History*, began when, as a sixteen-year-old Christian Bosnian, he had to flee to Constantinople after attempting to rape his sister-in-law. Having sold himself to a Jewish slave-dealer, he then became the property of Ali Bey, the notorious governor of Egypt, and was soon promoted to executioner. In this work in Cairo,

> he acquitted himself with such dexterity and cold-bloodedness that he acquired the surname of al-jazzar (the butcher), a surname in which he ever thereafter took pride and successfully tried to live up to. From Cairo he went to Damascus, joined the Syrian army and for his service was rewarded with the governorship of Sidon.

In Sidon he established himself in Acre, fortified the town by the use of forced labour, secured a monopoly of the Mediterranean ports and their trade, and established himself in luxury. The governorship of Damascus came to him in 1780 by a decree of the Sultan, and for 'about a quarter of a century thereafter this cut-throat ruled as virtual viceroy of Syria and arbiter of Lebanese affairs'. In Lebanon he pitted one party against the other and found in that rich and prosperous country a gold mine ripe for exploitation. His greed and love of money knew no limits. He demanded exorbitant tributes and tax contributions. The burden of these was loaded on to the shoulders of the people of Lebanon, who grew loud and bitter in their resentment.

The point came where Al-Jazzar's demands were impossible to meet, and Yousef Shihab supported a rebel movement against him. But the rebellion failed. Al-Jazzar sent his troops into Lebanon and in 1789 forced Yousef to abdicate and appoint his nephew, Bashir Qassim Shihab, in his place. Yousef surrendered to Al-Jazzar, and was later executed at the specific request of Bashir Qassim in an astoundingly ungrateful and disloyal gesture. Yousef Shihab had made Bashir Qassim welcome to his court and brought him up as a well-loved relative.

Bashir Qassim, better known as Bashir II, or Bashir the Great, at once became the tool of Al-Jazzar, obeying his orders and satisfying his every whim. Meanwhile, as Professor Hitti says, no major setback marred the career of Al-Jazzar, until it

ended in 1804 by natural death, a rather unique record in the annals of the period. The name of this usurper dictator has lived in local annals as a synonym of unscrupulousness and sadistic cruelty. A native chronicler reports that on a mere suspicion of infidelity he personally dumped all thirty-seven of his harem, dragged one after the other by his eunuchs, on to a burning pyre.

The death of Al-Jazzar left a gap within which Bashir II enjoyed full, despotic power, an advantage he swiftly utilized to rid himself of his remaining opponents. He began with Yousef's sons, who were, in the words of Dr Kamal Salibi, 'cruelly persecuted, and finally blinded and left destitute, while their supporters were hunted down or lured to their deaths'.

The Emir next turned against the Druze emirs and feudal sheikhs, robbing them of their wealth and prestige. The Arslans, Talhuqs, 'Imads, and 'Abd al-Maliks, one family after the other, were opposed and reduced to subservience, and only the Janbalats were left to enjoy their feudal privileges undisturbed.

Bashir II in fact went out of his way to befriend Sheikh Bashir Jumblatt, the most illustrious of the Druze feudal lords. He lulled his suspicions, heaped honours upon him and took no important decision without consulting him. Sheikh Bashir Jumblatt was substantially the more powerful of the two in the numbers of fighting men he could muster, as well as in wealth. He therefore made the perfect ally. The two

Bashirs were soon very good friends. They worked together and shared power for almost thirty-six years, and Sheikh Bashir Jumblatt's support kept Bashir II in power and was essential for the stability of his rule.

In assessing this partnership, Colonel Churchill said:

> Great wealth, combined with no inconsiderable degree of that tact and adroitness, these remarkable characteristics of the Druze character, had conspired to place the Sheikh Bashir Jumblatt in a position, which for many years gave him the chief direction of affairs in Mount Lebanon. In fact, the Emir Bashir II had even been under singular obligations to the family of Jumblatt, and the support he had on so many occasions received from that influential quarter, had been one of the main elements of his success, as a perusal of his past history will amply testify. The close friendship and intimacy, therefore, which sprung between Emir Bashir and Sheikh Bashir was but natural and the ordinary consequences of the antecedent alliance of their families.

The intimate friendship between the two Bashirs, and the mutual respect they had for each other, were misapprehended by many and gave rise to the popular expression, 'The Sheikh governed, the Emir only held the seal of office.' Even the traveller and historian Burckhart, renowned for his accuracy of observation, was influenced to write: 'The power of Emir Bashir II, however, is a mere shadow, the real government being in the hands of the Druze chief Sheikh Bashir Jumblatt.'

Regardless of the views of historians, the partnership between the two Bashirs was one based on mutual respect, admiration, appreciation of the value of true and genuine advice and, most important of all, real friendship. It was to last for nearly thirty-six years, which in the lives of men of power represents a record rarely equalled. Both were bound by the single objective of maintaining peace, stability and prosperity for Mount Lebanon. In this they were successful until the invasion and conquest of Syria by the Egyptians in 1833.

The Ottoman Turks, under Sultan Selim I, had, after invading and conquering Syria in 1516, gone on to conquer Egypt the following year. Syria, at the time, extended from the Taurus Mountains in the north to Suez in the south, the whole of that territory being better known as Bilad Ash-Sham (the 'countries of Damascus'). By the beginning of the eighteenth century, the Ottoman Empire was showing signs of disintegration as a result of corruption in its administration and European interference in its affairs. It was at this point that the Egyptians, under Mohammed Ali, rebelled against the Ottoman Turks and freed Egypt from their rule. They next planned an expansion to the north and took Syria from the Ottomans in 1833. Emir Bashir Shihab II quickly switched his allegiance from the Ottoman Turks to the Egyptians, and in fact went even further, in the opinion of Dr Kamal Salibi: 'For the duration of the Egyptian occupation of Syria, Emir Bashir II remained in power in Mount Lebanon as a vassal to the Egyptians.'

Even as a vassal to the Egyptians, Bashir II gained immense power and prestige, much enhanced when he recruited 7,000 Maronite Christians to rally to the aid of Ibrahim Pasha, Mohammed Ali's son, as he tried to quell a Druze revolt in Jabal al-Druze – an uprising that had already cost Ibrahim Pasha 15,000 casualties. But recruiting Maronites to fight the Druzes greatly angered Sheikh Bashir Jumblatt, and shattered to its foundations the long-standing friendship of the two Bashirs. It also deeply incensed the Druzes and sowed the first pernicious seeds of the Druze-Maronite feud.

There were other very grave errors of judgement committed by Emir Bashir II, but these had the effect of alienating the Druze and Maronite communities alike. The first arose from the crippling taxes and tributes he foisted on all his people so he could satisfy incessant Egyptian financial demands and meet the lavish expenses of the magnificient court and palace he built for himself in Beit-Eddine to feed his over-inflated ego. He increased threefold the dues the Ottoman Turks had levied and introduced many heavy new taxes that squeezed both Maronites and Druzes of possessions and property. But knowing the wealth of the Jumblatts, he targeted them especially for the major part of his levied tributes, setting out to bleed his erstwhile friend and supporter, Sheikh Bashir Jumblatt, of wealth and power.

His second action was to order the Druzes and Maronites to send conscripts to serve in the Egyptian army, an instruction he followed up by effecting the command of Ibrahim Pasha and ordering both communities to surrender their arms. Each community refused Emir Bashir II's orders. The Turks had taxed them heavily and drained their resources, but never had taken away their sons or asked them to give up their arms. To the Druzes this second command was tantamount to asking for their lives. The Egyptians wanted to take everything, and in this, it seemed, they had the approval and active assistance of their vassal, Emir Bashir II.

The Druzes, led by Sheikh Bashir Jumblatt, took up arms against Emir Bashir II, who with the help of the Egyptian military power succeeded in crushing the rebellion. The emir then took ruthless vengeance upon the Druzes, appropriating for himself their lands and properties. He razed the Jumblatt's palace to the ground and destroyed the houses of their supporters.

Sheikh Bashir Jumblatt fled the mountain to go to Jabal al-Druze, but on his way was arrested in Damascus, and sent to Acre, the seat of the Egyptian pasha. Here he was well received, a fact which greatly worried Bashir II, who wrote to Mohammed Ali in Egypt, urgently requesting Bashir Jumblatt's death. Mohammed Ali issued the order, and Sheikh Bashir Jumblatt was duly strangled in Acre.

Sheikh Bashir Jumblatt's rebellion had been against Emir Bashir Qassim Shihab II. It was in no way a war against the Maronites. The Druzes resented the emir's rule and the way he was systematically robbing them of their lands and feudal rights. They hated him, moreover, for having recruited 7,000 Maronite fighters to support the Egyptians in their counter-attack on the Druze uprising in Jabal al-Druze, and for his specific and treacherous request to Mohammed Ali for Sheikh Bashir Jumblatt's execution.

All in all, the Shihabs were to rule in Lebanon for 143 years (1697–1840), appointed by the Ottoman Turks and in general approved by the Druzes, without whose support they could never have maintained power. Two of the Shihabis, however, were responsible for the damaging decline of Druze power and influence in Lebanon. First there was Haydar, who engineered the massacre of the Yamani Druzes by the Qaysis at Ayn Dara and followed it up with the reform of the feudal system by distributing most of the Yamani Druze land to Maronite Christian feudal lords so as to achieve, for the first time in Lebanon, a balance of power between the Druzes and the Maronites. Secondly, there was Bashir II, who, with the help of the Turks and later the Egyptians, persecuted the Druzes, confiscated their lands and literally crushed them with the help of the Egyptian invading army.

It was these events that finally consolidated the Druzes' hatred for the Emir Bashir Qassim Shihab II and the Shihabs in general. Their confidence in that family had been deeply shaken when the Shihabs converted to Maronite Christianity. The Shihabs' subsequent rule then became a Christian Maronite rule of dominance, whose bias against the Druzes was demonstrated on every occasion.

For the Maronites, on the other hand, Emir Bashir II was the architect of the Lebanon they sought. He was certainly an ambitious and able administrator, a rigid disciplinarian, generous in his hospitality and a paragon of justice. But besides all these, he was also extremely ambitious, ungrateful, ruthless and cruel, and unforgiving in his enmities. He ruled over Lebanon as a despot whom the Christians loved and admired but the Druzes resented and never accepted.

He, in turn, hated the English and their missionaries, as well as the American missionaries. Of this aspect of his rule, and the influence of the Maronite clergy during the latter part of his reign, Colonel Churchill wrote in *The Druzes and the Maronites*:

> the Maronite patriarch and his clergy had acquired
> an influence and ascendancy most flattering to their
> aspirations. The emir, at their dictation, had sternly
> prohibited anything tending to religious toleration. The
> early efforts of Protestant missionaries were promptly
> crushed. Any one who was known to hold intercourse
> of any kind with Englishmen or Americans, was
> immediately put under the ban of excommunication.
> The idea was sedulously impressed on the minds of
> the Christians, that the English were freemasons and
> infidels, and as such, outcasts from the Holy Catholic
> and Apostolic Church. On the arrival of the British
> Fleet off the coast in 1840, a decree was issued through
> the mountain, that whoever went down to look on the
> ships should have his eyes put out. Every means that
> ecclesiastical ingenuity could invent was put into motion,
> to prevent the ingress of English ideas, political or
> religious, amongst the native Christian communities.

6. The Fomentation of Druze and Maronite Hostility

In due course, the leading European countries, worried about Mohammed Ali's ambitious plans, rallied to the support of the Ottoman Turks, and the Egyptians were ejected from Syria and Lebanon. With the Ottomans returned to power, Emir Bashir II feared the consequences of his collaboration with the Egyptians and in 1840 fled to exile in Malta. The Europeans now urged the Ottoman Turks to appoint as Emir of Lebanon a highly capable Sunni Moslem Shihab, but the Maronite patriarch strongly opposed such an appointment, insisting that only a Maronite Christian would be acceptable. When an equally capable Maronite feudal chief was proposed as emir, the patriarch also refused to accept him, and insisted that the post must be given to yet another Bashir, a Maronite Shihab. It was a well-known fact that this Bashir was weak, inexperienced and incapable of ruling, his one qualification being that he was the patriarch's protégé. But at this point France and Austria boosted the patriarch's intransigent stand with strong support, and as a result Bashir III was officially appointed in 1840 to be Emir of Mount Lebanon. The Druzes not unnaturally viewed the appointment of another Maronite Shihab with much apprehension.

Since I write as a Druze, I am aware that I may be accused of taking a partisan view of the historical consequences of the rule of Bashir II and that of his successor, Bashir III, especially since these consequences have continued to have an effect down to the present day in relationships between

the Maronites and the Druzes. Yet I may truthfully claim
that I am no hostile fanatic. My wife is a Christian, as
are the majority of my friends – most of them Maronite
Christians. From my father, likewise no fanatic, I learnt to be
not only a Druze, but also Lebanese. He was a firm believer
in Lebanese unity, and among his four closest friends, three
were Maronite while the fourth was a Shi'ite. To him they
were like brothers, and to us children they were uncles:
members of our family as much as we belonged to theirs.

My father always had a high regard for the Christians,
especially for the Maronites, though he was strongly critical
of their clergy. It was the latter, he believed, who had never
ceased to fan the flames of fanaticism and who nurtured a
hatred of the Druzes for inflicting defeats on the Maronites
in the civil wars of 1841, 1845 and 1860. Whenever I listened
to my father's fulminations against the Maronite clergy, I
used to feel that his opinions on their nefarious activities
were unreasonably exaggerated. As I progressed with the
research for this book, however, I discovered that many
independent historians have shared my father's suspicion of
their responsibility in promoting an undying enmity against
the Druzes among their own people.

It is probably impossible to escape accusations of bias
altogether in assessing the events of the nineteenth-century
civil wars, but to make my account as objective as possible,
I have chosen to base it directly on that of Colonel Churchill,
as an impartial witness who lived in Lebanon at the time and
had neither a Maronite nor a Druze axe to grind.* In his view,
the misgivings with which the Druzes observed the coming
to power of Bashir III, under the patronage of the Maronite
patriarch, were to be 'fully justified by subsequent events'.

There was at this juncture a chance for reconciliation with

---

* Unless otherwise stated, the quotations used throughout this chapter
are from Charles Henry Spencer Churchill, *The Druzes and the
Maronites under the Turkish Rule from 1840 to 1860* (1862).

the Druzes, who had suffered such injury under Bashir II, especially during the last stage of his rule. Unfortunately Bashir III had neither the tact, the personality nor the wish to pursue such a course.

> Haughty, arrogant, supercilious, and fancying himself able to carry out the iron policy of his predecessor, the Emir Bashir III seemed to take a delight in insulting all the Druze sheikhs who came into his presence. He constantly menaced them with a deprivation of their feudal privileges, declared his intention not to leave a Druze sheikh or the son of a Druze sheikh in the possession of even the shadow of authority, and to distribute the Druze feudal districts amongst the members of his own family.

The patriarch himself then stepped in to issue a decree, circulated to all the Christians of Lebanon, to the effect that each village or town should appoint by bond two representatives as their agents, who would take over the administrative powers up till then the exclusive preserve of the Druze sheikhs in their own fiefdoms. The intention was to supersede and overthrow 'the ancient and hereditary Druze feudal rights in the mountains ... [a] scheme – it may almost be said of conquest – to achieve which the patriarch and his colleagues were already prepared to draw the sword'.

It was a deliberately contentious act on the part of the patriarch. The Christians of the town of Dayr al-Qamar, which fell within the domain of the Druze Abou-Nakads (who had already suffered considerable privations under Bashir II), greeted the 'circular' with exultation, singing and firing off their guns in the streets. The Druze sheikhs looked on astonished at this demonstration, but it was only the beginning. The next move by the emir, under the patriarch's direction, was to order the Druzes to close the Protestant

115

schools recently opened in their villages, which held out
to them such opportunities for social advance. A respected
Druze leader, Naaman Bey Jumblatt, attended the patriarch
with a vain personal appeal that this swingeing and offensive
mandate should be withdrawn. As the patriarch gave him
a devious answer, the Bishop of Beirut was heard to boast
aloud that 'ere long the Maronites would drive the Druzes
out of the country'.

The European powers in general had endeavoured to
impress on Istanbul the need for an even-handed solution to
the artificially created tensions of the Lebanese communities.
But the French, for their own reasons, had decided to throw
the weight of their influence firmly behind the Maronites.
They now reinforced their standpoint with a grant of at least
20,000 gold *livres* to the patriarch, to 'enable him to carry out
his views, if necessary, by force'. The Druzes, observing this
development with alarm, began to come together and 'take
measures for self-preservation. With such feelings on both
sides,' wrote Colonel Churchill, 'it was clear that a collision
was merely a question of time.'

Matters initially came to a head in an incident at Dayr
al-Qamar on 14 September 1841. Dayr al-Qamar was
largely Christian, and stood across the deep and beautiful
valley which separated it from the largely Druze community
of Baaqline. On that day a party of Christians crossing
the ravine provocatively trespassed on a Druze shooting
preserve, only to be chased off by Druze watchers wielding
sticks. The Christians, instead of apologizing for the trespass,
at once summoned reinforcements, who arrived fully armed
from Dayr al-Qamar and opened fire indiscriminately on
the Druzes. It was clear they had been seeking a pretext
for launching a revolt, and the consequence of their vicious
attack was inevitable: the Druzes too sprang to arms and
began a counteraction.

As the Druze forces rallied from every direction, panic
seized the people of Dayr al-Qamar, as they realized they

had stirred up a hornets' nest. The town descended into chaos, with a Druze assault expected at any moment. It was only the intervention of the British consul-general, Colonel Rose, who rode out with a Druze sheikh and physically stepped between the two sides with 'reasoning and entreaties', that prevented this mêlée from marking the start of an immediate civil war. It left, however, the dangerous legacy of sixteen Druzes and five Christians killed, and sixteen Druzes and eight Christians wounded. Among the Druze dead were four senior sheikhs of the house of Amad, besides several women who had tried to intervene to stop the fighting.

For the Druzes, motives for revenge began to combine with an increasing sense that they must intensify defensive measures. Incidents against them continued, including the murder of three Druze rent collectors at Jezzine. In the meantime, the patriarch declared that 'if the Druzes persisted in demanding to be governed by a prince of their own sect, he and his clergy would head the Maronites, march against them and exterminate them'. And the Emir Bashir III worked 'to deprive the Druze sheikhs of their feudal privilege, and proceeded to levy a military force amongst the Christians, their feudal dependants, thus directly invading the hereditary rights of the "Druze feudal lords"'. Especially alarming was a rumour put about to the effect that the reinstatement of Bashir II was being considered.

The Druzes took the decision to make a pre-emptive strike at Dayr al-Qamar, Bashir III being then in residence at his palace there.

On the morning of the 13th October the feudal array of the Jumblatts, the Abou-Nakads, and the Amads, with their banners flying and kettle-drums beating, were seen, as if by enchantment, in possession of the various avenues leading to Deir-el-Kamar, and crowning all the surrounding heights. Never was a combination

more rapid or complete, or more characteristic of
that secrecy, energy and activity, for which the Druze
are so remarkable in their military movements. The
Christians, panic struck by the suddeness of the assault,
snatched up their arms and ran about in the utmost
consternation. The Druzes kept stealthily converging
on the devoted town. For some hours they met with an
irregular but vigorous resistance in the outskirts. These,
however, they at last succeeded in taking possession of
and burning. The Christians were finally driven back
into the central square, where all their families began
to congregate about sunset. Throughout the whole day
Beshir III remained shut up in a small room carefully
secured. Shortly after dark the principal suburbs were
in a blaze. During the whole of the ensuing night,
the town presented to view one grand but melancholy
spectacle; the sky being lighted up with rolling volumes
of flame, whilst every now and then might be heard the
desponding cries of Christians, the furious tolling of the
Maronite bells and the exultant yells of the Druzes.

For two more days the struggle continued, with 'considerable slaughter' in near-by Christian villages. 'When Druze
vengeance is once aroused,' wrote Colonel Churchill, 'it
is remorseless. They imbrue their hands in blood with a
savage joy that is incredible. Yet, as a general principle,
they never touch women.' The total destruction of Dayr
al-Qamar, with the massacre of its male inhabitants, was
averted only by another intervention from Colonel Rose,
who this time travelled from Beirut with the Turkish pasha.
The angry Druzes settled down to blockade the town, and
ensure there would be no escape route open to Bashir III.
   The patriarch had never imagined such a defeat for the
Christians at Dayr al-Qamar. Although he was ill at the
time, he 'loudly demanded to be carried in his bed ...
to the front of the Christian forces, "there to unfurl the

standard of the Cross, and die at their head"'. At Zahleh, the Greek Catholic bishop supported the patriarch with a proclamation declaring 'a holy war'. The Christians of the Greek Orthodox Church, on the other hand, as a rule joined the Druzes in attacks on the Maronites, and wherever conflicts occurred, it was usually the Druzes who triumphed. Within ten days the Maronites of the Druze domains were completely subdued and their villages and convents reduced to charred ruins. The Druzes 'prepared to carry the war into the purely Maronite districts, north of the Dog river'.

At this point Naaman Bey Jumblatt stepped in to use his prestige and influence in the cause of moderation, and announced that he personally would attack any Druze force that tried to cross the river.

> Sitting up day and night, surrounded by his secretaries, he wrote upwards of ten thousand letters to different influential Druzes and Christians, imploring them to cease from their fratricidal war. Thus was the triumphal course of the Druzes stopped by one of their own leaders. The Maronite patriarch, bewildered by the sweeping success of those he had thought to exterminate, shut himself up at first in a room in his convent, and finally negotiated for refuge on a British man-of-war.

The seige at Dayr al-Qamar was lifted on 5 November, when Bashir III agreed to the Druzes' terms of surrender, as ratified by the Ottoman pasha. His departure was 'one continued scene of mortification'.

> On leaving his palace, accompanied by some mounted attendants, his sword and dagger were taken from him with such violence as to wound his hands. He was deprived of his turban and the greatest part of his

dress. On approaching Beyrout he saw his own private
residence, the houses of the Shehab emirs, and those
of the inhabitants in the villages near Beyrout all in
flames. He beheld his Maronite subjects fleeing in the
greatest disorder along the front of the Turkish camp
of regular troops, who had been ostensibly sent to
restore order, but who all along remained tranquil and
even rejoicing spectators of every kind of outrage. The
Turkish irregular cavalry were charging, wounding, and
robbing the unfortunate fugitives, even to stripping the
very women of their clothes, which the Druzes in pity
had spared them. So keenly was the infamous conduct
of the Turkish troops felt, that the Maronites declared
'they would sooner be plundered by the Druzes than
protected by the Turks'.

This initial attempt of the Maronite patriarch and his allies
to establish an exclusive dominance in Lebanon had ended in
ignominy.

The emptiness of their boastful taunts and denunciations
were fully exposed. Their lofty and ill-judged schemes
of aggrandisement had completely miscarried. The vials
of wrath they had prepared for the Druzes had recoiled
fearfully on their own heads. All the bitterness of their
hearts had been fruitlessly exhaled, and nought was now
left them of the venom but the sting.

The rule of Bashir III was not to last much longer. He was
deposed in 1842 and dispatched to Istanbul. The damage
he had caused to Druze-Maronite relationships, however,
continued in its immensely harmful effects. These could
have been avoided, or greatly ameliorated, had he been
intelligent, competent and tactful, but he was none of these
things. They could have been avoided, too, had not the

Maronite clergy, headed by their patriarch and encouraged by the French and European Catholic missionaries, incited and fuelled the flames of fanaticism and hatred for the Druzes among the Maronites of Lebanon. The Christian historian Dr Kamal Salibi confirms the role of the European Catholic missionaries when he describes how they behaved at the time:

> The Lithuanian Jesuit Father Maximilien Ryllo went around the country inciting the Lebanese Christians to rise against the Druzes and vindicate their political claims by force. His campaign of fanatic zest, which bordered on frenzy, was so nefariously obnoxious that the French Consul in Beirut requested his immediate withdrawal from the country. It was European Catholic missionaries like Ryllo who were primarily responsible for the irreparable breach which came to exist between the Maronites and the Druzes of Lebanon.

Equally culpable were the Ottoman Turks, who intrigued and conspired to create hatred and dissent between the two communities to make the task of governing the quarrelling Lebanese so much easier. To take one example, the Turkish pasha, governor of Lebanon, sent five camel-loads of ammunition to the Maronites; simultaneously the Druzes received ample supplies of ammunition from the self-same source. Meanwhile the European powers, anxious not to be left behind by France, encouraged dissent by taking sides and openly interfering in the internal politics of Lebanon, so creating the tensions, sectarian hatred and political confusion that were mainly responsible for the frequent outbreaks of fighting between the two main Lebanese communities.

After the unhappy and premature end to Bashir III's rule, the Ottoman Turks appointed, as governor of Lebanon, a Christian Austrian who embraced Islam and had fought in their army against the Egyptians. He took the name of

Omar and was known as Omar Pasha. He was a failure in administration, but a master in intrigue and double-dealing. Having laboured in vain to establish his authority over the country, he decided to fall back on inciting the Druzes against the Maronites to create the hatred and dissension that would enable him to divide and rule. The Druzes realized that the pasha sought to use them as a tool to serve his own interests and refused to go along with his intrigues. He then made out that he would like to parley with the Druzes and asked five of their leading chiefs to dinner. After the meal he had them surrounded without warning and taken prisoner. This act of treachery provoked the Druzes to rebel. They called upon the Christians, who were equally dissatisfied with the pasha, to join forces with them, but the distrustful Maronites refused the appeal and purported to adopt a strict neutrality. The Druzes therefore went into action alone.

The Ottoman Turks, counteracting the Druze challenge to their authority, brought in a large military force which, assisted by a large body of Maronite cavalry, succeeded in subduing the rebellion. Nevertheless, they had been greatly alarmed by the event, and having realized the incompetence and mismanagement of Omar Pasha, they recalled him, released the Druze chiefs arrested by him and came up with a novel proposal.

The plan was to partition Lebanon into a Christian district in the north and a Druze district in the south. The Christian district was to be administered by a Christian, and the Druze district by a Druze. Each administrator was to operate under Ottoman Turkey's authority. The plan was designed, on the face of it, to resolve the Druze-Maronite problem, but in reality was a further reinforcement of the Turks' policy of 'divide and rule'. It had the approval of the European countries and was said to have been recommended by certain of them in the first place.

The scheme, however, never stood a chance of resolving

the steadily growing problems and ever more acute dissent between the Druzes and the Maronites. In seeing how it failed, and how it lead to the 1845 civil war, Colonel Churchill is once again our witness:

> This apparently equitable and satisfactory solution of a much vexed question, however, only gave rise to greater difficulties and fresh complications. Had the whole Christian population resided together in one part of the mountain, and the entire Druze population in another, within prescribed boundaries, the plan would have been as practicable as it was simple. But thousands of Christians, both Greek and Maronite, lived in the Druze districts, as feudal dependants of the Druze shiekhs, who exercised a right over them inherited from father to son, for ages. The direct rule of the Christian governor over the Christians, implying his absolute authority over them wherever they might reside, at once abolished this right, and struck at the root of those privileges which the Druzes regarded as the mainstay of their power.

For their part, the Maronites who lived in Druze territory saw the new arrangement as announcing their release from 'Druze bondage'. But in this atmosphere of heightening animosities, the position of the Greek Orthodox Christians remained a special case. They had no reason to love the Maronites, who had placed them under intolerable pressures to convert to Catholicism by attacking their civil and ecclesiastical rights, by depriving them of land and property through legal manipulation, and by various other intimidations. They feared the zealotry of the new Christian administrator and openly declared 'their preference for Druze rule', having 'found a refuge in the bosom of the Druze chiefs from the fierce bigotry and persecution of the Maronite patriarch' as he sought to further and promote 'his views of religious ascendancy over the whole of Lebanon'. It simply went to

123

show, said Colonel Churchill, 'that Druze resistance, and even violence, was not so much directed against Christianity as against Maronite ambition and presumption, and the domineering views of an intolerant priesthood'.

Week after week and month after month passed away in vain endeavours to find a common ground on which the two sects might merge their differences. Neither would resign their rights nor their pretensions. The Druzes, with natural and excusable pertinacity, refused to accept the arrangement which they clearly foresaw would ultimately reduce them, as a political body, to absolute impotence and insignificance. The Maronites, excited by their clergy, talked loudly of the intolerable yoke of Druze oppression, and declared their determination never to submit to it again.

All attempts at negotiation and mediation, including those sponsored by the European powers, came to naught. The new Maronite patriarch had learnt nothing from the humiliating experience of his predecessor, but declared, 'Maronite or Druze supremacy, the blow must be struck, and he who strikes first will have two chances to one in his favour.' The Maronites set in motion a cycle of assassination and reprisal that heralded the storm, much to the glee of the Islamic Turks, who anticipated nothing but advantage to their policy of divide and rule and expected the Christians to get the worst of any fighting.

Ever busy in the work of underhand intrigue, they warned the Druzes against yielding one iota to the contemptuous demands of Christian insolence; while, at the same time, so far from preventing hostilities, they absolutely encouraged the Maronites to attack the Druzes, openly telling them they had their leave to do so.

Full scope being thus given to their movements, the Maronites no longer made any secrets of their designs.

The Druzes looked on with apprehension and bitterness as the Maronites made military preparations and once again began to blazen the slogan: 'We cannot exist with the Druzes, either they or we must be destroyed or leave the country.' France and Austria had donated large funds for the relief of the Christian community after the previous civil war, and these the patriarch diverted into

the promotion of a second; authorizing his clergy to pay the combatants and to purchase arms and ammunition wherever they could be obtained. Knowing that the great body of the Maronites would not engage in a war, simply to destroy the political rights of the Druzes, the justice of which, indeed, the more dispassionate amongst them were ever ready to admit, he made a war of party a war of religion. The Druzes, the enemies of the cross, the infidels, were to be exterminated or driven out of the land.

At Dayr al-Qamar a self-constituted town council made it treasonable for a Maronite to associate with a Druze, and a Maronite priest who had contacts with a Druze sheikh was put to death. Christian tenants no longer dared to approach their Druze landlords, for fear of violence from their own people. As the bellicose Christian proclamations continued, the Christian Shihab emirs stepped into the forefront to declare their determination to fight, whatever the cost, to bring back from exile the old Emir Bashir II to rule all of Lebanon again. At Abeih the Shihabs formed a rallying point, 'whither all the Christians in the mixed districts were summoned to gather'.

By the end of January 1845 the principal Druze sheikhs were once again sinking their own differences and rivalries to attend a grand assembly at Muchtara, the seat of the Jumblatts, for 'in times of civil commotion' the Jumblatt family became for them, 'the grand centre of combination ... and of action'. That April, 'the long gathering storm burst, by a general attack from the Maronites on all the Druze quarters'. In the Shouf, they obtained the mischievous approval of a Turkish officer before launching an assault headed by their bishop brandishing a crucifix. Their onslaught and advance was so fierce that they burned fourteen Druze villages before being halted and thoroughly defeated at the walls of Muchtara, their main target.

The battle was fierce, too, at Abeih, and similarly ended in a total rout of the Christians, with the Shihab emirs blockaded inside their castle. They surrendered eventually, and were allowed to proceed to Beirut under safe conduct provided by Colonel Rose. All of this, and similar explosions throughout Lebanon, the Turkish forces surveyed with indifferent neutrality. Everywhere the result was the same: a repetition for the Christians of the fiasco of 1841, with 'villages in flames, property destroyed, and Christian fugitives pursued by Druzes and Turkish irregulars, plundered, mutilated and slain'.

Again the genius of diplomacy was taxed at Constantinople to find a conductor that might draw off the devastating elements of the periodical tornado of Turkish intrigue and treachery, Maronite priestly ambition, and Druze vindictiveness. A high ranking emissary was sent on a special mission to Syria towards the close of 1845, and after long enquiry and numerous deliberations, the government of Lebanon was settled on what was thought would prove a permanent basis.

It confirmed the principle of geographical partition, with two distinct administrators and two separate tribunals on which the different sects were represented. There was an acknowledgement of Druze feudal rights over those Christians who resided among them, with the proviso that the Christians should be permitted to appoint an agent to guard their interests. For the Christians of Dayr al-Qamar, the appointment of an agent was insufficient to neutralize their resentment at remaining under the yoke of a Druze sheikh, and the Turks secretly egged them on to petition for a Turkish governor.

> The boon was granted; but the insult offered to those Druses sunk deep into their hearts. They never forgave or forgot it. For years they lived within sight of, but exiled from that, their ancestral appanage. They saw it grow up and prosper, till it became a wealthy, flourishing Christian community. But within its precincts there were no revenues as of old, no feudal state, for them. They never passed it without gnashing their teeth. But they bided their time . . .

7. The End of the Ottomans and the Creation of Grand Liban

At the outset the Druzes were, unlike the Maronites, largely content with the new solution of a division of administration, for by their tenacity and ferocity in battle they had vindicated their rights and defeated the Maronite aggression. The Maronites, encouraged in their discontent by the Turks, their own clergy and France, remained far from happy meanwhile. They hated in equal measure the humiliating defeats they had suffered and the Druzes who inflicted them. The atmosphere of mistrust between both communities ran deep and prospects of reconciliation and peace looked highly doubtful, or even unattainable.

In the atmosphere of turmoil and turbulence which reigned, frequent isolated affrays and clashes continued all across Lebanon in the districts where the two communities co-existed. Since each community was in effect preparing for renewed conflict, the outbreak of war grew to be merely a question of time. It finally came in 1860, sparked off by the successful rising, in January 1859, of the Maronite peasants against the Al-Khazins, their feudal rich co-religionists who owned the land over which they sweated so hard for so little. Led by the Maronite, Tanious Shahin, the first Lebanese socialist leader, the peasants drove the Maronite feudal lords from their estates and took over the land. In this Tanious Shahin was encouraged and supported by the Turkish authorities in Lebanon and by the French. He was also secretly urged on by the then Maronite patriarch, himself of peasant origin,

128

and by his clergy. The fact that the Al-Khazins were known to be pro-British undoubtedly motivated the French and the patriarch in seeking to influence events.

News of the successful Maronite social rebellion swiftly spread throughout the countryside and raised the hopes of all the peasants, especially of those among the Maronites who worked as tenants of the Druze feudal lords. In a pre-emptive move to deflect from these ambitions, the Druze feudal lords, hoping to nip any challenge to their authority in the bud, stirred up religious fanaticism among their own peasants even as the Maronite feudal lords did the same among their Maronite peasants.

'It is said that 20 per cent of all agricultural land in Lebanon belongs to the clergy. They have never agreed to sell, despite repeated appeals from the Pope, who used to order them to do so and use the money to do good works,' wrote Kamal Jumblatt in his book, *I Speak for Lebanon*. The Maronite Church, as by far the biggest feudal landlord in Lebanon, now joined the fray and played a major role in promoting religious fanaticism and fear and hatred between Maronite and Druze. Families who had lived in amity for generations were turned against one another by carefully spread false rumours and tales of atrocity.

Tanious Shahin's socialist uprising was meanwhile a considerable success among the Maronites, and his personal prestige reached great heights. The success went to his head and he became autocratic in insisting that his commands be obeyed by all Maronites. Nevertheless his show of power was assumed to contribute greatly to his people's strength. When the Maronite Bishop of Beirut, Tubiyya Aoun, encouraged the Christians in the Druze districts to strike against the Druzes, they in turn, to be on the safe side, addressed an appeal to the new leader, Tanious Shahin, for assistance, and Tanious Shahin replied he could provide 50,000 fighting men if need be. Support was also promised from the Maronites of north Lebanon. The Druzes, with their far inferior numbers, appealed for help to the Druzes of Jabal al-Druze and other areas where Druzes resided. Characteristically, there was a general commitment to stand united in the face of an attack on any fellow Druzes or their land.

The rival communities thus accelerated preparations for a sectarian conflict. It was something the Turkish authorities might have halted, since they could have prohibited the importation of arms and ammunition. For reasons of their own, however, they chose to do nothing. The consequences are recounted by the Christian historian, Dr Kamal Salibi, in *The Modern History of Lebanon*:

> In the predominantly Christian villages and towns young Christians organized themselves in armed bands, each led by a *shaykh shabab* (fighting leader of young men) and adopted a special uniform; they roamed from one place to the other displaying their weapons and boasting of their determination to exterminate the Druzes. The Christian leadership in each distict went to a supreme *shaykh shabab*, who kept a record of the names of all the men under his command and maintained contact with other district leaders. In Beirut, Bishop Tubiyya Aoun organized a 'Maronite Young Men's League' and taunted the Druzes in the most irresponsible manner, while Maronites of wealth and means raised subscriptions for . . . arms and ammunition, which they distributed to their co-religionists in the mountains.

The secret preparations of the Druzes contrasted with the public posturings of the Maronites, but as it came to the eve of conflict, the Christians were eminently equipped for it and their leaders continually boasted of having under arms 50,000 men for whom overwhelming the 12,000-strong armed force of the Druzes would be no problem.

Yet the fighting in the Druze districts had hardly begun when the Christians were seized with panic. Whole families abandoned their villages in order to seek refuge in . . . Christian strongholds . . . The Christians of the Urqub district left their villages in a body and fled towards Zahleh . . . pursued and fired on by the Druzes.

From Zahleh, a retaliatory Maronite force of 3,000 set out to launch an attack on the Druze population of the village of Ayn Dara, east of Beirut, but were intercepted by a Druze counter-force of no more than 600. The fighting was fierce, but the day ended with the Christians in disorganized retreat and the Druze force descending on and burning down several Christian villages. It was a pattern of defeat for the Maronites that was to be repeated throughout Lebanon. The Druzes were outnumbered in many instances, yet invariably emerged as victors. Here is Colonel Churchill's comment on the subject of Druze fighting superiority:

The inferiority of the Christians in military organization to that of the Druzes, became apparent, as usual, from the first collision. The former advanced without the slightest order, dispersed themselves right and left, and seemed each to follow his own inspirations. In the battle near Ayn Dara, they actually fired upon each other, and while thus engaged, found themselves outflanked, and nearly surrounded by the enemy. The Druzes, on the contrary, moved steadily on given points, under the direction of their chiefs, to whom they yielded the most implicit obedience. Quarters menaced were carefully watched, and if attacked, reinforced with extraordinary celerity.

The sectarian conflict was warmly encouraged by the Ottoman authorities. They saw in it a chance to curb the Christians, especially the Maronites, who had been causing them problems by constantly appealing for aid to their Christian brethren in Europe and had become a painful thorn in the side of the Ottoman Islamic Empire. By fanning the flames of religious hatred between the Maronites and the Druzes, the Maronite clergy, supported by the European Catholic missions and the French government, were therefore inadvertently serving the Ottomans in their intrigues. 'The deadly enemies of the Druzes were not the Maronite aristocracy,' Colonel Churchill pronounced his verdict, 'but the Maronite clergy. The former never embarked heartily in any movement against them.'

The two relatively minor civil wars of 1841 and 1845 described in the previous chapter and the major one of 1860 were all started by the Maronites and all won by the Druzes. The explosion of 1860 was the most horrific, involving multiple ghastly bloodbaths. It started that May and lasted over two months, during which thousands of innocent people on both sides lost their lives, houses were burnt and villages devastated. The violence quickly spread to Damascus in Syria, where, on 9 and 10 July, thousands of Christian victims were massacred by fanatic Moslems. The European powers intervened vigorously with the Ottoman government to try to stop the fighting. The French landed troops in Lebanon to protect the defeated Maronites and retaliate against the Druzes. Warships of the British Royal Navy and other European fleets cruised at action stations off the Lebanese coast.

The Maronites and the French joined in accusing the Druzes of responsibility for the war and for the consequential killings and destruction, and demanded the execution of 4,600 Druze chiefs. It was now that the British came to the defence of the Druzes. 'For what,' asked Colonel Churchill, 'were the Druzes to blame?'

All they had done was in self-defence. Was it not the Maronites who started the war? Had they not also committed atrocities? Had they not coolly killed hundreds of Druzes, when following the French army into the mountains? Would they not, had they gained the day, have committed excesses at least equal to, if not exceeding, those committed by the Druzes? Had they not openly declared their intention to exterminate the Druzes?

The lives of the 4,600 Druze chiefs were spared, with two exceptions. One of these was executed, while the other died in prison. The British meanwhile gained the eternal gratitude of the Druzes for their intervention.

Various international solutions to the problem were discussed, and on 9 June 1861 a Protocol was signed, making Lebanon an autonomous province of the Ottoman Empire under the guarantee of the six signatory powers: Turkey, France, Britain, Russia, Prussia and Austria; in 1867, Italy joined the guarantors. It had taken a horrendously bloody civil war to make Lebanon officially a political entity for the first time.

The agreement stipulated that Lebanon was to be governed not by a Lebanese, but by a Christian Ottoman, whose appointment needed the approval of the Turkish government and the European guarantors.* The governor was to be assisted by a twelve-member council, representing the religious communities: four Maronites, three Druzes, two Greek Orthodox, one Greek Catholic, one Sunni Moslem and one Shi'ite Moslem.

Feudalism was to be abolished – or so said the Protocol. In practice, the Ottoman governor, to keep the feudal lords happy, made their traditional feudalism official by appointing them to leading government positions. And thus began the political feudalism in government administration

---

* The first governor to fill the post, it may come as no surprise to learn, was nominated by the French.

that has plagued Lebanese politics ever since. The Druzes, having won the war militarily, lost it politically, and had to be resigned to the establishment of an autonomous Lebanon in which they settled down to live peaceably, as a respected minority, alongside the Christians. As it happened, autonomy brought peace, happiness and distinct privileges to the new-born country, the most attractive of these advantages being exemption from military service in the Ottoman army. All of this helped to coin the proverbial saying: 'Happy is he who possesses a piece of land in Lebanon, even if small enough for a goat to sleep in.'

The serene phase lasted for over fifty years, until 1915, when Turkey joined in the First World War on the side of Germany, suspended the Protocol and stripped Lebanon of its autonomous status. In 1918, with the Allies victorious, France occupied Lebanon, as a result of which there was much rejoicing among the Maronite Christians. Two years later, France received a Mandate over Lebanon and Syria, granted by the Allied Supreme Council meeting at San Remo. And four months later still, on 1 September 1920, the French high commissioner proclaimed the creation of Greater Lebanon (Grand Liban). This action annexed to Lebanon, at the specific request of the Maronites, four districts taken away from Syria.*

The Maronites merely thought they had gained agricultural fertile land much needed by Lebanon. In the longer perspective, many of them have come to believe that the creation of Grand Liban was a grave mistake. In the first place, it brought within Lebanon's borders large numbers of Moslems, who, as a majority, were eventually to demand a more equitable share in the running of the country. In

* Syria has never either accepted the frontiers imposed by the French in 1920 or acknowledged Lebanon's sovereignty over the Grand Liban area. As a result, no official diplomatic relations have ever been established between Lebanon and Syria.

the second place, it caused great bitterness among the Syrians, who have continued to regard the 'lost districts' as their own.

The Druzes, for their part, were most unhappy with the French Mandate. They still remembered the inimical French attitude during the civil war of 1860 and France's prejudiced support for the Maronites. They therefore hated the French and were convinced that the hatred was reciprocal. They felt greatly let down by their British friends, who had, by the Mandate, agreed to deliver them to the French, their traditional enemies. They also resented the establishment of Grand Liban, for the advent of large numbers of Sunni and Shi'ite Moslems lost the Druzes their political status as an important minority in the Lebanon. They were helpless to do anything about it, but they were delighted when their Syrian brethren in Jabal al-Druze revolted against the French in 1925. Without the least hesitation, they went to their aid, sending large numbers of fighting men to assist.

The 1925 revolt came about in this way. The French had, under the Mandate, lost no time in adopting the tested and tried colonial policy of divide and rule. In Syria and Lebanon they established for the mandated territory several indigenous governments rather than one. The first was Grand Liban, later the Republic of Lebanon; the second the state of the Alawis in Syria; the third Jabal al-Druze. The remainder of Syria was divided into the states of Damascus and Aleppo, and the *sanjaq* of Alexandretta. The personnel of all these states were appointed by the French high commissioner and the most important posts were invariably given to French officers and officials.

The high commissioners appointed by the French government to administer the Mandate were army generals still flushed with their victory over the Germans and giddy with power. Their word was law and their whims stood above question. They were politically ignorant and expressed a strong contempt for politics and politicians. Their attempts at civil administration were hamstrung by attitudes of military autocracy. They felt and behaved like minor gods sent to chastise and discipline the colonials won from the enemy. They strongly believed that only the Christian sects were the friends of France and that all other religious communities were hostile, especially the Druzes, the traditional friends of the British.

One Druze chief whom the French disliked in particular was Sultan Pasha Al-Attrash, a member of the illustrious Al-Attrash family in Jabal al-Druze, and a fabled Druze warrior. Their dislike of him was mainly based on their awareness of him as staunchly pro-British. He had, in 1918, written a letter to the British command in Palestine to congratulate them on their victory over the Ottoman Turks and to offer his services and those of the Druzes. It dismayed and greatly disappointed him when a reply, dated 3 September 1918, arrived from the French Intelligence services. By tactlessly referring his letter to French Intelligence to answer, the British command had branded Sultan Pasha as pro-British and hence as anti-French. His attempt to contact the British afterwards continued to be deeply resented, while, for his part, he disliked and distrusted the French for their colonial oppressive methods in the Jabal and their ceaseless efforts to undermine and even destroy the long-established feudal rights of the Attrash family. Sultan Pasha was to have many scraps with the French, the most spectacular of which took place in 1922.

A Shi'ite notable, Adham Khanjar, who had led a rebellion against the French in south Lebanon, was at that time accused of attempting to ambush General Gouraud, the French high commissioner. Khanjar fled to Jabal al-Druze and sought refuge in Sultan Pasha's house, where he was arrested. He was then taken as a prisoner to Souaida, the seat of government in Jabal al-Druze, but it so happened that Sultan Pasha had not been at home when the arrest was made. As soon as he heard of the event he became very angry. The French action violated the hallowed Druze tradition of protecting all those who come in search of refuge. It also violated a Franco-Druze agreement of 1921, whereby the French had promised to respect and not to violate the long-established Druze customs, traditions and moral code, all of which the Druzes consider sacred. In Sultan Pasha's eyes the arrest was, moreover, a personal insult, blemishing his honour.

Accompanied by a group of his men, he proceeded to Souaida and demanded Khanjar's immediate release into his custody. When this request was rejected, he tried to solicit the support of his cousin, Salim Bey Al-Attrash, governor of Jabal al-Druze. But Salim Bey, under French pressure, refused to interfere in the matter. Sultan Pasha then telegraphed to the French high commissioner, who grossly misapprehended Sultan Pasha's request and angrily interpreted it as an outrageous challenge to France and its mandatory power. With all peaceful channels to secure the release of the prisoner closed, Sultan Pasha and his fighting men laid siege to Souaida, whose French garrison signalled to Damascus for help.

Reinforcements arrived from Der'aa, the nearest French army post, and engaged Sultan Pasha and his force in a ferocious battle, during which Sultan Pasha confirmed his reputation among the bravest of the brave and as a supreme leader of fighting men. With lightning speed, he charged on horseback one of the advancing French tanks, heedless of the bullets that sprayed about him. Arriving alongside the ironclad, he jumped from his horse's back to the top of the tank, whose turret was open because of the heat and because its occupants never dreamed such a daring attack might be attempted. Armed only with his sword, Sultan Pasha killed the officer and his crew member. It was an incredible feat of courage and a clear demonstration of the Druzes' fatalistic belief that, at birth, a Druze's age span on this earth is recorded in the book of destiny, that nothing which happens in this world may prolong or shorten it.

Sultan Pasha confirmed this belief not only by his courageous attack on the French tank but also in a lifetime of battles and warfare that began when the Ottoman Turks captured and hanged his father. In seventy years of continuous fighting, Sultan Pasha was never to be wounded or captured, nor did he ever have his horse killed beneath him.

The fearless assault on the tank rivetted the attention of his men and inspired them to emulate his example. In no time the French forces were routed, with many killed and only four surrendered prisoners. Sultan Pasha then proceeded with the siege of Souaida, while news of his feat of arms against the tank spread like wildfire. Poets composed songs in its praise. These came to be sung not only in Druze land, but also throughout most of the Arab countries.

Following the defeat of the French outside Souaida, a delegation led by Sultan's cousin, Salim Bey, governor of Jabal al-Druze, arrived on the battlefield. After a heated discussion, an agreement was reached to ensure the lifting of the siege, the safe passage of the Druze warriors back to their villages, the release of the four French prisoners and a promise that the delegation would return Adham Khanjar to Sultan Pasha at the earliest possible moment. Unfortunately, the last promise was never honoured and Adham Khanjar was subsequently executed by the French.

At this Sultan Pasha promptly left in indignation for Transjordan with his followers, and from there continued to raid the French posts in Jabal al-Druze. The French dynamited his house and the houses of his followers in retaliation, confiscated their land and livestock and tried to spread the news that Sultan Pasha was branded as an outlaw and a criminal committing crimes against his own country and against France. They even convicted him *in absentia* and sentenced him to death on 16 October 1922. But their efforts to discredit him failed utterly, and Sultan Pasha remained the hero and undisputed leader of the fighting Druzes.

The French then resorted to a two-pronged tactical plan to

stop his raids from Transjordan and eliminate any possibility of the British and Emir Abdullah of Transjordan using Sultan Pasha against them in Syria. They put pressure on the British to make it difficult for Sultan Pasha to remain in Transjordan, and at the same time sent intermediaries to invite Sultan Pasha to return to Jabal al-Druze, abrogating the death sentence and promising the return of his confiscated properties and those of his fighting men. As a result, the Transjordanian authorities made it abundantly clear that Sultan's further stay in Transjordan would be neither welcome nor desirable.

When the death sentence was abrogated on 4 April 1923, Sultan Pasha accepted the French promises and returned to Jabal al-Druze, where he was received with a grand ovation as a Druze national hero. But during his absence things had gone very wrong. The death of Salim Bey Al-Attrash, the governor, in 1923 at the age of thirty-one, had prompted many rumours of foul play. To fill the gap the French had appointed as councillor and acting governor a French officer called Carbillet, who had some African colonial experience.

According to the Franco-Druze agreement of 1921, it was for the Druzes to elect a Druze successor to the deceased governor, but Carbillet, hoping to retain the post for himself, succeeded in stirring rivalries between those Druze chiefs who aspired to the post. This effectively obstructed the election of a Druze governor indefinitely and left Carbillet at the helm. He then began to work to destroy the influence and prestige of the Attrash family, from among whom possible candidates for the position of governor would normally have been chosen. He closed the secondary houses they maintained in Souaida for when they came to the capital, he prohibited the people from visiting them and from participating in their funerals. He spread around them a net of spies to report back to him about them and their activities, he incited their tenants against them and encouraged them to refuse to comply with their requests. Finally, he prompted the ambitions of non-Attrash candidatures for the post of governor, previously the family's undisputed preserve.

Under the pretext of progressive social reforms, he was also quick to introduce harsh and authoritarian French colonial practices. Personal freedom was restricted, travel between villages controlled and visiting Damascus subject to a permit. Letters and telegrams were censored. Forced labour was employed on an unprecedented scale. A system of arbitrary fines for the most petty offences was introduced; a fine of twenty-five gold sovereigns being levied on the town of Souaida, for instance, for the disappearance of a cat belonging to one Lieutenant Morrel. He abrogated to himself the position of an authoritarian colonial governor and acted accordingly. The entire populations of villages and towns were required, against penalty of large fines, to come out *en masse* to greet him whenever he visited and were ordered to brandish French banners to signify their loyalty to France. His network of informers became vast, and he forced the schoolteachers, through a combination of bribes and intimidation, to undertake this abhorrent task. Punishments for trivial offences were harsh, even capricious. The sensitive Druze pride was repeatedly offended and the Druzes often publicly humiliated.

When Carbillet was informed that the elected National Council was unhappy with his actions and contemplated action to stop him, he at once dissolved the council and proceeded to engineer the election of a new one. The way he conducted this showed that he had a novel notion of free and democratic election. The entire proceedings took place within twenty-four hours. He visited the town of Shahba, for example, and was greeted outside its limits, upon his specific orders, by its whole population, men, women and children. Then he stood among them and delivered a short speech:

'I have come to liberate you from the despotism of your chiefs, who have long abused you and trampled on your legitimate rights. Provided you demonstrate obedience and loyalty to France, France will care for you, educate you and liberate you from the feudal yoke you are forced to carry.

'Now I must leave you. My time is very valuable. The list in my hand contains the names of the persons proposed to represent you as members of your new National Council. They will represent you well. Clap for them.'

The people clapped as commanded and the 'free and democratic' election by the people of Shahba of their representatives in the National Council was completed. The same electoral style was duplicated in every village and town of Jabal al-Druze. Small wonder that the election was completed in all the Jabal within twenty-four hours.

The first act of the new council was to vote unanimously to elect Carbillet as governor of Jabal al-Druze, so that finally he had what he wanted and had conspired for. He was now the absolute, despotic ruler of Jabal al-Druze. His governorship came to be characterized by a new ruthlessness and sadism, its main objective being to destroy the Attrash family and all the other traditional Druze feudal chiefs. This attempt to destroy the structure of Druze society was greatly and generally resented, except by those few vassals on whom he showered bribes and favours.

In April 1925, a Druze delegation finally sought an audience with General Sarrail, the French high commissioner, to submit complaints about Carbillet and his rule and remind the French authorities of how, according to the Franco-Druze agreement of March 1921, their governor should be a Druze. General Sarrail dismissed the agreement as valueless, saying it served merely as a historical document. He then praised Carbillet, the subject of their protests, and strongly implied that they were speaking falsehoods and certainly failing to appreciate this officer's splendid qualities. Carbillet in fact went on leave late that May, but was replaced by another French officer who followed in his predecessor's footsteps and rejected any complaints.

A second Druze delegation, made up of the most respected

personages of Jabal al-Druze, therefore travelled to Beirut once again, to submit their grievances to General Serrail. This time they were refused an audience. The high commissioner considered the delegation to be unrepresentative, since it did not include those few notables who were known friends of Carbillet and consequently pro-French. Humiliated, grossly offended and smarting with fury, the delegation returned to Jabal al-Druze. Serrail then dealt a final blow to French-Druze relations when he gave orders, in July 1925, that three Druze leaders of the highly influential Attrash family, members of the rejected delegation, should be lured by deceit to Damascus, under the pretext of discussing their complaints and possibly reaching a favourable consideration of their demands. On arrival, they were arrested and exiled to Palmyra.

At this point the old warrior, Sultan Pasha Al-Attrash, enraged by such an act of treachery, began to enlist young men to accompany him to the French governor to protest, from a position of strength, against the humiliation of the exiled leaders and demand their immediate release and return to Jabal al-Druze. The plan gained wide spontaneous support. The Jabal was by now boiling with anger and resentment at the betrayal of the three Attrash leaders and the insult it implied to the Druzes.

Informed of Sultan Pasha's activities, the French dispatched a machine-gun detachment of 200 or so Syrian and Algerian *légionnaires* to restore calm and order, and doubtless to apprehend Sultan Pasha and his leading aides. The detachment was ambushed by Sultan Pasha and his followers and all its troops were killed, with the exception of six Algerian *spahis* who sought refuge and sanctuary in the house of the local village sheikh. This event marks the start of the Druze revolt.

The angry French and General Serrail commanded General Roger Michaud, at the head of a force of 3,000 troops, to march into Jabal al-Druze, quell the uprising and punish its leader. This force in turn came under attack from Sultan Pasha and his relatively tiny force of Druze warriors, and was in turn completely routed. It panicked and fled, leaving behind more than 700 dead and wounded. One French commander of a company of Madagascan soldiers who bolted from the scene committed suicide, and General Michaud himself departed hastily and prematurely. Abandoned behind him were large quantities of canons, arms and ammunition, welcomed by Sultan Pasha as useful contributions to his cause.

The spectacular victory of Sultan Pasha and his Druze fighters over General Michaud greatly enhanced his prestige as a Druze fighting leader and rallied all the Druzes of Jabal al-Druze to his side while attracting support in both materials and men from the Druzes of Lebanon. The Druzes, wherever they live, as we have seen throughout their history, strongly feel themselves to be an integral part of the Druze community. Their religion demands that they help each other and come to the aid of the community to counter any threat to its land, independence and survival. Whenever they have needed to fight aggressors, they have fought back as one people, and so it came about in Lebanon and Jabal al-Druze in 1925. A strong contingent of Lebanese Druze fighters rallied to Sultan Pasha's support, while the rebellion against the French erupted simultaneously in south-east Lebanon.

The nationalists of Syria had long resented the oppression of the French and risen in many isolated rebellions against them. Now they lost no time in joining in the fray and proclaiming a general Syrian rebellion. The revolt spread beyond Jabal al-Druze until it covered the districts of Damascus and Homs as well as part of southern Lebanon. The Syrians referred to the uprising as the 'Syrian Revolt', and the term came to encapsulate both their and the Druze revolts. Nevertheless the French insisted, to the very end, on calling it 'La Révolte Druze'.

In his fury at the Syrian uprising, General Sarrail committed the gravest error of judgement when he ordered the aerial bombardment of Damascus, the oldest living city in the world, and reduced parts of it to ruins. It did nothing to subdue the revolt, but on the contrary, inflamed the hostility of Syrians everywhere. When Damascus was bombarded a second time, and substantial damage done, a loud and critical outcry arose from international public opinion, the loudest criticism being heard in France itself. Sarrail was recalled, and Mr Henri de Jouvenel, a senator and the editor of *Le Matin*, was appointed in his place. It had finally dawned on the French that a civilian would be more qualified than a military general to administer the Mandate.

Through this new and at least competent high commissioner, the French proceeded to satisfy a number of the Syrians' national aspirations while strongly reinforcing their own military forces, tanks, artillery and aviation power. The Syrian rebels had only rifles and swords, and their resources were soon exhausted, for they received no external assistance whatever. As a result, the Syrian Revolt was quelled and the large French military force could concentrate on Sultan Pasha and his fighters.

By the end of 1926, the Druze Revolt was over, except for several bands who continued guerrilla activities in some of the less accessible parts of the Jabal. These pockets of resistance were finally dispersed by the end of 1927, when Sultan Pasha and his principal aides once again sought refuge in Transjordan. Here they found they were unwelcome, so continued on to Wadi Sirhan in Saudi Arabia. Later they returned to Transjordan, only to be placed under locality arrest – the fighters in al-Azrak, Sultan Pasha and his closest relatives and aides in the town of Kerak. They felt a keen disappointment in the British, and in Emir Abdullah, for having so cuttingly spurned them, as they saw it, and let them down.

The Druze Revolt had lasted two years and cost the French

many humiliating defeats, heavy casualties and substantial losses of military equipment. The costs were staggering to both sides. The Druzes had lost some of their most gallant fighters, but won honour and prestige and regained their national pride. Dazzling feats of valour, courage and heroism had earned them the admiration of the world, but the accolades they most treasured had been those of the French military officers who fought against them and who went on record as paying their Druze adversaries the highest tributes for bravery and chivalry. Yet these well-deserved laudations did nothing to stop the French authorities using exceedingly harsh methods and meting out indiscriminate punishments on the innocent in putting down the insurrection.

In Lebanon, the Maronites rejoiced in the defeat of the Druzes, and the Lebanese National Council, dominated by France and the Maronite Christians, passed a resolution condemning the Druze Revolt and, with barely suppressed glee, expressing satisfaction at the defeat of Sultan Pasha and the collapse of what they called this treacherous disloyalty to France. The Druze members were outraged, and angrily voted against the motion, but since they were only a small minority, the resolution was overwhelmingly passed.

The Druzes in Lebanon continued to be greatly resented for the support they had given to Sultan Pasha's Druze Revolt.* There was nothing they could do about it except walk with heads held high, taking pride in the courage and bravery of the Druze fighters who had, during two years, inflicted many a humiliating defeat on French military forces that were superior in numbers and weaponry. The Druzes were accustomed to fighting alone against foreign

---

* As an Inspector of Education in Transjordan in the 1930s, I had to visit the schools of Kerak at least three times a year. During these visits I made the acquaintance of Sultan Pasha, his two brothers and his close aides. I had the privilege and honour of becoming their friend and of listening to fascinating first-hand accounts of their battles with the French: vivid memories I shall cherish all my life.

domination and had never yet been cowed by defeat. They settled to getting on with a quiet and peaceable life under the Mandate, resigned to the inevitable Franco-Maronite domination. They waited in hope to see what reforms the change from a military to a civilian high commissioner would bring about.

8. The French Mandate and the Seeds of War in Lebanon

The new high commissioner, Henri de Jouvenel, was a liberal, who appeared at first to show every indication of giving the French Mandate over Syria and Lebanon a liberal face. He decided to have National Assemblies for each of the two countries, freely elected and representing all the parties and religious communities. He proposed that these assemblies should formulate constitutions for Syria and Lebanon respectively, though their implementation was to be subject to French control and French veto. In other words, his policy was to seek to bring about an early political settlement of Syria's and Lebanon's problems while maintaining full respect and protection for French interests. But either he or his superiors in Paris never quite meant what they declared. For in practice, the politicians in Syria and Lebanon were encouraged to split into two factions: those who favoured a constitution and those who were against one. To add to the confusion in Lebanon, the Moslem population of the districts taken from Syria to create Grand Liban made it clear they wished to return to Syria and refused to be integrated into Lebanon.

Thus were political feelings in both countries diverted from resentment of the French to become resentments and squabbles between the various political and religious factions. In Jabal al-Druze, arguments raged between those who wanted autonomy in the Jabal and those who wanted to see it incorporated within Syria. The French encouraged the party which sought separation from Syria and decreed that Jabal al-Druze should remain autonomous but under direct French rule.

During the years that followed, successive civilian French high commissioners were sent from France to rule over the two countries. Constitutions were formulated by the French and a good deal of time was spent in discussing and arguing over the amendments the various national parties hoped to introduce. As time went on, the native presidents of Syria and Lebanon literally came to be appointed by the French. But peace and a kind of 'stable instability' did continue to reign in the two countries until the late summer of 1939, when the humiliating defeat of the French by the Germans in Europe lead the Syrians and Lebanese to hope for an end to the Mandate. The Franco-German Armistice of June 1940 dashed any such hopes, and the French continued to rule the two countries with reduced prestige but with a doubled political force that the war gave them, both as Vichy French allied with the Axis powers and Free French allied with the Allies.

The constitutions were suspended, a state of war emergency was declared and the French exercised direct rule even more intensively than ever in the past. An Anglo-Free French invasion of Syria and Lebanon, launched on 8 June 1941, lasted for thirty-four days after the Vichy French offered a far more stubborn resistance than was optimistically anticipated. The Free French intention, both before and immediately after this victorious operation, was to proclaim an independence for Syria and Lebanon, conditional on their conclusion of treaties to secure the 'rights and special interests' of France and exclude the British from any say or future interests in these countries. The actual proclamation was specific and unequivocal: 'A great hour in your history has struck: France declares you independent by the voice of her sons who are fighting for her life and for the liberty of the world.'

This unconditional promise contrasted strangely with the

later Free French assertion that the Mandate remained in force and would continue to do so until after the conclusion of the treaties to protect the rights, privileges and traditional strategic and commercial ties the French had enjoyed since after the First World War and even earlier. Regrettably the British supported the French in their quest for the proposed treaties, which were in reality a ploy to kill time and, essentially, the old Mandates masquerading as new deals. The high commissioner's title was to be replaced by that of a *délégué général*, but he had precisely the same powers disguised in flowery political language.

In the wake of the success of the Anglo-French invasion, most French in Syria and Lebanon remained. Some declared their loyalty and allegiance to the Free French, but many simply sat on the fence; nearly one third of the dyed-in-the-wool Vichyites were allowed to sail for home. The following months through to 1942 were marked by squabbles and dissention between the British and the Free French, the latter never ceasing to suspect the British of harbouring secret aims and ambitions for the control of Syria and Lebanon. Jabal al-Druze remained the most sensitive spot, since the French had always suspected the British, despite the facts in the case and the British repeated denials, of having aided the Druze Revolt of 1925.

Finally, in 1942, the Mandate in Syria and Lebanon went into its death-throes, marked by anti-French demonstrations and general strikes, some fighting by the Druze warriors in Lebanon, and the withdrawal of French troops under forcible pressure from the British. Jabal al-Druze opted for incorporation with Syria and gave up its autonomy, and the Maronites surprised the French by joining all the other communities in the bid to oust them. With the help of the British, this was achieved on 22 November 1943, when the French Mandate officially ended and French withdrawal from Lebanese affairs began. The French were never to forgive what they considered to be a gross act of treason

149

by the Maronites and a treacherous betrayal by the British, which thus forced them to depart the scene with graceless reluctance.

Following the withdrawal of the French, power-sharing was supposed to be distributed equitably among the communities in Lebanon, according to the unwritten National Covenant of 1943. This covenant had been hammered out between the feudal political leaders of the Lebanese religious communities and was based essentially on three principles: first, Mohammedan renunciation of an aspiration for Arab union; secondly, Christian acceptance of Lebanon as a part of the Arab Middle East and not an outpost of Europe, especially France; and thirdly, a reconfirmation, but this time with specific ratios, of the constitutional provisions introduced by the French in 1926 for the 'equitable' confessional distribution of seats and posts in the legislative and executive branches of government.

The covenant was a delicately balanced compromise which worked only so long as it served the interests of the political feudal lords from both communities. It was so ingenious that only the Lebanese could have conjured it up: Lebanon's identity defined as Arab yet not Arab, Western yet not Western. When Riad Solh, the Lebanese Sunni Moslem prime minister during the ending of the Mandate, made a speech to Parliament on 7 October 1943, he defined the country under the covenant in these terms: 'Lebanon is a homeland with an Arab face seeking beneficial good from the culture of the West.' Politicians defined the 'Arab face' as their interests dictated. When their interests changed, so did their definition. 'Beneficial good from the culture of the West' proved equally volatile in interpretation.

The covenant defined power-sharing as follows: the President of the Republic was to be a Maronite Christian; the president of the Chamber of Deputies, a Shi'ite Moslem; the prime minister, a Sunni Moslem. The Greek Orthodox were to have the deputy premiership and the vice-presidency

150

of the Chamber of Deputies. Although it was not clearly stipulated, the Druzes were to have the prestigious but in practice ineffective Ministry of Defence, for the Maronite commander-in-chief of the army held all the powers and the minister none. The director-general of security was a Maronite Christian. A ratio of six Christian Deputies in Parliament to every five Moslems was stipulated. This distribution of power according to religious persuasion permeated all the executive branches of government. The Druzes were allotted their quota in the feudal lords club – one Jumblatti and one Yazbaki.

The National Covenent in fact failed in its purpose and served only to divide the people into separate and discontented religious communities. It actually prevented the Lebanese from ever being Lebanese. Rather did it divide them more rigidly into factions: Maronite Christians, Sunni Moslems, Shi'ite Moslems, Greek Orthodox Christians, Druzes; and so reinforce the belief among the Lebanese that they are Christians and Mohammedans but never Lebanese.

The National Covenant hence endowed Lebanon with a hybrid democratic style of government, based on feudalism and religious representation. The feudal lords partitioned Lebanon into spheres of influence and controlled elections to Parliament. Each made his own list, and most of them sold the privilege of being on the list to candidates willing to contribute to what they called the 'election fund'. It was a Parliament of feudal stars, each circled about by his human satellites. There were, however, two genuine political parties, Kamal Jumblatt's Progressive Socialist Party and Pierre Gemayel's Kataeb (Phalangists). But neither party had, at the time, either the numbers or the power to be effective, and even they were feudal in their leadership, which passed from father to son.

Parliament was divided into two groups: those with the government and those against. Being with the government

151

depended on the number of privileges and favours allowed a political feudal lord. If he was denied the privileges that he felt were his due, he joined the Opposition, and thus would change his position at the same frequency as such privileges were granted or denied. Ministers were appointed not for their qualifications to manage a specific ministry, but to please the feudal lords and assure the newly appointed government of an adequate vote of confidence in Parliament.

A feudal lord's popularity depended on his ability to help his supporters flout the law and get unqualified members of his clan appointed to positions in the government and in Lebanese business organizations. The government's administrative services suffered most from this type of interference, and business organizations only slightly less. Reforming Lebanese society and the Lebanese system of government, and ridding it of the weaknesses of the confessional distribution of posts, proved consistently impossible, and thus did dual political and economic systems evolve in Lebanon.

Political feudalism continued mostly along the lines established by the French during the Mandate, while by its side there flourished a monopolistic system of financial control and exploitation by a handful of chosen traders. The ignorance of most of the political feudal lords of economic and financial matters, and their disregard for the national interest in favour of their own, encouraged the growth of what might be called a mafia of Lebanese traders, composed of merchants, bankers and entrepreneurs who colluded, regardless of religion, to exploit the country at the expense of the deprived Lebanese.

There was an unwritten understanding that the misdeeds of the political barons would be tolerated and never prosecuted. Article 80 of the Lebanese Constitution stipulates that a Supreme Court be formed with the power to prosecute the President of the Republic and the ministers should they be charged with treason, abuse of power or dereliction of duty.

Such a court was never convened. Conversely, a tradition developed to allow the incoming president to close the file on any misdeeds perpetrated by the outgoing president or his entourage. It also became the custom for a number of aides of an outgoing president to be appointed to positions of immunity as ambassadors or promoted to important positions in government. Naturally such a tradition, which guarantees heads of government safety from retribution, encourages mismanagement and corruption throughout the administration.

When corruption in government became endemic and over-obvious, a few political leaders, headed by Kamal Jumblatt and Raymond Eddé, forced through a law, passed by Parliament on 14 April 1954, requiring all public servants to submit a declaration detailing their families' assets to enable the authorities to verify additional sources of revenue. It was known as 'The law of where did you get this?' When it was filed but never applied, it came as no surprise and no one objected. In Lebanon there is no civil or national public opinion, because even that is sectarian. Occasions are almost unknown when the religious communities agree to act together as Lebanese. But it is not only sectarian differences which are responsible for the subservience of the Lebanese public. Through resistance to every invasion in the past, the Lebanese have mastered the art of survival, whose first axiom is to look after oneself. In order of priorities, a Lebanese places his personal interests first, then the interests of his family, then those of the religion he belongs to, and finally the interests of the particular political feudal lord whom he expects to protect his personal interests. Traditional attachment to a feudal political system and to religion have played a major part in bringing about the horrific conflict that raged for sixteen years from 1975.

*

The world never took Lebanese sovereignty seriously because Lebanon was not, in reality, a country with national unity. Ambassadors of foreign nations developed a habitual pattern of ostentatious intervention in Lebanon's internal national politics. After conducting frequent visits to political leaders to exchange views, these diplomats made political declarations which not only abused Lebanese hospitality but also mocked normal diplomatic practice and even violated the sovereignty of Lebanon. They appeared to believe that their letters of accreditation gave them authority to meddle in Lebanese affairs. Attachés, counsellors, Intelligence officers and spies from embassies all assumed the same rights. These curious patterns of behaviour and attitude were first established by the ambassadors of the Superpowers, but they were soon succeeded by a diplomatic free-for-all. It was to make it extremely easy for those same powers to play an active part in fomenting and fanning the flames of the war.

The weaknesses, imperfections and faults of the Lebanese were also to contribute in large measure to the war which transformed Lebanon from a beautiful country, famous for its trade and tourism alike, into a monstrous human slaughterhouse. But Lebanese imperfections alone could never have led to a bloodbath on such a drastic scale. The initial situation could have been resolved by a few skirmishes, even a short-lived civil war speedily ended by the usual Lebanese compromise, had it not been for two formidable underlying forces.

The first of these was Israel, with its desire to encroach on Arab lands and its plans to fragment the Arab countries to protect this expansionist policy. The second horrific force was oil, a commercial necessity at the root of modern civilization. Those who desire it and covet the power it brings, as well as those who already have it and abuse the power it has given, are constantly engaged in policy games of catch-as-catch-can.

Unfortunately for Lebanon, it was ideally placed to serve

the objective of these two powerful forces. Israel targetted it as seeming to be the easiest neighbouring country to fragment. The West resented having to pay realistic prices for oil and was jealous that the Arabs should have in their hands the fortunes it formerly reserved for itself. It was determined to get the money back, the easiest way being to foment trouble in or adjacent to the countries which produced the oil – especially in the Third World – and then to stand by to sell them all the arms needed to enable the dissension to continue. This process has cynically been termed the 'recycling of petro-dollars', and the Arab-Israeli conflict was encouraged and used for that purpose.

The seeds to the war in Lebanon were actually sown in 1957, when the Americans, with the help of some of their European allies, rigged the parliamentary elections to secure a pro-American, pro-Western majority in the Lebanese Parliament. They also sought to get rid of any Deputies who strongly objected to the Eisenhower Doctrine, which Lebanon's government was the first country to adhere to. The doctrine was proposed by President Eisenhower in January 1957 and passed as a joint Congressional Resolution authorizing the President of the United States to commit American troops to the defence of any government in the Middle East threatened by suspected communist aggression from within or from outside its boundaries; and to give economic and military aid to the threatened state to build up its own defences. It was mainly designed to halt the Arab nationalist wave of Nasserism, then beginning to sweep through the Arab world. To achieve their objective of rigging the votes, the Americans utilized the Central Intelligence Agency (CIA) and its funds.

The rigging was successful, and all the Mohammedan political feudal lords who had opposed the Eisenhower Doctrine, including Kamal Jumblatt, the Druze leader, lost the parliamentary seats they had held in successive elections since Lebanon's independence in 1943. These ousted political feudal lords then ganged together to seek revenge by plotting a rebellion to overthrow the rigged Lebanese government. They looked to Syria for help, promising in return that Lebanon would be incorporated within the United Arab Republic (UAR). Since Syria was at the time freshly united with Nasser's Egypt in the recently formed UAR, the promise inspired them to provide the rebels with financial aid and to supply arms and ammunition while seeing many valid reasons for going along with the planned rising.

Syria was naturally strongly opposed to the Eisenhower Doctrine and to the machinations of the CIA, which had, in 1956 in Syria, planned a military *coup* that failed miserably. Syrian army officers, assigned a major role in the projected *coup*, had in fact gone to their government, paid in the bribe money the CIA gave them and handed over the names of the CIA agents who contacted them. The Syrians were furious, but could do nothing against the might of the United States. In any case, they had from the beginning resented the use of Lebanon by the CIA as a base for its activities in the Arab Middle East. Furthermore, they had never forgotten nor forgiven the loss of the four Syrian districts annexed by France to Lebanon in 1920 to create the 'Grand Liban'.

Kamal Jumblatt and his followers, however, did not approve of the plan to take Lebanon into the United Arab Republic. While Kamal Jumblatt shared in the craving for revenge for the election rigging, he had a far loftier and nobler objective. As a socialist and reformer, he had the vision of uniting sectarian Lebanon into one non-sectarian socialist state, friendly to Syria and the United Arab Republic but definitely independent and free from its domination. His Progressive Socialist Party had been founded in 1949 with objectives of social justice and anti-imperialism. Its members were, in the great majority, Jumblatti Druzes, but they also included Christians, Sunni Moslems and Shi'ites. Thus it was Kamal Jumblatt's Progressive Socialist Party and not the Druze community as a whole who joined the rebellion of 1958 to overthrow the government which rigged the 1957 elections.

In May 1958, when fighting broke out in Beirut and within days plunged Lebanon into a state of rebellion that paralysed the country, the Yazbaki Druzes, who formed 50 per cent of the Druze community, took no part. Their feudal political lord at the time, Emir Majid Arslan, had not lost his seat in the 1957 elections. In fact he was a staunch supporter of the government and of the Maronite Christian Lebanese. He even attempted to halt Kamal Jumblatt and his Druze fighters when, at the head of a force of Yazbaki Druzes, he proceeded to a village east of Beirut and engaged the Jumblattis in a futile battle that left some of his most valiant fighters dead and forced him into a hasty retreat.

The rebellion blossomed Lebanese style. There was prolific shooting in the air, a setting up of barricades in the streets, a burning of old tyres, a lot of noise and daily declarations from the rebel leaders censuring the government, but still there was no real fighting; except by Kamal Jumblatt and his socialist Druzes, who fought fierce engagements in the mountains against the well-armed 'Syrian Popular Party' (PPS), a right-wing faction violently opposed to President Abdel Nasser. (Ironically, many PPS members were Druzes.) The other Lebanese communities' casualties in the rebellion remained relatively few, and the commanding officer of the Lebanese army, the Maronite Christian General Fouad Shihab, refused to support the government and use the army against the rebels. This refusal he justified by a desire to avoid the shedding of Lebanese blood. The government appealed to the United States for help, and in July 1958 American marines landed on the beaches of Beirut.

The marines stayed three months, without on this occasion firing a shot. The rebellion was ended, but a stalemate soon developed since American policy was far from clear and was divided on what it hoped to achieve by intervention. The stated aim was to rally to the aid of the 'legally and democratically elected' government in response to its appeal. But other Americans favoured a more even-handed approach that sought at the same time to maintain links with the rebel feudal lords by aiding them as well. In fact Mr Robert Murphy, sent by the State Department to resolve the rift between the American officials in Beirut, had his first meeting not with the democratically elected President of the Lebanese Republic, who had appealed for American assistance under the Eisenhower Doctrine, but with one of the feudal leaders of the rebellion.

It was General Fouad Shihab who, with the support of the Americans, was next elected President of Lebanon. The appointment angered the Maronites since they considered General Shihab a traitor for refusing to perform his duty and use his army to support the former Maronite president. General Shihab then aggravated the situation further by calling on one of the Moslem rebel leaders to form his first Cabinet, which, it came as no surprise to find, was dominated by the rebels and their supporters. This infuriated the Maronite Christians and confirmed their suspicion that Mohammedan communities in Lebanon, having never believed in an independent Lebanon and, in their opinion, never ceased to use every effort to incorporate the country with Islamic Syria, had scored a victory and could well be on the way to achieving their objective. General Shihab was spitefully referred to in the Maronite community as 'Mohammed Fouad Shihab'.

The behaviour of the Americans, their dialogue with the rebels and their evident support for them was all to cause alarm to the Christians and to have a lasting and damaging effect on Lebanon. It legitimized the use of an armed uprising against a legally elected government as an alternative to dialogue in the processes of democratic political opposition, and once it was established that, by taking up the gun, a faction could obtain political advantage without fear of the consequences, then the gun became the most powerful force in Lebanese politics. And, in the words of a top CIA executive:

Within days of the end of the crisis, groups of all religions and political colour were arming themselves with the idea that 'We must fight for what is ours'. Prior to the crisis of 1958 American diplomats as well as American business men firmly believed that the way to forestall violence was to ensure that it did not pay. This was further enforced by a conviction, held by the same people, that those who resort to violence, however right their cause, cannot be trusted in any circumstances.

So wrote Miles Copeland in *The Game of Nations*.

During the Lebanese rebellion of 1958 and the years that followed, the American reversed their policy of 'the way to forestall violence was to ensure that it did not pay' and instead favoured and encouraged violence and made sure that it did indeed pay. With American backing, violence and the gun were to pay off handsomely for those rebels who took up arms against democratically elected Lebanese governments. The Eisenhower Doctrine was murdered and buried in Lebanon.

The turn-around in American policy was no doubt at the behest of the arms manufacturers, who had built huge armament factories during the Second World War and as a result reaped enormous profits. Once the war was over, they were left with idle factories, large work forces and soaring losses. To remedy the situation, they worked on two fronts: to encourage regional wars and armed confrontations world wide, and to frighten the American people and their allies into arming themselves against the communist menace.

An incident I witnessed at first hand throws a light on what the arms manufacturers in the United States suffered after the fall in demand for their wares after the war as well as how they were able to remedy these heavy losses. I was privileged to know and to have gained the friendship of Colonel Sosthenes Behn, the chairman and, with his brother, founder of the International Telephone and Telegraph conglomerate (ITT).

On one of my visits to the States, Colonel Behn invited me to accompany him to an outing to Federal, an ITT company in New Jersey. Federal was a large radio manufacturing works, very modern and highly equipped with outstanding skills, both human and technical. The buildings stood in a large park, and I thought it the most beautiful factory I ever saw. On the return journey to New York, I was profuse in my compliments and admiration. Colonel Behn smiled and said, 'Yes, it is beautiful, but Najib, we are in the red with it this year to the tune of 20 million dollars.' The subject was changed and we spoke no more of Federal. Two years later, on another of my trips to New York, I was invited to lunch by Colonel Behn in the famous penthouse he kept above his offices. After lunch, as we were having coffee in his office, I asked the colonel about Federal. 'Najib,' he said, 'we are fine and the company is very much in the black.' I asked him how this came about. 'The war in Korea,' he replied.

Yet not even the wars of Korea and Vietnam, and between the Arabs and the Israelis, and all the other armed conflicts we have seen, were enough to satisfy the output of the arms manufacturers and their greed. So they embarked on feeding the scare of communism and the Cold War, which diverted huge portions of their countries' national budgets to fuel an arms race of which they alone were the beneficiaries. Now that the menace of the so-called Cold War has disappeared, they will doubtless redouble their efforts to enflame existing regional wars and confrontations and effectively oppose all efforts to bring about settlements. At the same time, they will try by every means to promote more such conflicts to keep their trade booming. They are working hard to find a symbolic enemy to take the place of communism as a focus for the fears of the peoples of the West. It has been rumoured that Islam is nominated for the role!

It will be clear from what I have written that the war in

Lebanon actually started in 1958. There was then a long uneasy period of 'wait and prepare', which continued until 1975. Scores of books and hundreds of articles have been published about the Lebanese war. The purpose of the remainder of the present book is to describe the role the Druzes played in it and how it came about that a minority of less than 10 per cent of the population of Lebanon could have held such an important and dominant position in the fighting and claim a decisive say in all matters related to the political future of Lebanon. It will also expose certain aspects of the war in Lebanon which have not, in the author's opinion, been adequately dealt with previously.

Part Two
The Bitter Fruits of Conflict

9. The Drawing of the Battle-lines

Soon after the initial victory of arms over democracy in Lebanon, all the major communities in the country were encouraged to begin arming themselves in preparation for what, it was said, must be the inevitable confrontation arising from the seeds sown in 1958 through the wish shown by the Mohammedan communities to be incorporated with Syria. The Maronites continued to accuse the Druzes as a whole of being party to the plot to have Lebanon taken over by Syria, notwithstanding the fact that it was only the Jumblatti Druzes of the Progressive Socialist Party who were involved in the 1958 rebellion and despite Kamal Jumblatt's repeated declarations that he sought no more than a socialist Lebanon, completely free of foreign domination.

The Phalangists, the Maronite Christian militia, were reported to number between 6,000 and 8,000. The Druzes were born warriors, and had proved time and again that they were among the best fighting forces in the world. They needed no training to become an effective militia force and they all went armed. A Druze house is considered shamefully under-equipped if it lacks arms to defend the independence and rights of the Druze community.

Only a small militia was maintained by the Sunni Moslems, but they believed they could always count on Syria and the Palestinians for help. The Shi'ite community, subjected to an orchestrated campaign, were meanwhile made highly conscious of being the most deprived group in Lebanon.

And so they were, though the great gap between rich and poor was not confined to the Shi'ites alone: 'In Lebanon, at the time, 4 per cent of the population retained 60 per cent of the country's gross national income. Ninety-six per cent of the Lebanese had to make do with the 40 per cent that remained.' Overall, however, the Shi'ites were the poorest of the communities. Their awareness of their position made them ready to accept arms from anyone willing to supply them as they prepared to fight for their legitimate rights.

The consequence of all these tensions was that the Lebanese communities came to be psychologically prepared for confrontation. They then needed only a pretext, and this the Palestinians readily provided, in particular those who had been driven out of Jordan in 1970 by King Hussein's army. They had not been settled long in Lebanon, their new host country, before they began to act with arrogant disdain for the Lebanese government's authority and took the law into their own hands in a number of incidents, mostly in Moslem West Beirut. One of the most flagrant was a battle fought by Palestinian commandos with a gang of Moslem Lebanese smugglers. Several gang leaders were killed, and others captured and executed by the Palestinians, yet no one objected to this irregular vigilante action. The Palestinian Resistance Movement therefore proceeded to take over the policing of all the Moslem armed gangs, not only in Beirut, but right across Lebanon. They assumed a responsibility for dealing with the illegal activities of these gangs that amounted to setting up an independent police force.

In 1973, the Palestinians' overbearing behaviour provoked a confrontation with the Lebanese army. After two weeks of sporadic shooting, the opposing sides came to an arrangement. By the standards of what would happen two years later, it had been a very modest affair, but the resentment against the Palestinians in Lebanon was by now universal. Even Kamal Jumblatt, a firm supporter of the Palestinians, described their behaviour in these terms in *I Speak for Lebanon*:

It has to be said that the Palestinians themselves, by violating Lebanese law, bearing arms as they chose and policing certain important points of access to the capital, actually furthered the plot that had been hatched against them. They carelessly exposed themselves to criticism and even to hatred. High officials and administrators were occasionally stopped and asked for their identity papers by Palestinian patrols. From time to time, Lebanese citizens and foreigners were arrested and imprisoned, on the true or false pretext of having posed a threat to the Palestinian revolution. Such actions were, at first, forgiven, but became increasingly difficult to tolerate. Outsiders making the law in Lebanon, armed demonstrations and ceremonies, military funerals for martyrs of the revolution, it all mounted up and began to alienate public opinion, especially conservative opinion, which was particularly concerned about security. Industry and commerce, the main activities of the Christians and especially of the Maronites, required a stable society. I never saw a less discreet, less cautious revolution [than the Palestinian].

It is nevertheless a mistake to speak of the Palestinians as the sole cause for the start of the present war in Lebanon. Those who say so forget it was the Maronite Christians, not the Moslems, who were responsible for the large Palestinian presence coming about in Lebanon and for the Palestinians being given freedom of action against neighbouring Israel. The first Maronite President of the Lebanese Republic, Sheikh Bishara el-Khoury, in fact allowed large numbers of them to enter in 1948 – numbers by far exceeding the share tiny Lebanon should have accepted in proportion with the numbers accepted by other very much larger Arab countries. Sheikh Bishara made this concession in return for Moslem support for an unconstitutional plan he put forward to renew his presidential mandate for a further term of six years.

It was another Maronite President of Lebanon, Charles
Hélou, who approved the signing in 1969 of the Cairo
Agreement between Lebanon and the Palestine Liberation
Organization. This was the authority that gave the PLO
uncontrolled and unrestricted freedom to attack Israel from
Lebanon. It implied, moreover, a point of no return for
Lebanon's sovereignty, and virtually established the PLO
as a state within the Lebanese state. The organization also
acquired Arquob, a piece of Lebanon (Fath Land), from
which to operate unhindered against Israel.

Even worse than the signing of the Cairo Agreement was
the way in which it was approved and ratified by the
Lebanese Parliament without its contents being commu-
nicated to the parliamentary Deputies. As the Maronite
Christian political leader, Raymond Eddé, declared in an
interview printed on 6 October 1989 in the Arabic magazine
Al-Hawadeth:

When President Charles Hélou asked the Speaker of
the House not to disclose the contents of the Cairo
agreement to the members of Parliament, he, Mr Eddé,
had spoken for two hours, trying to dissuade Parliament
from ratifying such an important agreement without
knowing its contents, but to no avail. A parliament
that willingly accepts being ordered by a so-called
democratically elected president to ratify an agreement
of vital national importance without being allowed to
know its contents is a bizarre novelty in democratic
procedures.

The Palestinians who were chased out of Jordan were able to
flock freely with their arms into Lebanon as a result of the
Cairo Agreement, promoted and forced through Parliament
by a dominant Christian Maronite administration. By 1975,
however, the Christians had been manipulated into firmly
believing that the intruding Palestinians sought to overthrow

the traditional Lebanese system of government and replace it with a Moslem-dominated socialist state to be incorporated with Syria. (The fact that nearly all the Lebanese and Syrian gurus of communism and radical socialism were not Moslem but Christian throws an interesting sidelight on this aspect.) The Palestinians, on the other hand, were simultaneously led to believe that the Maronite Christians were, as friends of Israel and King Hussein, determined to liquidate the PLO. No declarations to the contrary by leaders on either side had the slightest effect in damping down the rising tension and increasing hatred of one faction for the other.

The radical forces in Lebanon therefore sought to equip themselves better to confront the internationally supported rightist Christians. They grouped themselves into the National Movement, of which Kamal Jumblatt was elected leader and chief spokesman. The Palestinians promptly associated themselves with the movement, thus inextricably entangling their political disputes with domestic Lebanese problems. As a result, the line-up of hostile groupings developed into Lebanese rightists *versus* Lebanese leftists and ceased to be the Lebanese *versus* the intruding Palestinians.

The National Movement was a coalition of Kamal Jumblatt's Progressive Socialist Party and twelve other radical factions, including the Nasserites and the Communist Party. All had differing radical aims and objectives, differing sponsors and financial providers, differing religions and differing power-loving leaders. With the exception of the Druzes in Kamal Jumblatt's Progressive Socialist Party and the members of the Palestine Resistance Movement, many of the balance of parties had no or only a few trained fighters at their command. It was the powerful and charismatic personality of Kamal Jumblatt that held them together.

The Palestine Resistance Movement was made up of the PLO (Palestine Liberation Organization or Fath) and eight other well-known Palestinian resistance groups. (It is said that, besides these eight, there came to be as many as fourteen other splinter groups with claims to being part of the movement.) The PLO and the eight groups in turn had differing political and ideological aims and objectives, differing sponsors, differing financial backers and differing methods of action. Their main qualities in common were and are being well-trained, well-armed and determined effective fighters. At times the other groups have acted in unison with the PLO, but on many occasions they have acted unilaterally.

It was therefore a stupendous feat on the part of Kamal Jumblatt's National Movement to carry on effectively despite the enormous difficulties arising from this conglomerate of different parties with varying aims and objectives, and with so many group leaders who were utterly enamoured of their independent powers of leadership. When the fighting finally happened, the most efficient actions would be those of the Druze fighters of the Progressive Socialist Party and the armed forces of the Palestine Resistance Movement.

First, however, there came an intensifying of tensions when Rashid Karami, hereditary Moslem political boss of Tripoli, announced that he intended to present himself as a candidate for the presidency, the sacrosanct post reserved in the National Covenant for the Maronite Christians. This deepened the suspicion that not only the radical National Movement with its Palestinian allies but also the Moslems were joining in the plot to destroy Lebanon's traditionally accepted pattern of government and instal a Moslem leftist radical state willing to be incorporated with Syria.

By the summer of 1974, there were clashes and disturbances throughout the country: explosions in Beirut, a raid on the Bank of America by a group belonging to the Arab communist organization, strikes by students, night-watchmen and firemen, and violent student demonstrations. Workers in Tripoli, Beirut, Sidon and Tyre took industrial action over the rising cost of living. Threats were heard of a general strike to demand changes in the Lebanese Labour Law.

Political demonstrations against Henry Kissinger's visits to the Middle East degenerated into riots. The students of the American University in Beirut occupied the university buildings to demand student participation in running the university and protest against a proposed increase in tuition fees. These clashes, demonstrations and strikes were by no means haphazard and spontaneous, but were directed by political forces inside and outside the country.

Lebanon was by this time flooded with foreign secret agents who practised their trade and recruited Lebanese nationals to the country's detriment. It became impossible, when talking to a foreigner, to guess whether he was what he claimed or a spy working for one or more foreign powers. In fact it was the spies of foreign powers who would orchestrate the Lebanese war. The diplomats fled Lebanon and left the field to their Intelligence services, who were expected to act upon instruction, though most of the time they acted on their own.

The writing on the Lebanese wall was clear. Sophisticated weapons poured in and intensive preparations for a major confrontation were under way. A bloody battle was about to be waged that would affect the life of every Lebanese citizen. With the battle-lines drawn for the resumption of the 1958 civil war, the first violent tremors were felt on 13 April 1975, when Pierre Gemayel, head of the Maronite Phalangists (Kataeb), was on a visit to Ayn al-Rummaneh, a Christian suburb of Beirut, to attend the consecration of a new church. A car with covered number-plates drove towards the church and sprayed the crowd with automatic fire, killing four men, two of whom were Kataeb (Phalangist) party members – one a bodyguard of Pierre Gemayel himself. The killers escaped.

On the same day, a bus full of Palestinian commandos, returning to camp from a meeting in West Beirut, was passing through Ayn al-Rummaneh as gunmen, presumed to be Christian, opened fire and shot dead thirty, of whom twenty-six were Palestinians. It later transpired that these killers were not Christian militia, in the view of Elias Khalil Zakharia, director-general of justice in Lebanon, who was charged with investigating the incident. In an interview published in July 1983 in the Lebanese weekly *Al-Afkar*, he claimed that agents of the foreign power which had the 'greatest number of agents in Lebanon' were responsible and that the shooting came from inside not outside the bus. He also disclosed that the bus, which displayed all the evidence, disappeared from the municipality garage while in police custody and it was never afterwards possible to trace it or find who caused its disappearance.

From this point the war began to rage, and despite incessant political activity, Lebanon was henceforward to know no more than brief periods of calm invariably shattered by fresh clashes and attacks with rockets, cannons, missiles, bombs, explosive devices as well as the newly introduced tactics of terror: sniping at civilians and kidnapping. Government authority disintegrated; lawlessness prevailed.

Elias Sarkis, President of Lebanon for six years during some of the darkest days, never doubted where responsibility lay. On 31 January 1982, the Lebanese journal *An-Nahar* quoted him as saying: 'The solution of the Lebanese crisis is not in the hands of the Lebanese but in the hands of Brezhnev, Reagan and Begin.' Chafic Wazzan, then prime minister of Lebanon, was even more specific. In a speech reported by *L'Orient-Le Jour* on 12 March 1982, he said: 'Les États-Unis sont responsables de nos malheurs' ('The United States is responsible for our misfortunes').

The United States may or may not have been responsible. What is beyond doubt is that, had the United States wished, it could have ended the Lebanese war within forty-eight hours of it starting. (The Arab-Israeli war would take a bit longer.) Yet in blaming the Americans alone for what was being done in Lebanon, Prime Minister Wazzan was forgetting the others: the Russians, the Europeans, the Arab countries, the Israelis and the Palestinians. All bore their share of guilt for what happened, not only in Lebanon but throughout the Middle East. All were to pursue their own interests; and thereby, separately and collectively, they brought death and destruction.

The United States, in seeking to support Israel, fight international communism and protect the Arabian oil fields (its primary interest), repeatedly assured the Lebanese of support for their continued independence, sovereignty and geographical integrity, and displayed its readiness to lend a powerful hand to those who opposed leftist influences. President Reagan himself described Lebanon as part of America's 'vital interests'. The end result of those assurances is the Lebanon of today: a country occupied by the Syrian and Israeli armies and an entity remote from being sovereign and independent. If this is how the Americans guard their 'vital interests', then one can only despair for the developing world as it looks to America for protection and wise leadership.

The USSR, for its part, wanted to combat imperialism, support the Palestinians, destabilize the region and encourage the Arab socialist states. Israel wanted, in the short term, to annex south Lebanon and fragment Syria, with as many other countries as possible, in numerous mini-states, hopefully as Israeli satellites. In the longer term, the Israeli dream of a Greater Israel is far from being abandoned.

The Syrian objective all along has been to regain the districts they claim were taken from them under the 'Grand Liban' conspiracy of 1920 and to help the Palestinians and convert Lebanon to their own, Ba'athist, version of socialism. The Palestinians, supposedly there to fight Israel from Lebanon, were drawn into the plot to destroy Lebanon and came to believe they possessed the right to play a dominant role in events as the militia force of the Moslems. They claimed that the road to Jerusalem lay through Jounieh, when Jounieh is a town that lies in the heart of Maronite Christian land, north of Beirut, in quite the opposite direction from Jerusalem!

France supported Lebanon, and proclaimed its sympathy for the Lebanese, especially the Maronites. The Vatican fervently supported the Maronite Christians, fearing their extermination by the Moslems. The British, too, played a part, presumably to assist the United States, though no one knows for certain what their role has been in reality. Certainly they wished to preserve their Middle East markets. Nearly all the other European states maintained an active presence in Lebanon, but no one understood what they truly wanted or what they were doing there.

The Arab oil-producing countries supplied funds and arms to almost all the fighting parties under various pretexts: aiding the Palestine cause; helping rightists against leftists, leftists against rightists; protecting Moslems from Christians, Christians from Moslems. Kamal Jumblatt and his Palestinian allies had in fact hoped that the Arab states would come to their assistance and help the Palestinians to regain their lands and homes lost to Israel and save Lebanon the horrors of war. In this ambition they were greatly disappointed. The Arab governments were determined to confine the Palestine Resistance Movement to Lebanon and keep it as far distant as possible from their own countries, even as they continued to maintain, for public consumption, accounts of how they were helping the Palestinians in their rightful cause. They were, as keenly as the United States, determined to crush communism, which, they were convinced, had begun to show its satanic face in Kamal Jumblatt's National Movement.

In *I Speak for Lebanon*, Kamal Jumblatt expressed his feelings about the Arab states when he wrote: 'No state or empire in history has had at its disposal so much money, power, energy and prestige as these Arab oil states, and no government or state in history has used it so badly.' Kamal Jumblatt was not the first Druze fighting chief to express resentment and disillusion at a lack of Arab support. When, on his death-bed, Sultan Pasha Al-Attrash, the illustrious Druze warrior, heard how Israel had annexed the Golan Heights in June 1967, he exclaimed, 'God curse them, not the Israelis who did it but the Arabs who did nothing. Their land is taken and they do not react. They have the armies, they have the tanks, they have the war planes and they have the money and they do nothing. I despise these rich Arabs.'

No country with an arms industry failed to be highly active in selling its wares to the various factions, either directly or through the arms merchants who descended upon Lebanon like jackals scenting a carcass. But while each of these countries must take its share of the blame, the Lebanese cannot escape their own responsibility. Other countries were certainly to play vital roles in the devastation, but they could never have succeeded unless certain of the Lebanese had proved to be more than willing partners in their schemes.

As a result, between 1975 and the present, no less than 180,000 Lebanese were destined to be killed in the two Israeli invasions and the never-ending fighting that would also leave hundreds of thousands maimed and badly injured. For the most part, the great army of the dead was to be recruited from innocent victims, trapped in the cross-fire through no fault of their own in conflicts nurtured by international intrigue.

10. The Role of Kamal Jumblatt's National Movement

Kamal Jumblatt's National Movement, backed by the Palestine Resistance Movement and supported by the Syrians, was a successful force. By the early summer of 1976, it was poised to occupy the Maronite Christian land and capable of achieving such an aim. Strangely enough, at this point, the leftist Syrians reversed their policy and came to the rescue of the rightist Christians. Even more strangely, it was a case of Moslem Syria rallying to the aid of the Christians in Lebanon against both the Moslems and the Palestinians for whose cause Syria was constantly at war with Israel. The Syrian forces that invaded Lebanon in June had by September defeated Kamal Jumblatt's leftists and halted them short of their objective. This intervention was prompted by an appeal from the Maronites to the Syrians that had the approval of the United States, Israel, the Vatican and many European states. It also received the blessing of many Arab countries.

The reason given for the Syrian government's dramatic change of policy was outlined in a statement issued from Damascus:

> The Syrian Arab Republic rejects confessional fighting, and it rejects the killing of nationals because of their religious affiliations. This is not part of the manners, values or principles of the Arab people. Additionally, confessional killing is contradictory to the spirit of love and forgiveness that characterizes Islam and Christianity.

Accordingly, the Syrian Arab Republic cannot in
any way be a party to confessional conflict, but will
steadfastly fight against it.

There were two other reasons given by the Syrians for their intervention in Lebanon, the first being their deep-rooted belief in the indivisibility of Syria and Lebanon. Secondly, there was President Hafez Al-Assad's fervent wish to convince the Maronite Christians that they no longer needed to turn to Europe and the United States for protection, but could look to the Arabs, and to Syria in particular.

'Listen,' President Assad told Kamal Jumblatt, 'for me this is a historic opportunity to re-orient the Maronites towards Syria, to win their trust, to make them realize that their source of protection is no longer France or the West. They must be helped to stop going to beg for help abroad.' This conversation was recorded in *I Speak for Lebanon* by Kamal Jumblatt, who went on to comment that, in his opinion, 'this was a bad calculation and a total lack of understanding of Lebanon's problem. President Assad felt it was his national duty as an Arab to disengage the Maronites from the magic protective circle of France and Europe.' Kamal Jumblatt then asked further:

Was President Al-Assad sincere? At the time, he
seemed to be, but who would say so lately? Politics
is not charity. At first, admittedly, his *tour de force*
succeeded, but eventually Maronite suspicions prevailed.
Arab-Muslim occupation always frightens the Maronites,
especially if the occupying forces are the Syrians,
whom they have always considered their worst enemies.
The Maronites' nightmare is that, once the Syrians
have entered the region, they will not leave it again.
There was an outcry when the Syrians marched into
Beirut and the Metn. In fact, it is neither the Muslims
nor the patriotic Christians who express the greatest

reservations about the Syrian aggression; the Maronites are the ones who are the most appalled by what has happened. Especially now that the Syrians are here, they (the Maronites) can forget their dreams of partition and a little Maronite state. The isolationists (Maronites) are often slow to understand the consequences of their actions.

In the light of all that has happened in Lebanon subsequently, who could deny that Kamal Jumblatt was a prophet in Lebanese and Syrian politics? If the Syrians had held other concealed aims and objectives in Lebanon in 1976, what was there to prevent them exacting these as the price for saving the Maronite Christians at the time? The Syrians would have been granted any concessions, for the Maronites had no choice except to give in and the Sunni Moslems and the Shi'ites would have agreed readily. Only Kamal Jumblatt and the Druzes would have stood out in opposition. The Syrians, however, never made any such demands, but changed their role later from 'saviours' to 'squatters', encouraged in this by the Lebanese politicians and the spectacle the latter presented with their political intrigues, personal ambitions, corruption and sectarian hatreds. Above all, there was the manifest Maronite desire for alliance with Israel, which, the Syrians believed, could seriously endanger their national security.

Despite all the justifications given for the Syrian presence in Lebanon in 1976, the Druzes objected and were the only Lebanese community openly to do so. Their viewpoint was affirmed in a letter to President Assad from Kamal Jumblatt:

I beg you to withdraw the troops you have sent to Lebanon. Carry on with your political intervention, your mediation, your arbitration. You were about to succeed, one might even say you have succeeded already. But you want unanimity and that is impossible. The two sides both want peace now and an agreement is imminent. Your political arbitration will then be even more unlikely to be effective. But I must advise you against military means. *We do not want to be a satellite state. We want to be independent.* We do not want the sort of federation preached by your Ba'ath Party representatives in Beirut. In any case, the Israelis would eventually turn upon such a federation; perhaps they will conquer large areas of Southern Lebanon (the Israeli intervention has already begun; Christian enclaves are being set up along the frontier) in order to create the secure frontiers they want, leaving you with only a part of Lebanon and with a Maronite state somewhere in the Mountain. Or else they will attack you directly, because a 'Greater Syria' is a danger to Israel. Furthermore, Europe will not welcome this partition of our little country, like some new Poland or Czechoslovakia.

Do not think we are opposed to the Arab union, on the contrary. We are the only party to have presented a rational federative programme and constitution to all the Arab leaders – but we want a federation which guarantees us our freedom. We do not want the great Syrian prison. *When you have moved towards political democracy in Syria, when you have created a real democracy on Western lines, then we will be the first to ask that Lebanon become part of a Syrian federation.*

Kamal Jumblatt's letter to President Assad, written a year before his own assassination, had no effect at all and the Syrian army remained in Lebanon, later to be transformed by an Arab Summit into an Arab Deterrent Force. It is in Lebanon still, and there it will stay indefinitely, or so long as the United States and Israel allow it to remain.

Kamal Jumblatt was assassinated in March 1977, but that year also saw a rapid return to normal and plans were put in hand to start repairing the damage. But any hopes that the lull would hold proved too good to be true. The troubles resumed early in 1978 when fighting flared up all over the country. The pretexts of rightists fighting leftists, Christians fighting Moslems, Christians fighting the Palestinians, the have-nots fighting the haves and other proclaimed reasons were transparently exposed. Behind them loomed the real and even more sinister reason for the war: a plot to destroy Lebanon and its economy and turn it into a Christian state friendly to Israel; failing which, the scheme was to fragment the country into small sectarian cantons capable only of fighting between themselves.

In all the fighting before and after 1978, the Druzes as a whole community took no part. Only the Druzes of Kamal Jumblatt's Progressive Socialist Party participated, a fact that Kamal Jumblatt, and his son Walid after him, repeatedly affirmed. Nevertheless the Maronite leaders and their foreign supporters still declined, for their own reasons, to be convinced.

It suited them better to continue to believe firmly that the Jumblatts, as Druze leaders, involved all the Druzes in whatever they undertook. In holding rigidly to this belief, they ignored the fact that the Yazbaki Druzes, constituting 50 per cent of the Druze community in Lebanon, not only took no part in the fighting but openly declared their friendship and support for the Maronite Christians. Instead the Maronite leaders incited frequent acts of provocation against the Druze community as a whole in efforts to bring about a general Druze involvement in the war.

Hundreds of Druzes were murdered at the check-point barricades manned by Maronite Christians, simply because they were Druzes; for a novel method of murder was introduced by the Maronite Christian militias, the Phalangists – a practice termed 'murder by religious identity'. In Lebanon, religion is an item clearly recorded on everyone's identity card. Militiamen at the check-points, set up in various locations, would therefore ask a passer-by for his identity card.

180

So long as the religion specified was Christian, the passer-by could continue to his destination. But if it was Moslem, Shi'ite or Druze, the unfortunate holder was slaughtered on the spot.

This barbarous practice, subsequently adopted by the Phalangists as a legitimate fighting tactic in the Lebanese war, began on Saturday, 6 December 1975, better known in the history of the war in Lebanon as 'Black Saturday', when hundreds of Moslems, Shi'ites and Druzes were massacred and large numbers kidnapped and later killed. The justification given by the Maronite Christian militias for the massacre was that it was in retaliation for four Phalangists found murdered in a car at the roadside.

The populations of two Druze villages in Maronite Christian land were summarily murdered, men, women and children alike. The two villages had been in that area of Lebanon since its creation, and had lived peacefully alongside their Maronite Christian neighbours for centuries. The Druzes preferred to believe that the murderers must have been in the pay of a foreign power, intent on inciting the Druzes to fight the Maronite Christians. It was this belief that kept the Druzes in check and held them back from retaliation, for they could never imagine their Christian acquaintances and neighbours, with whom they had co-existed so long, suddenly taking or approving such action.

Kamal Jumblatt's sister was herself assassinated by members of a well-known Maronite Christian militia. She was of noble birth and had devoted her life to acts of charity from which Lebanese of all sectarian beliefs benefited. She had never been involved in Lebanese politics, unless, in terms of Lebanese politics, her non-sectarian charity was a political crime. The cowardly act outraged the Druzes, but Kamal Jumblatt wanted no retaliation. He saw in the assassination of his sister yet another provocation designed to draw the Druze community as a whole into a war he had never regarded as sectarian but wholly as a struggle for the social reform Lebanon needed so badly.

After Kamal Jumblatt was, in turn, assassinated on 16 March 1977, more than a hundred Christians were killed in retaliation, despite a plea from his son Walid to stop reprisals. It emerged that the Druzes who went on this revenge rampage were very few in number, since they did not exceed ten persons, and that these few were neither especially loyal to Kamal Jumblatt nor members of his Progressive Socialist Party. Conversely, most of the Christians killed were sympathizers of Kamal Jumblatt and his party, and included his personal secretary. As a result, many inferred that the so-called retaliations had been engineered by those who sought to provoke an all-out war between Christians and Druzes by using the assassination of Kamal Jumblatt and the subsequent killings of Christians as incitement. It was a ruthless plot, but it failed because of the wisdom of Walid Jumblatt and his effective intervention and because the Druzes did not, in any case, want all-out war with their Christian friends and neighbours.

A year later, in March 1978, Israel invaded south Lebanon. That April the United Nations, in certain areas only, forced Israel to withdraw and be replaced by United Nations Forces (Unifil). Israel refused to evacuate its forces from what it claimed was its security zone in southern Lebanon. It then proceeded to adopt a major role in stoking the fires of war by supplying arms, ammunition, military training and expertise to the Lebanese Maronites. Four years later, on 6 June 1982, in collusion with the Maronite Christians and with the approval of the United States, Israel again invaded Lebanon, naming its operation 'Peace for Galilee', or, as others in Israel called it, 'Litani II' ('Litani I' having been the invasion of Lebanon in 1978). Exhaustive accounts of the invasion of Lebanon have filled several books, the most accurate and best documented of which is *Error and Betrayal in Lebanon* by George Ball, an under secretary of state during the Kennedy and Johnson administrations. If I repeated less than half that George Ball wrote, I would be accused of anti-Americanism and anti-Semitism, neither of which would be true.

When the second invasion started, Israel announced that its aim was to drive the PLO beyond a line forty kilometres from its northern border, so 'that Israel would no longer be within PLO artillery range'. In actual fact, the Israeli army pushed the whole way to Beirut, destroying everything in its path. As soon as I read that Israel's prime minister, Menachem Begin, had declared that Israel did not 'covet one single square inch of Lebanese soil', I shuddered, remembering the words of Levi Eshkol, a previous Israeli prime minister, on the first day of the Israeli-Arab war in June 1967: 'Israel has no intention of annexing even one foot of Arab territory.' Within fifteen years of that earlier declaration, Arab Jerusalem, the Golan Heights and much of Gaza and the West Bank had all been annexed, and remain today on the verge of total annexation.

By October 1982, according to a report in the *Guardian*, Begin was saying, 'Arab lands will never be surrendered.' In March 1984, Prime Minister Yitzhak Shamir stated: 'Israeli troops are likely to stay in Lebanon for all time'; and, according to a report in the *Jerusalem Post* of 16 August 1986, Brigadier-General Tat-Aluf Danny Rothschild, commander of the Israeli liaison unit in Lebanon, had declared there was 'no choice but to stay' in south Lebanon.

The invasion, it was claimed, was sparked off by the attempted assassination of the Israeli ambassador in London, but this was soon dropped even as a pretext, to be replaced by an allegation that the cease-fire of July 1981 between the Palestine Liberation Organization and Israel had been violated 150 times. Yet, as the British foreign secretary told the House of Commons on 9 June 1982, three days after the invasion, there had been no attacks by the PLO across Israel's northern border between the cease-fire of July

1981 and May 1982 when the Israelis broke the cease-fire themselves and attacked Palestinian positions in Lebanon. This was confirmed from within Israel on 5 July 1982 when *Haeretz* published a letter from Ya'kov Guterman, son of the Zionist Simha Guterman, who died in the Warsaw ghetto rising, and father of Raz, one of the first Israeli casualties in the attack on Beaufort Castle in south Lebanon. Ya'kov castigated the Begin government in these words: 'Cynically and shamelessly you declared the "Peace for Galilee" operation when not one shot had been fired across the northern frontier for a year.'

As Israel's eminent historian, Professor Yehoshua Porath, has declared:

> The decision to invade Lebanon resulted from the
> fact that the cease-fire had held . . . Yassir Arafat had
> succeeded in doing the impossible. He managed an
> indirect agreement, through American mediation, with
> Israel and even managed to keep it for a whole year . . .
> this was a disaster for Israel. If the PLO agreed upon
> and maintained a cease-fire they may in the future agree
> to a more far-reaching settlement and maintain that too.

The implication of Professor Porath's statement is that Lebanon was invaded, not because the PLO was attacking Israel and the Israelis, but, strangely enough, because it was not. It seems curious that Arafat's ability to maintain the cease-fire was considered a disaster for Israel, when that cease-fire implied the security of the northern borders so frequently claimed as Israel's main concern. And why should the Israelis fear that the PLO might, in the future, agree to maintain a more far-reaching settlement? Could it be that any peaceful solution to the Arab-Israeli conflict appeared to the Zionist hawks a disaster for Israel?

The trumped-up pretext that the 1982 invasion was necessary to safeguard the security of Israel's northern borders simply camouflaged a long-planned invasion, the real objective of which was later announced by Menachem Begin in the Knesset: 'To establish in Lebanon an independent and sovereign state friendly to Israel and to push the PLO out of Beirut.' Or was this perhaps a manifestation of Begin's 'divinely ordained war', as reported in *The Times* on 16 July 1982: 'More than five weeks after the Israeli forces launched their massive invasion, the resulting war has been officially described as being divinely ordained by Mr Begin. Until now, he has preferred to rely on the argument of self-defence to justify Israel's widely criticized tactics.'

There was nothing divine about the invasion of Lebanon. By 14 June, the Israeli army had encircled Beirut and laid siege to its Moslem western sector where the PLO fighters were dug in. The siege was fierce and lasted until 12 August. Electricity and water were cut off. Food supplies were not allowed through and medical and other forms of aid were barred.

West Beirut was shelled and bombed to pieces, some 60,000 shells being fired into the city. Cluster bombs were used, every one of which could destroy an area the size of a football pitch, tearing to shreds any human being within range. The United States had first provided cluster bombs to Israel during the 1973 Yom Kippur War, but, because of their barbarously inhumane effects, their use was curtailed, not only by the law limiting American-supplied weapons to self-defence, but also by specific special restrictions. Israel had signed an agreement, pledging not to use these bombs unless attacked by two or more of the countries it had fought in 1967 and 1973. Even then, cluster bombs were to be used only against fortified military targets and never 'against any areas where civilians were exposed'.

This last restriction was introduced after the American Central Intelligence Agency (CIA) reported that Israel had violated the agreement, when, in 1978, it 'saturated south Lebanon with United States cluster bombs – mainly against

185

civilian refugee camps'. During the 1982 invasion, Israel nevertheless used cluster bombs widely and indiscriminately against civilians. According to authentic American reports, there were nine types of cluster bomb used in nineteen locations in West Beirut as well as in fifty-one others throughout Lebanon. In the face of such indisputable evidence of wanton misuse, the United States suspended further supplies of cluster bombs to Israel, but only temporarily. President Reagan lifted the suspension during Prime Minister Shamir's visit to Washington in 1983 – not surprisingly, since the Pentagon confirmed that the United States was itself by then using cluster bombs against Syrian positions in Lebanon.

Eventually, the PLO forces were evacuated on 21 August under the supervision of an International Peace Keeping Force, made up of American marines and French and Italian troops. There was an undertaking that this force would also protect civilian Palestinians left behind after the departure of the PLO fighters. Israel, however, showed no real desire to destroy the PLO. The invasion only forced the PLO fighters in West Beirut to quit the city, leaving the rest of their forces intact in the mountains, in the Beqaa valley and in north Lebanon. Even before the PLO left West Beirut, Eric Silver reported in the *Guardian* of 30 June 1982 that, 'Prime Minister Begin offered to let the Palestinian guerrillas leave Beirut with their personal weapons.' And so they did, to reappear shortly after in north Lebanon and the Beqaa valley. Before long, Arafat's PLO fighters were chased from the Beqaa valley and north Lebanon, not by Israel but by Palestinian dissidents. Israel, in fact, did its utmost to prevent the PLO's departure.

The media all over the world reported fully on the invasion, its killing of tens of thousands of innocent people, the destruction of Tyre, Sidon, West Beirut and scores of Lebanese villages, the ruthless bombing and shelling, and the use of cluster bombs, phosphorous bombs, vacuum or suction bombs and other American-made instruments of destruction, probably being tested in Lebanon for their effective killing capacity. The world condemned the invasion, but in words only. The UN Security Council produced on 9 June 1982 a resolution condemning and threatening Israel with sanctions unless it agreed to a cease-fire and unconditional withdrawal from Lebanon. The United States vetoed the resolution as not 'sufficiently balanced'. The fact that the invasion had US approval – or, at least, that of Reagan's secretary of state, Alexander Haig – only emerged later.

At the outset, President Reagan was reported as being angered and outraged, though this did not stop him, according to the *International Herald Tribune* of 3 August 1982, sending birthday greetings to Menachem Begin the previous day, at the very moment when Israel was conducting 'the heaviest Israeli shelling and bombing of the war'. Other Western heads of state, equally outaged, presumably sent no birthday greetings. The Soviet Union, apart from blaming the United States, made low-pitched noises of protest, and the US secretary of state, Alexander Haig, described the Soviet Union's attitude as 'encouragingly cautious'. Even in the Arab world, voices were muted. Perhaps there were secret hopes that at last they might be rid of the Palestinians and their problems, and that Israel would take the blame.

According to Lebanese government casualty figures, the human cost of the invasion by the end of August 1982 stood at 18,000 dead and 30,000 wounded, 90 per cent of whom were civilians. Bashir Gemayel, Israel's ally during the seven years of Lebanese fighting preceding the invasion, was elected on 23 August 1982 to be president of what was left of the Lebanese Republic. Only twenty-three days later, he was assassinated in a huge bomb explosion at the Phalangist party headquarters in East Beirut, before he could even officially assume his presidential post.

Two days after Bashir Gemayel's killing, the world witnessed the brutal massacres of the Sabra and Chatilla camps.

The Peace Keeping Force, supposed to guarantee the protection of civilian Palestinians after the departure of the PLO, had itself departed suddenly and inexplicably a few days before the massacre and before the end of its mandate. Nobody knew why, and no one asked the reason, but the slaughter of over 2,000 innocent Palestinian and Moslem Lebanese civilians, including many women and children, sent waves of shock and revulsion throughout the international community, and had a particular impact within Israel itself.

The Israelis and their Phalangist allies at once accused each other of committing this atrocity. The world's official response was confined to verbal condemnation, but the Israeli people's extremely critical reaction compelled their government to appoint a Commission of Inquiry. When the true facts were disclosed, the government was forced by Israeli public opinion to admit its culpability in the massacres and take disciplinary measures it would have preferred to avoid. The resignation of Colonel Eli Geva and that of the energy minister, Yitzhak Berman, because of the Israeli government's initial refusal to hold a public inquiry into the massacres, together with the Israeli people's sincere reaction to the crime, should have given the Arabs at least some measure of real hope that peace with the Israelis might be a possibility despite the Zionist hawks.

Meanwhile the Druzes, as a whole community, had continued to refrain from joining in the fighting, even after the 1982 Israeli invasion of Lebanon and despite the Israelis urging the Lebanese Forces (as the Maronite Christian militia was by now termed) to invade the Druze land. The Israelis had in fact kicked the bona fide Druze troops of the Lebanese army out of its barracks in Druze land and handed the buildings over to the Lebanese Forces. The pretext given by the militia for this invasion of Druze land was to protect the Christians living in villages scattered across Druze land.

The fact of the matter is that the deplorable and bloody

fratricidal battles of 1841, 1845 and 1860 have, to a large extent, continued to be the source of the potent hatred so long nurtured for the Druzes by the Maronites. The Druzes had not forgotten the fighting between 1841 and 1860, but as victors it was easier for them to free their memories, over the years, of vindictive bitterness. It was quite otherwise for many Maronites and their clergy. They neither forgot nor forgave, but kept the fires of vengeance alive in their hearts. When the Lebanese Forces invaded the Druze land in 1982, their objective was to settle scores dating back more than a century.

Jonathan Randal has described the Maronite invasion of Druze land in these terms in *The Tragedy of Lebanon – Christian Warlords, Israeli Adventurers and American Bunglers*:

The Lebanese Forces, following in the Israeli Army's footsteps, almost without exception opened old wounds and produced a predictably bloody settling of accounts wherever they went. The Israelis, by design or through ignorance, were upsetting Lebanon's precarious balance among minorities seething with mutual hatred and revenge. And willy-nilly they were indulging in that classic imperial principle of divide and rule so familiar in Lebanese history: by either stirring up or tolerating trouble, the outside power could demonstrate its usefulness by sending in troops to separate the combatants. By the fall of 1982, Shuf mayors in neighbouring Maronite and Druze villages were catching on when Israeli officers offered them arms and warned them of the other's evil intentions. A simple telephone call often got to the bottom of the skulduggery, but not often enough – as the steadily lengthening list of incidents, and casualties, bore witness. By the end of 1982, hundreds of Druze and Lebanese Christians had been killed.

With many scores of their own militia dead, the Lebanese Forces had also suffered severely, and it was clear that their strong-armed tactics had gained nothing. Far from being an effective shield to allow 'dispossessed Christians to return to their former homes', they had created so violent a situation 'by their presence', says Mr Randal, 'that many Christians who had stayed put since since 1975 left the Shuf'. While the 'Lebanese Forces sheepishly admitted their errors in going into these areas', they 'did little to mend their ways'. They were themselves largely recruited from among 'young men whose families had been forced to flee their homes during the civil war and seek refuge in the Maronite heartland' in the south. The fact that they were intent on vengeance had led to their recruitment in the first place.

> It was child's play for the Israelis to manipulate the situation. The whole business was a drearily familiar rerun not just of the 1976 'events' but of the Druze-Maronite slaughter between 1840 and 1860 – complete with an intergenerational struggle and interfering foreign powers.

Back in Israel, meanwhile, the Israeli authorities had made problems for themselves among their native Druze minority, which perceived the Israeli army supporting the Maronite Lebanese Forces against the Druzes of the Shouf, and became loud in its protests. There was a population of 50,000 Israeli Druzes, represented in the Knesset by their own elected deputy, and a further 13,000 who lived on the recently annexed Golan Heights. The Israelis, moreover, relied on their Druze recruits for tough army assignments and border police patrol work, to help maintain a hold over the occupied territories, including the Gaza Strip. In the Hasbaiya area they had allowed the formation of a Druze self-defence region, equipped with Israeli-supplied weapons and overseen by a Druze military governor. A similar autonomous arrangement, they implied early on in the invasion of Lebanon, might be possible for the Lebanese Druzes. This overture was scorned by the Druzes of Lebanon, but even more disconcerting for the Israelis was the fact that, during sporadic outbreaks of shooting in the Shouf, there were some Israeli Druze troops who 'sided with their coreligionists despite army orders against such entanglements'. 'In short,' says Mr Randal, 'the strife between Druze militiamen and the Lebanese Forces inevitably undermined the Israelis' power in Lebanon – where they were now the only organized force capable of maintaining law and order.'

The Israelis were about to make the same discoveries that the Syrians had before them, with the extra complication that the high casualty rates running into thousands, which never worried the Syrians over the years, would be politically unacceptable to the Israeli public. They would also find themselves the scapegoats, cheerfully blamed by every Lebanese faction, for any violent incident in the Shouf, whether they had played a part or not.

The Syrians had been welcomed as peacekeepers in 1976, but had failed to keep the peace. They were blamed for keeping the country divided, and finally were regretted by virtually no one when driven back to the Beqaa and north by the Israeli invasion. The Israelis copied them in things great and small – all the way down to their efficiency in looting private homes. If anything, the Israelis went further. Quite apart from 520 tons of arms and material eventually hauled away from West Beirut, Israeli soldiers took private cars, telephones, telex machines, video cassette machines, even wooden school benches. Israeli Arabists had warned the government of the dangers of the Lebanese quagmire and of the almost infinite potential for error and bloodshed. But Ariel Sharon [then Israeli minister of war] and his group paid them no more mind than the US government had the views of American specialists on Iran during and after the Iranian revolution.

The Druzes of the Progressive Socialist Party never for one moment accepted the pretext offered by the Maronite militia for their invasion of Druze land. They knew there had been no harassment or molestation of the Christians living in Druze villages, who existed at peace alongside their Druze neighbours. Instead they detected a clear inference that the invasion was intended to drive the Druzes from their land as a prerequisite to establishing, with Israeli support, a Christian state in Lebanon. It was reported that Ariel Sharon, presumably reflecting the intention of the Israeli government, had promised Bashir Gemayel, the supreme chief of the Maronite Lebanese Forces, the control of all Lebanon. It was unclear whether the Israelis subscribed to the Lebanese Forces' intention of chasing the Druzes out of Lebanon or merely expected to see them subjected to absolute Maronite rule.

The Yazbaki Druzes, who constitute 50 per cent of the Druze community, had chosen, under the guidance of their feudal chief, Emir Majid Arslan, not to share the suspicions of the Progressive Socialist Party Druzes, but to remain loyal to the Maronite Christians and their Lebanese army. After the Maronite Lebanese Forces' invasion in the autumn of 1982, Emir Majid called a meeting of his followers, to which the Druzes of the Progressive Socialist Party were also invited. Upon his personal intervention, and following guarantees he received from the Maronite-dominated Lebanese army, a truce was declared and the Lebanese army allowed to take up positions at key strategic points.

In no time the Druzes discovered that the guarantees of the Lebanese army to Emir Majid were never intended to be honoured. Atrocious massacres of the Druzes – the Yazbaki followers of Emir Majid not excepted – followed, carried out by the Lebanese army, or with its full approval. Sheikh Massoud Gharib, an eminent Druze judge who had trusted the Lebanese army and its guarantees, was brutally murdered with all his family and other members of his village, the latter having made the fatal error of sharing the judge's confidence in the Lebanese army and its promises. The holiest of the Druze shrines, Maqam Es-Sayyid Abdallah, was razed to the ground, and was not the only Druze shrine to be so destroyed. The tragic fate of Sheikh Massoud and his family and other subsequent atrocities finally provided evidence to convince all the Druzes that the Maronite Christians were, by their invasion, intent on driving them from their land.

At this point the Druzes as a whole community became enraged by the atrocities. But they stood no chance of mounting a successful all-out counter-action against the invading Maronite forces while the powerful Israeli army still maintained a presence. They therefore bided their time and accelerated preparations to defend their land and long-established traditional rights.

Once the Israeli government had failed in its invasion objective, ordered its army's withdrawal from Lebanon and departed from the Druze land, the Druzes rose to fight like tigers for their heritage. *Uqqals* and *Juhhals* alike, men, women and even children, took up arms under Walid Jumblatt's leadership and, in no time at all, drove out the Lebanese Forces and the Maronite-controlled Lebanese army.

On many occasions in their history, the Druzes have demonstrated that fear of death does not exist for them when they fight for survival. In their combat with the Lebanese Forces, hundreds of examples of exceptional bravery and valour on all fronts were cited and were mainly responsible for their rapid routing of the opposition, despite the sophisticated weaponry and well-planned and well-built defences they faced.

In all these confrontations the Druze warriors adhered to

their traditional codes of chivalry and to the most important dictum of clean man-to-man fighting. They never indulged in or resorted to the atrocities perpetrated by others in the Lebanese war: no sniping, no kidnapping, no torture, no raping, no setting of bombs or booby-trapped cars, no shelling of residential areas. They never attacked the Maronite Christian residents of Druze land, or harmed them or their women and children. Regrettably, many Maronite Christian villagers in Druze land panicked and fled to Maronite Christian land east of Beirut, but other Maronite Christians chose not to panic, but stayed put in their communities, the most important of which was the Maronite Christian town of Dayr al-Qamar, across the valley from Baaqline, the largest Druze town in the Shouf. In 1120 the founder of the house of Ma'an chose Baaqline to be his headquarters, though in 1613, nearly five hundred years later, the Ma'ani seat moved to neighbouring Dayr al-Qamar, which was, like Baaqline, inhabitated jointly by Maronite Christians and Druzes, as were most of the villages of the Shouf. For over 250 years, Dayr al-Qamar continued with its mixed population of Druzes and Maronites living in undisturbed peace and friendship until the troubles of the mid-nineteenth century culminated in the massacres of 1860, the tragic history of which was told in Chapter 6 (see pages 115–27). After those events, a process of voluntary rehabilitation made Dayr al-Qamar essentially a Maronite Christian town, while Baaqline became overwhelmingly Druze. Nevertheless Christian families long continued to live in Baaqline.

I vividly remember, for example, Said Haddad, the last male representative of a remarkable Christian family who was and felt more Baaqlini than I. Despite the factional hostilities, Said continued to live in Baaqline until 1981, when he died of old age. His coffin and the crosses in his funeral procession were then carried by the Baaqline Druzes, his fellow villagers and friends. The church bells were tolled by young Druze men and the church in Baaqline continues to stand intact, respected and well cared for to this day. On important occasions, visits continue to be regularly exchanged between the Maronite Christians of Dayr al-Qamar and the Druzes of Baaqline, and nothing has so far been able to destroy the atmosphere of tolerance, friendship and peace between the two communities.

11. The Four Stages of the War

In making an analysis of the war in Lebanon, we may say that it underwent an evolution of four stages. Stage one was fought and confusedly settled in 1958. Stage two began in 1975, when the political feudal lords, representing the various religious communities of Lebanon and encouraged by foreign powers, loudly proclaimed that they were defending what they considered were the legitimate rights of their own communities. Hence the Maronite Christians sought to preserve the power given them under the French Mandate, and later in 1943 by the National Covenant, despite the fact they had subsequently become in Lebanon a minority relative to the Moslem communities. They also hoped to drive the Palestinians out of Lebanon, among the various motives for this being the wish to deprive the Moslems of the ability to use the Palestinians as their armed militia. Some of their leaders, moreover, saw in war the chance to establish their dream of a Christian state in Lebanon.

The Shi'ites meanwhile demanded their legitimate rights as Lebanese citizens, together with social justice, being genuinely the country's most deprived community. The Sunni Moslems, on the other hand, wanted a larger share in government power, and certain of them still hankered to return to Syria, their country before the creation of Grand Liban by the French in 1920. As for Kamal Jumblatt and his Progressive Socialist Party with its majority of Druze members, they hoped during this second stage to reform the government structure in Lebanon by creating a non-sectarian socialist state.

The Palestinians themselves saw Lebanon as providing an ideal base for attacking Israel. Some of their leaders additionally dreamed of settling the Palestinians in Lebanon, knowing full well that the Israelis would never allow their return to Palestine. Lebanon, after all, was a pleasant country in which to live, and by establishing themselves there they would become a substantial minority of its population. To settle in any other Arab country would mean resigning themselves to being an insignificant minority and never breaking free of the status of poor relations.

All the political war-lords of every community imagined they were manipulating foreign powers and interests to help them attain their objectives. They congratulated themselves on their cleverness, but were being too clever by half. As they soon came to realize, they were in reality being themselves manipulated by those same foreign powers to serve quite different ends. The political feudal lords were quickly reduced to being their masters' voices, enthralled to the foreign powers who supplied them with the funds to pay the salaries of their militias. All the combatants were salaried men, who commanded moreover substantial salaries. They also needed to be kept supplied with arms and copious amounts of ammunition, for, quite apart from the fighting, all hell tended to break loose at the slightest pretext. Weddings, funerals, feasts, circumcisions, recoveries from illness or wounds, elections to office, promotions – all were celebrated by automatic weapons, rockets and cannon pumping thousands of rounds into the sky. The prodigious amounts of ammunition so wasted were proclaimed as emblems of the potent firepower of the militias concerned.

Thus were the destinies of the political war-lords removed from their own hands and reluctantly surrendered to the foreign powers who supported them financially and materially. Their vociferous proclamations consequently came to be inspired and dictated by those same powers, and whatever was proclaimed ceased to be either genuinely Lebanese or in the interests of Lebanon. The conflict was transformed from a war to achieve Lebanese political aims to a war fought between foreign powers seeking to settle their differences by using Lebanon as the battlefield and the Lebanese to fight on their behalf. It heralded the start of stage three in the war in Lebanon, when the foreign powers took over and began to intervene openly and directly in the country's affairs.

In August 1982 the PLO forces left Beirut. In the same month, Bashir Gemayel, Israel's staunchest ally, was, with Israeli help, elected President of the Lebanese Republic. The Israelis now hoped to turn the republic into a Christian state friendly towards them. That September, Bashir Gemayel was assassinated and his brother Amin elected to replace him; and in January 1983 negotiations for a security treaty between Israel and Lebanon were set in motion. In May, Israel and Lebanon signed the security treaty, and in August 1983 Israel withdrew partially from Lebanon, to be replaced by American, French, Italian and British forces, who moved in to help maintain law and order. By September, the Druzes had driven the Maronite forces from Druze land. And in October, 239 United States marines and 59 of their French colleagues were blown up in Beirut – a spectacular outrage, the perpetrators of which were never exposed or punished. Soon after this, the American and European forces, having made a glorious mess of a task they seemed incapable of defining clearly, departed from Lebanon, leaving the country to its own devices in continuing with its own wars. In this way, the scene was set for stage four: an open season in Lebanon for the activities and enterprises of the international arms dealers and drugs barons.

In 1984, Lebanon, under pressure from Syria, denounced the security agreement it had signed with Israel. The latter, however, remained ensconced in south Lebanon, claiming a security zone was essential to safeguard its northern borders. Why it was necessary to establish this security zone on Lebanese rather than Israeli territory may be seen as an example of the incomprehensible logic used by the powerful when dictating their will to those in a weak position. Israel was adamant in denying the United Nations Force, Unifil, any access to the zone. Meanwhile the Israelis greatly strengthened what they termed the South Lebanese army, set up in 1978 under Major Sa'ad Haddad, a Lebanese Maronite Christian officer, seconded to them for this task by the Maronite-controlled Lebanese army with the approval of Elias Sarkis, the then Maronite Christian President of Lebanon. It was reported that Major Haddad was paid his salary and emoluments by the Lebanese army. After his death, he was replaced by Brigadier-General Antoine Lahad, another Maronite Christian officer from the Lebanese army.

The Syrians, who had vacated Beirut and the mountains at the time of the 1982 Israeli invasion, remained in the Beqaa valley (later, in 1987, to be invited by the Lebanese government and the inhabitants of West Beirut to come to their rescue and maintain law and order in that section of the city). Lebanon was thus left with two invading armies within its borders: the Syrian and the Israeli, alongside the ineffective and discountable United Nations Force (Unifil). The picture was further complicated by Iraq, which chose to fight Syria in Lebanon, and Iran, which sent units of its national guard to Lebanon to form Hizbollah, with the aim of fighting Israel, the United States and the West by taking their nationals as hostages to be kept in Lebanon. It was now that the war in Lebanon entered its fourth stage, with the last semblances of control by Lebanese political lords and foreign powers being lost to a whole repellent medley of profiteering gangs. These, in the names of the politicians and the foreign powers sponsoring them, and sometimes with their approval, went to work to transform Lebanon into a lawless, uncontrollable field of pickings for the world's 'mafias' of evil. The picture darkened beyond belief as arms and ammunition bazaars proliferated, as drug-producing plants were cultivated and harvested for processing and unrestricted export, as hostages were taken for political reasons, or simply for ransom money. There was smuggling and counterfeiting, extortion and blackmail, and a booming trade in the export of terrorist mercenaries. For a price, it was possible to recruit the services of professionals, using Lebanese passports, to perform any criminal terrorist act in the repertoire.

Certain of the politicians and foreign powers entered into devil's pacts with the mafias and took their cut from the profits. For the most part, they did not want to see an end to the war; it was making fortunes for them. Profit-sharing with the mafias produced an abundance of millionaires in Lebanon, until it is estimated today that there are per capita more than a hundred times as many millionaires in Lebanon as in the United States of America. By contrast, the majority of the innocent Lebanese were barely living at subsistence level.

Stages two to four of the war in Lebanon had been conceived and plotted as parts of a progressive, demonic conspiracy to destroy Lebanon. In retrospect, the first stark storm warnings were there as early as 1966 when Intra Bank, by far the biggest Lebanese and Arab bank, was slaughtered by foreign interests, aided and abetted by a number of Lebanese who were willing to sell themselves and their country to the highest bidder. Intra Bank had attracted Arab deposits from the oil-producing countries and was certain to attract more. It followed a positive policy of financing Arab industries and Arab economic projects, but also helped to nationalize Lebanese and Arab enterprises that were owned and controlled by foreign interests. The fear grew among certain Western interests that Intra might convince the oil-rich Arabs that they should invest in sorely needed Arab development ventures and so keep Arab money within Arab lands. Thus was Intra condemned to death, its slaughter being the first nail in the coffin of Lebanon and the Lebanese economy.

That this event marked the beginning of a conspiracy which led to sixteen years of bloody war and the total destruction of Lebanon is indeed no mere conspiracy theory or fantasy to form the material for a novel by John Le Carré. In *I Speak for Lebanon*, Kamal Jumblatt recorded that Dr Edmond Rabbath, the prominent Lebanese jurist, had warned him, even prior to Intra's destruction and well before the onset of the civil war, that while he was in Switzerland American friends told him, 'You will shortly witness the destruction of the structures and institutions in Lebanon. An international conspiracy is under way.'

The massacre of Intra was followed by similar attempts on Lebanon's Middle East Airlines. In December 1968, its fleet was destroyed by an Israeli military attack on Beirut international airport. But like the phoenix it rose from the ashes, to become stronger, more efficient and even more competitive. Subsequent plots and intrigues against the airline were for the time being successfully deflected. The crime that made it a target had been to prove beyond argument that it was one of the most efficient airlines in the aviation world; its unforgivable sin had been to work to form a united Arab airline with the ultimate potential of carrying the lion's share of all air transport to and from the Middle East. This would have placed it in the strongest possible position to bargain for the purchase of aircraft, for to be able to buy, say, eighty aircraft for a united Arab airline must be to gain a far more favoured position than could ever be possible for smaller airlines buying only five or six each. The capital expenditure on spare parts would likewise have been greatly reduced and hundreds of millions of dollars a year saved.

At the very start of the war in Lebanon, Beirut's commercial centre seemed to be targetted for total destruction. Working through the wreckage, various foreign-backed militias then began, with the help of foreign professionals, to loot the safe-deposit boxes in every bank in Lebanon, whether it was Lebanese or foreign. It was an act calculated to destroy confidence in the Lebanese banking system.

Prior to the outbreak of the war, hundreds of thousands of oil-rich Arabs had flocked into Lebanon each year in pursuit of pleasure and investment possibilities. The sight of so much bounty remaining to Lebanon was intolerable to Western predatory interests, who wanted it for themselves and saw the ideal chance to divert it away by fomenting a war in the country and frightening off the Arab visitors. The tactic worked. In 1976, rather than going to Lebanon, over 500,000 Arabs travelled to Europe, where they found ample fields for leisure and investment and spent billions of pounds sterling in each area. Year by year their numbers increased as the war in Lebanon continued, their extravagant expenditure representing one of the rich rewards for the success of the foreign conspiracy.

Another offence by Lebanon had been to provide an example where seventeen religious sects contrived to live together in peace, so long as they remained free from outside interference. This fact was resented by its neighbours, who believed that sovereignty of the state resides in an exclusive and monolithic religion and that harmony and tolerance between communities of different religious sects was not an example to be countenanced. Their interests therefore coincided with those of the arms vendors in seeing Lebanon's multi-sectarian communities driven apart. Lebanon's strength thus paradoxically became its weakness, for the arms dealers were able to exploit this vulnerability by promoting sectarian dissent and so create a market place for their wares.

12. The Druzes and Israel

The most remarkable event in which both the Druzes and the Israelis were involved took place during the fighting between the Druzes and the Maronite Lebanese Forces. This was the defection of a number of Israeli Druzes serving in the Israeli army that invaded Lebanon and their going across to their Druze brothers to help them in their battle for survival. Whether they 'defected' or 'went on unauthorized leave', the fact remains that many Druze soldiers in the Israeli army ardently wished to aid the Druzes of Lebanon in their fight, and did so. Israeli Druze soldiers had, in any case, sided with the Druzes in Lebanon despite Israeli army orders to the contrary.

There have been Druzes living in Palestine (now Israel) since the start of the Druze Faith and the proclamation of the Divine Call – a fact confirmed by many historians who have written about the Druzes in Safed (Palestine) from the early years of the eleventh century. Their numbers increased greatly at the time of the Ma'anid dynasty in Lebanon, and especially during the reign of Fakhruddin II, who encouraged a policy to settle Druzes in Palestine for the defence of his southern frontiers. The Druze presence in Palestine was most intensive during the Ma'anid rule, though during the years that followed there were many migrations, this way and that, between Syria and Lebanon and the Druze settlements in Palestine, depending on internal crises and political upsets. Most notable among these were the arrival from Lebanon of some of the Yamanites after their defeat by the Qaysi Druzes in the battle of Ayn Dara in 1711, and migrations from Aleppo and northern Syria in 1811. These were followed by minor migrations, such as that from Jabal al-Druze after the collapse of the 1925 revolt.

The Druzes of Israel have historically differed in their situation from the Druzes of Lebanon and those of Jabal al-Druze in Syria, in part from having enjoyed no citizenship privileges of any kind and in part from their small numbers. They had a constant struggle for survival against the successive governments that ruled Palestine and with the non-Druze communities among whom they lived. They had, in their past history, been without protection and needed to battle on alone against persecution.

It is estimated that there are over 50,000 Druzes in Israel today, a majority of them living in Western Galilee and on the slopes of Mount Carmel. They built their villages mostly in the mountains in inaccessible locations they could easily defend. Their strength has always stemmed from their fierce resistance to persecution and an ability to fight for survival. They drew strength, too, from their deep-rooted assurance that they could depend on the two other branches of the Druze nation in neighbouring Lebanon and Syria for spiritual and material support. The Druzes of Galilee were exceptionally friendless and isolated in their own land, but the wonderful Druze talent for organization gave them, wrote Lawrence Oliphant in the 1880s, 'a cohesian, a unity, and a power for combined action which the Christian sects, with their jealousies, bigotry, and internal dissension, do not enjoy'.

The Druzes in Palestine were persecuted both by the Ottoman Turks and their Moslem neighbours, a fact that inspired a tendency among them to ally themselves with other minorities and which, in turn, provided a strong motive for cultivating good relations with the Jews throughout their history. When the state of Israel came into being, the Palestine Druzes refused to leave their land and were heavily criticized in this stance by the Palestinians, who got up and departed *en masse*, leaving homes and lands for the Israelis to take with the utmost ease. It is one of the great ironies of history that, after more than forty years of the Palestinian diaspora, the Palestinians, who criticized the Druzes for refusing to vacate their homes and land, should be actively demanding the right to return to Palestine to live, like the Druzes, in peace alongside the Israelis. One cannot help but wonder how different history would have been had the Palestinians, like the Druzes, refused in 1948 to be driven from their homes and land.

It was never, however, easy for the Druzes to co-exist with the Israelis, as the new citizens of Israel flocked in from all over the world, hungry for land to settle and power to govern this complex and geographically restricted state which, from its founding, has never ceased to be at war with its Arab neighbours. The Druzes, like all other non-Jewish communities in Israel, lost part of their land and had their freedoms greatly restricted. But they declined to take the process lying down and fought back for their rights and won a partial success. In *The Druzes in Israel*, Gabriel Ben-Dor describes their campaign to stop the Israelis from taking over all their land:

> The availability of land is limited not only because of the mountainous location of the Druze settlements, but also – according to many Druze complaints – because of the policy of the Israeli Government, encouraging large-scale Jewish settlement in the Galilee, and ensuring land for that purpose. For this purpose, the Israeli authorities decided to check the title to land, and all those unable to prove their rights of ownership had to give up land that they considered theirs for generations, some of it fertile, some of it uncultivable rocky plots. Recently, following a constant stream of complaints, the policy of

expropriations was halted, and a commission of inquiry set up. Nevertheless, it is quite clear that the chances of further land being available for the Druze community are few, and would be so even if governmental land policy in the Galilee were to change.

The Druzes in Israel have been strongly criticized for accepting service in the Israeli army, despite the fact that such service is compulsary by law. Since 1956, Druze males aged eighteen and over have been subject to the same rules of conscription as other Jewish citizens. In *I Speak for Lebanon*, Kamal Jumblatt vigorously spoke up against all those who criticized the Druzes for serving in the Israeli army:

> As for the question of Druzes in Israel – who are so often slandered by our detractors – I would point out that of the 8,000 Muslims who used to serve in the Israeli armed forces, many were Sunni; strangely the Sunnis here – who are always prompt to criticize the Druses – seem to have forgotten the fact. Their sectarian spirit notices the mote in the eye of others, not the beam in their own. In any case, it is unimportant: Druses have given sufficient proof of their nationalism.

The Druzes in Israel have been pragmatic realists. They recognized they could never successfully take on the Israelis, with their strong army and unlimited Western backing, especially of the United States. (This, after all, is a fact which all the Arab countries have come to realize at the cost of repeated wars and humiliating defeats.) The Druzes instead opted for co-existence from the first and campaigned vigorously for equal rights to match those enjoyed by the Jewish citizens of Israel. The important role they came to play in the Israeli army reinforced their demands and inspired a listening ear on the part of the Israeli authorities.

Their presence in the Israeli army, though obligatory by law, has promoted other communities in the Arab world to accuse them of committing atrocities against Palestinian communities in Israel. All such accusations have, without exception, been shown as fabricated and malicous. A massacre of fifteen Palestinians in the village of Nahalin by Israeli border guards was immediately claimed to have been the work of Druzes. The Druzes vehemently denied responsibility; they had not been involved and were not even present. Despite their vigorous objections and strong resentment at being constantly falsely accused of such deeds, it seems it has become a reflex with the Palestinians and other Arabs, without evidence or proof, to accuse Druzes serving in the Israeli army of acts of brutality and savagery done by others.

The Druzes in Palestine were never given community status by the Ottoman Turks. The succeeding British Mandate authorities likewise recognized all the other communities in Palestine which had existed during Ottoman times, but refused the Druzes judicial autonomy, repeated requests notwithstanding. The Druzes tirelessly continued to ask for autonomous community status after the establishment of the state of Israel. Their requests were eventually granted in 1957, when the government of Israel approved the drafting of a law recognizing the Druzes as an autonomous community and establishing a Druze judiciary system. For this system, the Druze spiritual leaders chose to adopt the Druze Religious Law of Lebanon. Furthermore, the Israeli authorities approved in 1967 an exclusive measure to give the Druzes a right to put requests directly to government offices without the need to go through the intermediary agencies established for Arab or other minority problems in each office.

The Druzes also campaigned for the application of Israel's Proclamation of Independence of 14 May 1948, in particular its third operative clause, which declares: 'The State of Israel will devote itself to developing the Land for the good of its inhabitants.' This, they claimed, must mean *all* the country's inhabitants, not its Israeli inhabitants alone. They asked, too, for the application of that part of the proclamation which promised that Israel 'will maintain complete equality of social and political rights for all its citizens, without distinction of creed, race or sect'. They were also successful in obtaining voting rights, and as a result now have two elected Druze members to the Knesset, the Israeli Parliament. Both are ready to speak vigorously in drawing attention to acts of discriminatory treatment by the Israeli authorities against not only the Druze community but other Arab communities as well.

The Druzes in Israel remain deeply devoted to their religion and its teachings, and also maintain the tradition of loyalty to other Druze communities wherever they are found. They publish a monthly magazine recording all the important news from the world's Druze communities and the work of Druze personalities who have contributed to the welfare and prestige of those communities or the countries of which they are citizens. They are, in fact, the only Druze community to perform this important Druze informatory service. Thus they are very well informed on what is happening within the Druze nation everywhere and seek to play their part in any conflicts involving the Druzes whenever possible.

The defection of Druze troops from the invading Israeli army in 1982 to help the Druzes of Lebanon gave a boost to that community's already high morale, besides providing a startling eye-opener for the Israeli authorities. As a result, they realized they would have to pay serious heed to the reaction of the Druzes in Israel should they fail to follow an even-handed policy regarding the Druze community in Lebanon. In an editorial in the *Jerusalem Post*, International Edition, 18–24 September 1983, entitled 'Why the Druses are Formidable', the views of the Jewish Arabist, Moshe Sharon, were called on to explain the reason why they indeed were, then further to stress

> that the entire Lebanese Druse community, including the religious leaders, who had been opposed to Jumblatt, supports the current struggle to clear the Shouf of the [invading] Maronites. More than that: the Druse 'communal identity' guarantees the involvement of Israeli and Syrian Druses. [Moshe Sharon] likens their communal link to that which binds Jews throughout the world. The Israeli Druses, many of them members of the Israeli Defence Forces, who have requested permission to fight alongside the Lebanese Druses, are similar to the Diaspora Jewish veterans who volunteered to fight in Israel's War of Independence. When it comes down to Druse survival, the communal bond cuts through national boundaries.

'Israel begged Jemayel (Amin) to enter into an agreement with the Druse,' the editorial article then quotes Sharon as saying, adding that such an agreement would have brought about a complete change in the atmosphere and could perhaps have held off the imminent blood-letting. But in Sharon's opinion the Maronite Phalangists were refusing to listen, 'trapped in their own bravado'. 'All they wanted was to get their revenge,' he said, alluding to the massacres of the mid nineteenth century. They had been under the impression that there would be Israeli backing for any action they chose to take. The Israelis then made a fatal error, in Sharon's view, by letting the Lebanese Forces enter the Shouf, where their presence was an affront to the Druzes. 'They strutted around in their fatigues, brandishing Kalashnikovs, smelling of the latest French aftershave,' was how he described their posturings.

In 1982, Sharon had been in Lebanon for four months in an official role, so had gained a first-hand view on which to base his conclusions. His experience had left him 'scornful of the Maronites'.

> His attitude appears to reflect the change of Israeli policy in recent months. He does not criticize Israel's dependence on, and confidence in, the Maronites prior to last year's invasion, but says that, with hindsight, that confidence was misplaced. It is clear that, in his view, the Maronites have proved themselves to be less than fit partners for Israel.
>
> Sharon has great respect for the Druses and their abilities. He describes them as 'quiet but warlike, and very courageous'. In this he appears to mirror the even-handed approach which observers say now characterizes Israeli policy in Lebanon. The Maronites are no longer 'natural allies'. Israel's interests come first.

In May 1983, four months before this *Jerusalem Post* item was published, Israel and Lebanon had concluded a security treaty between the two countries. Moshe Sharon evidently did not foresee how, under pressure from Syria, Lebanon would the following year denounce that same treaty.

13. The Devil's Playground

The silent majority of the older generation of Lebanese, of all the country's sixteen religious sects, had never wished for the anarchy, killing, destruction and misery the war brought with it. But they found themselves intimidated and terrorized by the various militias, and since they dared not speak out, were forced to keep silent. They longed ardently to see the insane fighting end and for a solution, any solution, to be found and restore to them the Lebanon they once knew. The destiny of Lebanon, however, ceased to be in Lebanese hands from the moment they accepted manipulation by foreign powers and allowed their country to become a battlefield on which those same powers could settle their differences.

They also surrendered their former God-given paradise to the modern world's mafias of evil, especially the arms vendors and the drugs barons. It is estimated today that billions of dollars'-worth of drugs – cannabis, cocaine and heroin – are freely grown, processed and exported from Lebanon each year, and that the volume is steadily increasing. Ever greater areas of land, especially in the Shi'ite and Christian districts, are being planted, and the profitable drug trade booms. Trade in drugs is now said to constitute more than 60 per cent of Lebanon's gross national revenue. Before the civil war, some relatively small and remote areas in the Beqaa valley were planted with modest quantities of *Cannabis sativa* or Indian hemp, the plant from which marijuana and hashish are produced. In the 1960s, the government of President

211

Fouad Shihab launched a scheme to persuade and compensate farmers if they would plant sunflowers instead of hemp. The scheme was partially and only briefly successful. It is currently estimated that Lebanon's production of marijuana amounts to about half the world's supply in the illicit drugs markets.

The Beqaa valley, nicknamed the 'Narcotic Valley', is a highly fertile bowl of land, 150 kilometres in length by 20 wide. It forms the eastern boundary of Lebanon with Syria. Once it was planted with vines, fruit trees and cereals. Today it is completely covered with hemp, opium poppies and every kind of drug-producing plant. The Shi'ites and Christians cultivate the crops, the Maronites process and export the drugs. There are reported to be eight heroin-processing laboratories on Christian land east of Beirut, ten more in the Beqaa valley, but so far none in Druze land or in south Lebanon. The Syrians, firmly established in the Beqaa valley, cannot avoid being aware of the booming drugs trade, and it is rumoured they take their share of the profits in protection money.

One effect of the drugs boom has been to generate the funds to keep the Lebanese war going. Reciprocally, the war has kept the drugs boom flourishing. The profits thus generated are shared by most of the war-lords, besides being used to finance terrorist activities, both national and international. The mafia octopus is deeply ensconced in Lebanon, and its tentacles reach to every corner, while neighbouring countries are also very much involved. Drugs money is used to purchase arms and drugs are at times bartered for weapons and ammunition. As a result, Lebanon is not only an important importer but also an active exporter of arms.

There has been no way that the American Drug Enforcement Agency and European drug control and prevention agencies can observe at first hand what is going on, because if they dared to set foot in the area they would certainly be kidnapped and taken as hostages. The fact that

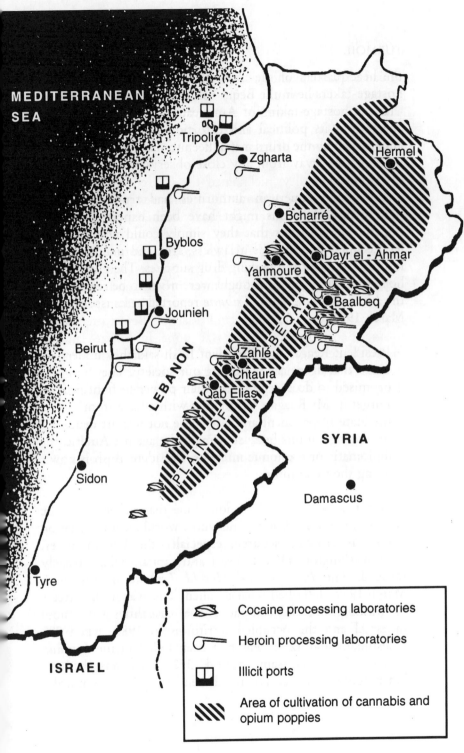

MEDITERRANEAN
SEA

Tripoli

Zgharta

Hermel

Bcharré

Byblos

Dayr el - Ahmar

Yahmoure

Baalbeq

Jounieh

BEQAA

Beirut

LEBANON

Zahlé

Chtaura

Qab Elias

SYRIA

PLAIN OF

Sidon

Damascus

Tyre

ISRAEL

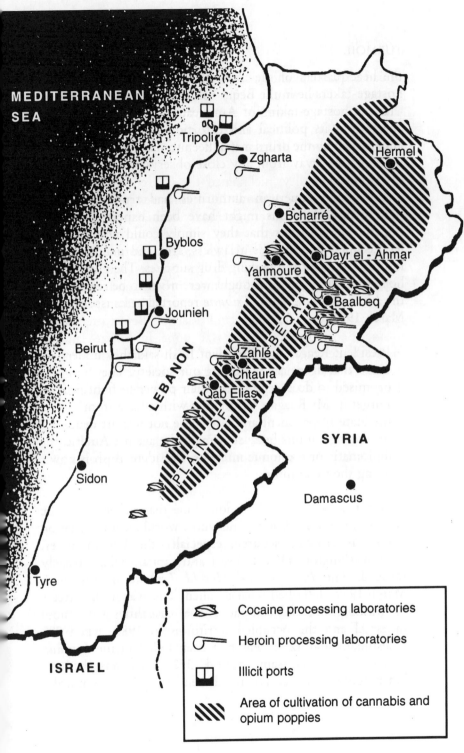	Cocaine processing laboratories
	Heroin processing laboratories
	Illicit ports
	Area of cultivation of cannabis and opium poppies

Drug production and export in Lebanon

the headquarters of the most active and dangerous of the hostage-takers lie in the Beqaa valley gives rise to a suspicion that the hostage-taking of Americans and Europeans, quite apart from its political and extortion objectives, has been encouraged by the drugs mafia, keen to scare Western control investigators away from any close observation of Lebanon's drugs boom.

Yet if the American authorities had truly wished to fight drugs, then this might have been expected to raise hopeful anticipations that they simply could not afford to let Lebanon continue as a lawless, free and uncontrollable leading source of burgeoning drug supplies. The glimmers of hope offered by such a thought were never to be realized. As the *International Herald Tribune* reported in its issue of 4–5 March 1989:

> President Reagan and President Bush said they under-
> stood that drugs are poisoning our society. They
> promised to do everything in their power to fight drugs.
> Forget it. Mr Reagan went along with advice from
> the State Department and elsewhere not to hurt drug
> producing nations because it might be against America's
> diplomatic or economic interests. President Bush is now
> doing the same thing.

It is not, as we know, Lebanon alone that suffers from the effects of the drugs boom. The whole world faces devastation from this growing scourge, especially the United States, with Washington, DC, its heart and capital, being savagely ravaged. The *International Herald Tribune* of Friday, 3 March 1989, described what it called 'The War in the Streets of Washington', and compared local casualities with those in Israel and the occupied territories in 1988, when 280 Palestinians and 12 Israelis had been killed in the *Intifada* (uprising). In that same period, 372 Americans died on Washington's streets; and by the end of 1989, this murder rate had nearly doubled. It seems that the end of the world is more likely to be brought about by drugs than by nuclear fission. Nuclear weapons may be deterred, but not, it seems, the disastrous proliferation of drugs.

At every stage of the Lebanese war, the arms manufacturers and vendors laid pressure on the fighting factions and the foreign powers behind them to prolong the war in Lebanon indefinitely, the objective being to promote the highly profitable sales of the products of their industries, not only in Lebanon but in all other countries of the Middle East. Yet greed knows no limits, and not even the Arab-Israeli wars and the war in Lebanon were thought to provide adequate stimulants for the arms bazaar. The long-term Iran-Iraq conflict was therefore encouraged, with arms vendors busily selling wares to both sides.

The seeds for the Iran-Iraq war were indeed sown when the late Shah of Iran, encouraged by his American advisors and the arms manufacturers, especially the American, deliberately began to build his military forces into the strongest in the Middle East by exchanging oil revenues for arms. In 1975–6, Iran's expenditure on arms, and what it termed defence, exceeded $10 billion. And while the Shah often stated that Iran had no designs on the land or wealth of others, its neighbours distrusted his declarations. Saudi Arabia, Iraq, the Arab Gulf states and Israel were thus encouraged to start their own military build-ups to match that of Iran. The arms race was therefore on, and where Saudi Arabia, the Arab Gulf states and Iraq were concerned, the exchange of oil revenues for weaponry provided the necessary funds. In the case of Israel, the United States was the provider, though it must also be said that Israel feels itself under no obligation to its patron for the generous loans and grants it receives annually. These are equal to, or even overshadowed by, the commissions due to Israel on the sales of arms, ammunition and war equipment generated by the

215

Israeli-Arab wars and supplied by the United States to Arab countries.

Prior to the Iran-Iraq war, Iraq had three arms suppliers; with the war in progress, it had twenty-one. Iran, having had five, during the war had twenty-nine. In all of this, the West and the Soviet bloc co-operated. North Korea also supplied arms to both sides, and China became the most recent participant. Since Iran and Iraq had the oil to pay for the arms to pursue their senseless war, no other aspect mattered.

It has been estimated that, before the Gulf War to liberate Kuwait, the Middle East hosted over 25,000 tanks and more than 4,000 military aircraft. It has also been calculated that Iraq was spending on arms 50 per cent of its annual national revenue, Israel 27 per cent and Saudi Arabia 21 per cent. By comparison, the United States was spending 6.9 per cent, the United Kingdom 5.1 per cent, the former Federal German Republic 3.1 per cent and Italy 2.7 per cent. In the light of such figures, how is it possible to believe seriously in the constant lip-service paid by all the arms-exporting countries to the need to advance peace initiatives to settle the conflicts in the Middle East?

On 4 November 1986, a Lebanese journal triggered the scandal of 'Irangate' in the United States, revealing how President Reagan's men had been involved in a massive sale of arms to Iran, despite the 1979 embargo placed on such sales by President Carter. It was further reported that the United States was also supplying arms to Iraq. The European public followed the shocking revelations of 'Irangate' with close interest, unaware that there existed in Europe a far vaster scandal. Sales of arms from Europe to Iran were in progress, despite an embargo on such sales by all European countries, also levied in 1979. The scandal involved Belgium, Sweden, Denmark, the former Federal German Republic, Holland, France, Portugal, Spain, Italy, Greece, Turkey, Britain and even Switzerland – all countries which had officially declared their hopes for peace between Iran and Iraq. On the one hand, they unreservedly and officially approved the efforts of the United Nations to achieve peace between these two countries, starting with a proposal for a cease-fire from the Security Council as early as September 1980. On the other hand, unofficially and clandestinely, they also approved massive sales of arms to Iran and Iraq, for no sales on such a scale could have been achieved without the tacit agreement of the governments of the exporting countries. The amounts of money involved were powerfully tempting. Up till 1987, the costs of arms for the Iraq-Iran war were estimated to be running at over $700 billion. Evidently the loss in human lives, exceeding one million, was not a statistical cost to be taken into consideration by the arms vendors.

When a cease-fire proposal was eventually agreed under the auspices of the United Nations, and even before a final peace settlement had been reached, the states which had supplied Iran and Iraq with arms for mutual destruction were falling over one another in a frantic rush to appropriate the two countries' oil revenues by offering to rebuild what their arms had helped to demolish. The costs of rebuilding what the war had destroyed were set to exceed by far the total costs of the war itself. They also hoped and planned to promote a second cycle of hostilities, to enable them to arm, destroy and rebuild yet again. In motivating the war to liberate Kuwait, they may be seen as having landed a very considerable *coup*. Wars will continue to occur in the Middle East so long as extractable oil deposits exist beneath its sands and rock.

The *Financial Times* in London, as far back as December 1974, condemned what was happening and predicted what was likely to happen in the future in the oil-rich Middle East. There could hardly have been a truer judgement or a more accurate forecast:

217

There can be no more distasteful aspect of the contemporary world scene than the way in which the industrialized countries of the West and the Soviet Bloc are effectively collaborating to enable the Arab oil-producing countries to devote a sizeable part of their increased wealth to financing massive armament programmes. And it is surely high time that all advanced countries recognized that they have a collective duty to stop getting profit for themselves by providing the bullets for small countries – rich and poor – to fire at one another. It is a sombre fact that all the major armed conflicts since World War II have taken place in the Third World. No doubt the willingness of so many advanced countries to pour arms into this major theatre of war can be set down to their wish to ensure that their respective spheres of influence are suitably supported and rewarded. But it is difficult to escape the impression that the current determination to reduce oil deficits by hook or by crook is playing a major part in seeing that the Middle East gets all the arms it needs to enable its dissensions to go on flourishing. Whatever the reasons, it is abundantly clear that, if the Middle East does go up in flames once again, it will be because the advanced countries have effectively 'willed' it to do so by furnishing it with the fuel to support another massive conflagration.

The long years of the Lebanese war, the Iraq-Iran war, the repeated invasions of Lebanon by Israel and the war to liberate Kuwait have all confirmed the *Financial Times*'s prediction. The sale of arms has become a highly valued commercial export operation designed to balance government budgets and used as a self-justified and legitimated means to recycle petro-dollars.

When, in March 1989, British Aerospace announced that a deal they had signed to supply military aircraft, air bases and naval ships to Saudi Arabia could prove to be the biggest export deal in United Kingdom's history, worth up to £150 billion sterling, they provided a prime example of such recycling. Beside it we may place the fiction of 'arms for peace', first proclaimed in 1978 by the Camp David Agreement, when the United States, to celebrate the cessation of hostilities between Egypt and Israel, provided the two countries with $4,500 million in military grants and loans and, by contrast, very little in economic aid. And then there is the use of arms 'as an instrument of foreign policy', as declared by the American administration in a startling front-page news item in the *International Herald Tribune* of 3 May 1988. The White House, it stated 'seeks a 28 per cent increase in weapons sales' and the State Department had 'listed potential sales to 33 countries'.

The *International Herald Tribune* of 6 June 1988 quoted from a study made by World Priorities, a Washington research institute. The most relevant conclusions were:

That there were 25 wars still going on. The study did not include countries in which uprisings and confrontations have taken fewer than 1,000 lives a year. Many of the present wars were fuelled by the United States, the Soviet Union and other industrial countries. The news of the present wars is limited by indifference, censorship and unwillingness on the part of major governments to share what information they have with the public. To a large extent, therefore, these are the forgotten wars, neglected even by those countries that preach the precious value of every human life. More wars were fought in 1987 than in any previous year on record. Present nuclear arsenals, scattered worldwide, alone represent more than 26,000 times the explosive force of all armaments used in World War II. The United States and the Soviet Union together spent about 1.5 billion dollars a day on military defence.

The *International Herald Tribune* of 30 August 1988 recorded some figures on United States poverty: '32.5 million Americans continue to live below the poverty line. A fifth of all American children are now poor and two fifths of the poor are children.' These seem like alarming statistics for a country believed to be the richest and most powerful in the world. No comparative statistics were available for the poverty in the former Soviet Union, but it is certain these would have been far worse. Nevertheless both these mighty countries, leaders of the world, allowed themselves to spend $1.5 billion a day to deter each other from mutual destruction while high percentages of their populations continued living below the poverty line. It seems a clear example of the distorted logic of insanity, but the developing countries (also called the Third World) have been manoeuvred into a far worse situation, where they spend almost four times as much on arms as they do on the health care of their people. The price of one modern aircraft bomber would build a thousand homes for the destitute, and the price of a naval ship equipped with nuclear capability would build a hundred universities or thousands of schools and educational institutions. And what could not done with $1.5 billion a day to ease the situation of the poor, the starving and the needy throughout the world? Who can honestly claim we live in a world where the balance of sanity prevails?

We may be sure meanwhile that all the industrialized countries of the West and East will continue, for a handsome return, to help Israel and the Arab countries to build more and more factories to produce arsenals of nuclear, chemical, biological and other weaponry. They will also continue to promote the causes of hatred, fear, schism and anger between the Arabs and the Israelis so as to keep the arms bazaars booming. They will moreover shamelessly persist with manipulating the United Nations into being their hypocritically moral mouthpiece as it advocates and advances peace initiatives for the Middle East, but never turns to lay the blame at the doors of those who carry the fundamental guilt. The mockery stands revealed through one incontrovertible fact: that there will be no peace in the Middle East so long as the oil is there and the industrialized nations remain resolutely intent on bartering arms and other destructive weaponry to obtain it, meanwhile exploiting the Arab-Israeli wars as well as other conflicts in the area to achieve their objective.

Without the unholy scramble to sell arms, the Israeli-Arab war would never have been encouraged to develop into what it has become. Israel and the Arabs would very probably have agreed on a national home for the Jewish people without prejudicing the civil and religious rights of the existing non-Jewish communities in Palestine, as the British government specifically intended in its Balfour Declaration of 1917. Lebanon would have been spared a mindless war, the Israeli invasions, the destruction of its towns and villages as well as the savage wrecking of its economy and social structures.

If there had been no war in Lebanon, and no Israeli invasions, many Druze villages would have escaped destruction from the wanton bombardment of the US navy, the Israeli and French air forces, and the sectarian Lebanese army. Neither would the Christians in 1982 have been goaded by the Israelis into invading the Druze land; this in turn sparing the Druzes the agony of having no choice except to fight back against the Christians, alongside whom they had lived in friendship and peace since the civil war of 1860. The Druzes would also have been spared the heavy loss of life their fight for survival cost them, as well as the pain of watching helplessly as their beloved country disintegrated before their eyes. The world, too, would have been spared the horrific spectacles of the Iraq-Iran war and

221

the war to liberate Kuwait along with all the attentive terrors and scandals.

Yet still the scramble to sell arms intensifies, as does the driving greed behind it. The prospect, as things stand, is for the wars in the Middle East to continue, with no hope for an end to them in view.

14. The Ambitions of General Aoun

President Amin Gemayel, only hours before the end of his term of office in September 1988, appointed General Michel Aoun to be prime minister of a Maronite military Christian government in Lebanon, pending the election of a new president. General Aoun, a United States trained artillery officer, was commander-in-chief of what was left of the Lebanese army, consisting by that stage mainly of Maronite Christians, most of the Moslem, Shi'ite and Druze elements having split away and left. Its troops numbered 15,000 and its combat brigades were largely trained by the United States and equipped with US tanks and artillery. Its arsenal had, under General Aoun, also been greatly increased by heavy weapons and ammunition sent by Iraq.

The appointment of General Aoun as prime minister was unanimously rejected by the Moslem, Shi'ite and Druze communities. They considered it an illegal act of sectarian provocation. There already existed in Lebanon a legally constituted government, headed by Salim el-Hoss, a Moslem prime minister appointed in June 1987, by President Amin Gemayel himself, to replace Rashid Karami, the Moslem prime minister assassinated in June of that year. Karami's assassin, reported to be a Christian member of the Lebanese army, was never brought to trial or punished for his crime, nor were the reasons behind the outrage ever disclosed.

President Amin Gemayel had governed in successful co-operation with Salim el-Hoss's government from June 1987 to September 1988. There was therefore no need for any new government at the end of his term. Consequently, the Salim el-Hoss government continued in office and appointed a high-ranking Moslem officer to head a Moslem army and so create sectarian military balance within the country. President Amin Gemayel had originally, after the assassination of his brother Beshir, been elected to the presidency of Lebanon by a unanimous vote of Parliament, representing all the Lebanese communities. Their hope had been that he would be the man to find the ardently desired solution to the Lebanese crisis. Not only did he fail to find any solution, but now he crowned his turbulent, much-criticized rule with this last-minute act, so producing a *de facto* partition of Lebanon: two prime ministers, two governments, two armies, two administrations.

The reason for President Amin Gemayel's appointment of a rival Maronite military prime minister was the traditional conviction among the Maronites that power in Lebanon is theirs (despite the fact that they represent less than 30 per cent of the population), and that power must never be entrusted to the Moslems, even for short transitional periods. In the event, it did not take long for General Aoun to abandon his newly proclaimed position of prime minister of Lebanon. Instead, he assumed the title of Christian leader of Lebanon.

In a show of military muscle, General Aoun clashed with the Christian Lebanese Forces and took control of their movements. He also occupied the clandestine seaports held by Christian militias, and sent his army's gun-boats to blockade those ports held by the Moslem militias. His objective was to control all imports, especially of arms and ammunition, and all exports, especially of drugs. The Moslems objected, first because their ports were their only gateway for the supplies they badly needed for survival, and secondly because they suspected that the seizure of the Christian militia ports was not to stop their illegal trades but a ploy to blockade and close those in Moslem hands. They saw the general's credibility as highly questionable, for in their opinion he headed an exclusively Maronite sectarian government already rejected by the Moslems as illegally constituted and representing none of the other Lebanese communities. He was also commander-in-chief of a wholly Maronite-controlled Lebanese army.

Enraged by the reaction of the Moslem communities to his bid to control the ports, General Aoun retaliated by shelling the residential areas of West Beirut and the Druze villages. He also forced Lebanon's international airport to close by threatening to shell it if it operated. At this point he declared a war of liberation against Syria and its army in Lebanon, and continued to shell the residential areas of Moslem West Beirut and the Druze villages, sheltering behind a claim that he was shelling Syrian positions. He vowed to liberate Lebanon by chasing the Syrians and their army out of the country regardless of any cost to Lebanon and the Lebanese.

The Syrians had originally withdrawn from Beirut and the mountains following the Israeli invasion of 1982, but in 1987 they were begged to return and re-establish law and order at a time when West Beirut was ruled by total anarchy as militias fought for local power and gangsters killed and looted. This desperate request originated from the legally constituted government of the time, with Amin Gemayel as its Maronite Christian president, and had the full approval of Sunni Moslems, Christians, Shi'ites, Druzes and other sects as well as the beleaguered inhabitants of West Beirut.

As we have seen earlier in this book, Lebanon is not for the Maronite Christians alone. More than sixteen religious sects live there, and any request for the Syrians to leave should have come from a legally constituted government, representative of all those sects. It is true that many of them may have wished to see the Syrians leave Lebanon, but they should have been allowed to express that wish for themselves, and they had the right to demand guarantees that they would receive an adequate level of law-enforced protection in their place. General Aoun possessed no authority to speak for them any more than he had authority to declare war in the name of Lebanon. His only contribution to debate in these matters was to open fire with high-explosive shells on residential West Beirut and the Druze villages.

The strangest aspect was that the general and his Maronite supporters seemed to have completely forgotten who initially invited the Syrians to enter Lebanon: not the Moslems or the Druzes, but the Maronite Christians themselves when, in 1976, they faced imminent defeat by Kamal Jumblatt's National Movement and its Palestinian allies. First the Maronites had appealed to the West, and especially to France, but received no response. Only the Syrians would agree to come to their rescue and halt the advance of the National Movement fighters. Some say the Syrians were asked directly by the Maronites to rally to their aid; others that the Syrians came because they were told, by the Americans, that if they did not, then Israel would. The Druzes were the only Lebanese community to object to the invasion of Lebanon by the Syrian army; hence Kamal Jumblatt's famous letter to President Assad of Syria (see pages 178–9).

General Aoun's Maronite forces continued their daily indiscriminate bombardment, on the pretext, in the case of the Druzes, that they were Syrian allies. He never ceased to claim that he was shelling the Syrians and their positions, but very few Syrians were killed and few hits on Syrian positions were scored by the thousands of shells fired nightly. The shells instead killed hundreds and wounded thousands of innocent Lebanese. The hospitals, clinics, schools, electricity generating plants, water works, apartments, houses and finally complete streets in Moslem West Beirut were coldly and systematically razed to the ground. All Druze villages within range of the general's cannon were shelled regularly and many houses and properties destroyed. As for those Druze villages which his cannon could not reach, he requested, as an Israeli radio report confirmed, the ex-Lebanese army Maronite Christian brigadier-general, Antoine Lahad, the officer commanding the Israeli-sponsored South Lebanese army, to shell and destroy them on his behalf. Fortunately, the Israelis did not approve and the villages were preserved from attack.

It has been estimated that more property was destroyed during the seven months of Aoun's shelling between 1988 and 1989 than in all the sixteen years of Lebanon's war, including the 1982 Israeli invasion. It has also been recorded that each day saw the firing of thousands of large-calibre shells. The daily costs of that lunatic deadly extravaganza came to millions of pounds sterling, and one can only ask where such huge sums of money originated. Possibly certain Arab oil-producing countries were active conspirators in what was happening in Lebanon, or perhaps they came from Iraq and Iran financing their own private war in Lebanon, or the revenues of drug traffic, or revenues derived from all these sources. A contribution could also have been made by Western powers intent on the destruction of Lebanon. The truths lie deeply concealed.

In the early days of the Lebanese war, the Western powers and Israel had imposed red lines around the Christian enclave and the Christian positions, prohibiting Syria or its allies from attempting ground or air attacks across the lines. General Aoun was therefore confident that he would be safe from military defeat by the superior Syrian forces, which could have finished him off in a few hours if allowed to take him on. He was also certain that, so long as his supply of arms and ammunition from Iraq and other interested parties remained assured, he could safely declare a war of liberation against the Syrians and their army while continuing as long as he pleased to shell Moslem West Beirut and the Druze villages, publicly stating meanwhile that he was shelling Syrian positions. The presence of the American

Sixth Fleet and of a French fleet off the shores of Lebanon was taken by him and his supporters to guarantee both the inviolability of the red lines and their own invulnerability.

Some interpreted the general's war of liberation and his request for the immediate withdrawal of the Syrians from Lebanon as bargaining tactics to ensure the maintenance of the status quo and preserve the power to rule Lebanon unchallenged in the hands of the Maronite minority. This was not, however, the general's aim, as events would prove. He sought to focus international attention on what he strongly claimed to be the serious plight of the Christians menaced by the oppressive presence of a Moslem Syrian army in Lebanon and its Moslem and Druze allies. In this way he hoped to provoke an urgent demand for an internationally backed solution to the Lebanese crisis that would give him and his Maronite supporters their Christian state in Lebanon. The general in fact behaved and acted as though he were already elected president of that non-existent state.

It is understandable that the Maronite Christians should in the past have wanted a state of their own, free from Islamic domination. Islam is a very compassionate and tolerant religion, but, historically, certain governing Islamic powers have not been so, and especially not the Ottoman Turks, under whose rule the Christians suffered wounding persecution and humiliation. But it also needs to be said that the Christians themselves contributed in large measure to the generation of hatred for them among the Islamic Ottomans. They aided the Crusaders against Islam by supplying them with scouts and fighters. They never possessed or showed allegiance to the ruling Ottoman Empire. Their loyalty was always to the Vatican, to Europe and the Europeans, and especially to France. If the Maronite Christians of Lebanon went out to greet the arrival of a new Ottoman governor, they carried and waved French flags. It only made matters worse when constant pressure was applied on the Ottomans by the European states, foremostly by France, which furiously supported the complaints from the Christians of being badly treated by the Ottoman governors. Such high-handed pressure drove the Ottomans to regard the Maronite Christians of Lebanon as a goading thorn in the thigh of their Islamic Empire and a cancer that needed to be excised. This they tried to achieve when they helped to foment the hatred and dissension that played a major part in the fighting of 1841, 1845 and 1860 between the Maronite Christians and the Druzes.

Nevertheless the Maronite Christians suffered ugly persecution and vicious discrimination in the towns and on the plains in Lebanon, especially in the time before the ascendance of the Druze Ma'anid dynasty to power and in particular of Prince Fakhruddin II, under whom persecutions were abolished, discrimination ceased and Christians came to be treated as equal citizens with the Druzes and other communities. They even ruled Lebanon during the latter part of the eighteenth century, and after the massacres of 1860 were given, by the intervening European powers, a dominant position in the administration. From 1918, they ruled under the French Mandate, and went on doing so after the independence of Lebanon in 1943. Yet having been a party to the creation of Grand Liban and the annexation of the four districts from Syria, they were themselves responsible for creating a Moslem majority. They continued to rule none the less, despite being a minority, through to 1975, when the Moslem majority claimed an increased share in the government of Lebanon. At this point the Maronites obstinately declined to relinquish their absolute power, an attitude which provided a major pretext for the start of war in Lebanon. They refused to acknowledge that, in a democratic world, the minority cannot rule the majority for ever, that change must occur to give the majority its democratic rights. The Moslem majority asked for no more than a trimming back in the undemocratic power privileges of the Maronite Christian minority, but the Maronites persisted in clinging to absolute power and to wanting to secure the whole of Lebanon as their sovereign Christian state.

Despite all that has happened, they have continued to entertain the illusory belief that some external force will help them to retain, even as a minority, this absolute power. France, after all, did it in 1861 and 1920, and there were attempts to do it by the United States in 1958 and by Syria in 1976. Israel, too, invaded Lebanon in 1982 with that objective much in mind. But the Maronites had made overtures to the Zionists and Israelis to ask for help in establishing their Christian state in Lebanon on many previous occasions, as is known from the diaries kept by Moshe Sharett, secretary-general of the Zionist Agency for many years, later minister of foreign affairs when Israel was first established, then its prime minister from 1953 to 1955. This important document first appeared as *Personal Diaries* in Hebrew in 1978, after Sharett's son had beaten off all attempts by the Israeli establishment to place an embargo on its publication.

The diaries turned out to contain many entries, back to as early as 1920, mentioning the Maronites' sympathy for the creation of a Jewish state in Palestine and their repeated requests seeking Zionist and Israeli support to enable them to establish their Maronite Christian state within Lebanon or in place of Lebanon. Most of Israel's leaders were sympathetic to the idea of providing such help, but Sharett, one of their wisest, remained highly cautious and insisted on prudence and restraint. As Jonathan Randal records in *The Tragedy of Lebanon*, Sharett more than once complained of General Dayan that he favoured 'hiring some (Lebanese) officer who would be ready to serve as a front man so that the Israeli army can appear to be responding to his call to "liberate" Christian Lebanon from the burden of its Moslem oppressors'.

This scheme in Dayan's mind became reality when Israel formed the South Lebanese army under Major Sa'ad Haddad (later promoted to colonel). Israel additionally trained hundreds of Phalangist fighters and delivered to them arms and ammunition worth more than $150 million. Nevertheless the Israelis failed in their partnership with the Maronites, despite all the military aid, the formation of the South Lebanese army and the 1982 invasion. It would be interesting to have a Maronite reaction to the news item recorded by Jacobo Timmermann in *The Longest War* to the effect that, during Israel's invasion of Lebanon, 'the army's Chief Rabbi, General Gad Navon, is distributing a map on which Lebanon is marked as the territory that was occupied in antiquity by the Jewish tribe of Asher. The city of Beirut has been hebraized, appearing as Be'erot.' The fanatics among the Maronite Christians, who want to see Lebanon a free and independent Christian state, are outmatched, it seems, by the fundamentalist Zionist Jews, whose voice in Israel booms louder by the day and who would like that same Lebanon to be incorporated within their concept of Greater Israel.

Lebanon, Syria, Jordan and Palestine (now Israel) belong to that part of Asia Minor always known as Syria until its occupation by the Allies during the First World War. It then fragmented into four separate states and was shared out between the British and the French under the Sykes–Picot Agreement, which under the so-called Mandates gave Syria and Lebanon to the French, Palestine and Jordan to the British. Syria therefore remains convinced of its historical indivisibility with Lebanon and its right to an assurance that there will be no use of Lebanon to threaten its own national security. This is the basis for the Syrian military presence in Lebanon, even as national security gives the Israelis their alibi for occupying the buffer zone along the southern border.

By 1989, General Aoun had evidently become convinced that a plot existed against Lebanon. That April, the British newspaper, the *Independent*, recorded his views in an interview and summarized his beliefs as follows:

Long ago, perhaps in the era of Kissinger diplomacy, the United States decided to acquiesce in the silent destruction of Lebanon. 'Now they are allowing Israel and Syria to hold two zones of hegemony here. The southern part of our country, from Sidon to the border, is under Israeli hegemony. From Sidon to the north is meant to be under Syrian hegemony. But Israel is going to be allowed to keep the West Bank and the Syrian Golan Heights and half of Lebanon; the Syrians and the Palestinians – instead of getting back Golan and the West Bank – they will just get the other half of Lebanon. And we Lebanese are supposed to disappear. The Plot will be at our expense.'

'The man ready to destroy this complex, almost manic conspiracy,' the *Independent* added, 'is, of course, none other than the general himself.' Oddly enough, the first country to which Aoun appealed for help with chasing the Syrian army out was the United States, the power he had accused of acquiescing in a conspiracy for the silent destruction of Lebanon. Failing to secure American support, he then looked elsewhere. As the broadcast on Israeli radio confirmed, General Aoun telephoned four times within two successive days, to request that Brigadier-General Antoine Lahad, the Maronite Christian officer commanding the Israeli-sponsored South Lebanese army, ask the Israelis to help him in his war of liberation against Syria. The Israelis refused and made it clear they had no wish to be dragged back into the Lebanese quagmire. They were still smarting under their disastrous experience with the Maronites in 1982. Furthermore, they were not enamoured of the general's declaration that he also wanted to get their army out of Lebanon.

As he next cast around for other interested parties, General Aoun found the Iraqis anxious and willing, not to help him or Lebanon, but to engage the Syrians on the Lebanese battlefield. According to reports, the Iraqis supplied General Aoun with fighting men, gun-boats, missiles, arms, large quantities of ammunition and possibly chemical warfare weaponry. They also supplied tanks and other military equipment, especially missiles, to the Lebanese Forces militia. The Iraqis claimed that by so doing they were preventing the Maronites from seeking help from Israel, but the basic result was that Lebanon was again being used as an arena for feuding foreign powers. For the Iraqis to combat the Syrians in Lebanon was an outstanding act of calculated cynicism, since Iraq and Syria have vastly extensive common borders. If the Iraqis wished to fight the Syrians, why not do so openly on adjoining Syrian territory? Why seek to take them on in Lebanon? Doubtless they saw this option as economical in arms and men. The saying circulated widely that Iraq intended to fight Syria to the last Lebanese Christian.

In the meantime, the Shi'ites in Lebanon had already requested the Iranians to supply them with missiles for use against the Iraqi missiles supplied to General Aoun and the Lebanese Forces. During the hostage crisis in August 1989, and the intensive international efforts to find a solution, President Rafsanjani of Iran laid down as one of the conditions for the release of Western hostages the ousting of General Aoun from power in Lebanon. What was more, the Iranians were growing to be more involved in Lebanon following Iraq's open and unlimited support for General Aoun, coupled with Iran's ardent desire to transform Lebanon into a fanatic Moslem state like their own.

During all the preceding years, the situation in Lebanon had grown so complex and confused that the world could no longer fathom out what was going on in the country: a sectarian war that was not sectarian; a civil war that was not civil; an Arab responsibility that the Arabs were loath to admit; a threat to its Christian inhabitants that was a constant worry to the Vatican and the Christian West; a haven for drug producers and traffickers, hostage-takers, smugglers, counterfeiters, blackmailers, mercenaries and criminals from all over the world. Who could wish to call to mind such a country? Better to forget it, pretend it never existed. That is what actually happened. As the *International Herald Tribune* reported in its issue of 25 October 1988: 'There is an argument in the United States to forget about Lebanon. It claims that Lebanon is a pleasingly open and democratic but still an artificial state that was created by the French to preserve a Western outpost in the emerging post colonial order, and that this state simply failed to take root.' This argument was not confined to the United States. Many Europeans, most Arabs and a number of others, some openly, others less so, believed it to be true.

General Aoun's achievement was to make the world remember Lebanon after it was long forgotten. He did this by his indiscriminate shelling of innocent people, his extensive destruction of property and his outcry of fear that a Christian genocide was imminent, and so delivered to the world a jolt that temporarily returned Lebanon to the news. But, in the world's interests, Lebanon ought never to be forgotten. It should be remembered for having provided the world with two perfect examples of what may happen when there is a failure to settle regional conflicts promptly and they are left to linger. The first of these lessons is the breeding, within the fighting factions, of a younger generation nurtured on hatred, fanaticism, vindictiveness, love of killing and a total disregard for human life and moral and social values. It will in the future be virtually impossible to persuade such generations to live together in peace and friendship.

This is now the case in Lebanon, and a parallel consequence is clearly demonstrated in Israel. There, too, a younger generation has been nurtured on fanaticism, anger and vindictiveness. In their example the focus of hatred is on the Palestinians, whom they blame for the repeated wars against Israel and who, they are convinced, wish only to exterminate them and destroy their state. They do not see how they can possibly expect to coexist peaceably alongside people who, they believe, harbour such motives.

And a further mirror image of the problem is provided by the younger generation of Palestinians, many of whom have grown up in the miserable living conditions of the refugee camps and seen themselves, their families and people treated as undesirables in their own country (and often in their host countries), knowing that their heritage has been stolen from them by the Israelis. Those who remain in former Palestine have to suffer daily from deprivation, maltreatment, persecution and the fanatic determination of Zionist extremists to exterminate them or drive them too into exile. Nor do they see how they can be expected to coexist in peace alongside the younger Israeli generation which has currently come to represent the majority in Israel. The Israeli-Arab conflict has been allowed to continue far too long and it is hard indeed to be optimistic about the emergence of a peaceful solution acceptable to both sides.

The second example for which Lebanon should be remembered is its demonstration of the incontrovertible certainty that any regions where conflicts occur and are allowed to linger will be taken over by the profiteering mafias, political and financial, who will do their best to ensure that any settlement of the conflicts remains impossible to achieve.

15. The Casablanca Summit and the Al-Taif Agreement

The Arab states, claiming that there existed a rising tide of fear at the danger to the whole Arab world should the war in Lebanon continue to blossom and grow, put on a show of belated and long-overdue sympathy for Lebanon and the Lebanese. After receiving a most effective nudge from the Superpowers, they called for a summit meeting of the Arab League to be convened in May 1989 to explore solutions to the Lebanese dilemma. The meeting gained the immediate support of the Superpowers and many West European countries, who placed the emphasis on it being an Arab problem requiring an Arab solution. The Lebanese received the news with a sigh of relief, not unmixed with scepticism regarding the mission's prospects of success.

At the summit meeting in Casablanca, all the Arab heads of state were present, except for those of Lebanon, whose two squabbling governments remained unrepresented. They had not been invited for fear that any invitation might be construed as an admission of the legality of either one or the other. Even the Lebanese ambassador to Morocco was obliged to sit far from the meeting hall, humiliated at being prevented from attending a gathering that purportedly sought a solution to his country's problems.

After several days of heated discussion, the summit emerged on 26 May with two unanimous resolutions: first, warmly to welcome Egypt's readmission to the Arab League; secondly, to back without qualification the PLO's decision to make a bid for a peaceful settlement of the Palestinian conflict with Israel. The summit had never been destined to solve the Lebanese crisis, which in fact received quite a secondary role in the deliberations. Its purpose had been to pass these two very important resolutions required by the Superpowers.

The implication of the second resolution – the PLO's decision to try to gain a peaceful settlement of the Palestinian conflict with Israel – was that the PLO for the first time recognized the existence of Israel. The Superpowers saw this resolution as a necessary first step for the process of peace talks, which were to begin in Madrid after the Gulf War.

The actual exploration for a solution to the Lebanese problem, originally put out as the main reason for calling the summit at Casablanca, was entrusted to a highly placed and illustrious committee of the three heads of state of Morocco, Saudi Arabia and Algeria: namely, Their Majesties King Hassan and King Fahd, and His Excellency Chadli Benjedid. The committee was to examine the Lebanese crisis in depth, then recommend to the Arab League an appropriate policy of action. It accepted the challenge of what appeared an impossible task, and appointed a sub-committee of its ministers of foreign affairs to study the problem and report its findings. The distinguished committee of the heads of state then proceeded to exert pressure on the Superpowers to elicit their genuine co-operation. The Superpowers responded by issuing, with the full approval of the committee, a joint statement to the effect that no military solution should be contemplated for Lebanon. All the red lines imposed by the Western powers to keep the fighting parties apart and protect the Christian enclave and the Christian defence positions must remain in place as drawn.

The Druzes lost no time in announcing support for the Arab committee, declaring an ardent wish to co-operate fully in its aims, but expressing grave doubts on the likelihood of the mission's ultimate success. These doubts were soon justified when the Maronite Christian Lebanese Forces, upheld by General Aoun, demanded the withdrawal of all foreign armies from Lebanese soil before they would agree to any talks with the committee. It was a sentiment that would have been shared by most Lebanese, except that it begged one most important question. If the Syrians left Lebanon, who was to take their place in the maintenance of law and order? Surely the Lebanese Forces could never expect the Sunni Moslems, Shi'ites and Druzes to accept the replacement of the Syrians by General Aoun's sectarian Maronite Lebanese army, so deeply implicated in the indiscriminate shelling of non-Christian communities, the killing of innocent people and the destruction of their houses and property on an unprecedented scale.

Besides this, the Lebanese Forces and General Aoun told the committee they would want to see the Israeli army leave Lebanon at the same time as the Syrian army departed. But they did not specify who they thought should put such a request to the Israelis. Was it be the Lebanese Forces themselves, known to be Israel's closest allies, or the Moslem communities who were fighting the Israelis? Or was it to be the Arab countries, who remained at a state of war with Israel; or perhaps the United Nations, for whom Israel had never shown one iota of respect, any more than it had ever abided by its resolutions? And, in the face of such a request, would Israel actually leave Lebanon?

The Druze position on these issues was outlined by their leader, Walid Jumblatt, in a speech delivered on Saturday, 22 July 1989. It seemed perfectly clear to the Druzes that General Aoun's indiscriminate shelling of the Druze villages was an attempt to drive them off their land as part of a preconceived plot to establish in Mount Lebanon the Maronite dream of a Christian state. In the light of this, the general's declared war on Syria and his plans to free Lebanon from the Syrian army could only be regarded as a ploy. His true objective was to drive out the Druzes and establish a Maronite state, though this time with Iraqi rather than Israeli help. The Druzes, however, were not to be driven off their land, and would stand firm and fight to the last man, woman and child to retain it.

Walid Jumblatt directed strong criticism at the moderate Maronite Christian politicians, who, while always declaring their allegiance to one Lebanon for all the Lebanese and rejecting previous plans for partition or the establishment of a Maronite state in Lebanon, had kept silent. Such silence implied their support for General Aoun and his policies. He similarly lambasted the PLO for assisting General Aoun and fighting on his side, reminding the Palestinians of the PLO that it was to chase them out of Lebanon that the Maronites had begun the war and that his father, Kamal Jumblatt, had given his life in defence of their cause. He further declared that the Druzes desired nothing more than to be able to live at peace with their Christian friends and neighbours.

As the committee of Arab foreign affairs ministers continued its tireless shuttling, the United Nations continued to maintain silence; the Superpowers and their allies continued to express faith in the Arab League effort; Israel continued in the role of interested spectator; Iraq continued to supply General Aoun with arms, ammunition, missiles and other military equipment. And the world as a whole continued to care little, if at all, for what became of Lebanon and the Lebanese.

General Aoun's daily indiscriminate shelling of Moslem West Beirut and the Druze villages was unceasing. The innocent Lebanese continued to pay for this deliberate homicidal lunacy with lives and property. Beirut was emptied of 75 per cent of its population while the Druze villages within range of the general's fire-power were emptied of all inhabitants. And where did most of these fleeing refugees go? Believe it or not, most of the Beirutis sought shelter in the Israeli-occupied security zone in south Lebanon. The Druzes, however, moved southward to Druze land, ready, if

239

need be, to consolidate their community and fight and die for land and survival.

The Arab committee had meanwhile begun to realize, after unceasing flurries of shuttle diplomacy and exhausting contacts between all the interested parties, that the complexities, national and international, of the Lebanese problem were immense. The most basic contention remained the withdrawal of the Syrian army from Lebanon in the current anarchic situation. If the Syrians were to withdraw from Lebanon before the formation of a national government and army representative of the Lebanese as a whole, who would then disarm the militias and maintain law and order? Furthermore, if the Syrians were to withdraw from Lebanon, then the presence of the occupying Israeli army in the south could not be ignored. And, it was known, the Israelis would never leave south Lebanon unless a solution to the Israeli-Palestine conflict was finally agreed and implemented.

The Superpowers and their allies therefore agreed to allow both the Syrian and Israeli armies to stay in Lebanon pending a solution to the complex Middle East problem. Before any solution to the Lebanese crisis could be found, the Lebanese would first have to agree to patch up their differences and elect a president, then a government, to represent all the communities. After that they must reach agreement on the much desired reforms, the most important being the elimination of political and administration sectarianism, and free themselves from the clutches of the foreign powers. A truly Lebanese army would have to be built to defend the Lebanese borders and the interests of all Lebanese, to maintain law and order and rid Lebanon of its underworld of drugs and arms dealers and disarm the militias. Only then would their democratically elected government be legally, constitutionally and effectively in a position to ask the Syrians and the Israelis, and any other foreign forces, to pull out. This was the somewhat utopian solution that the distinguished Arab committee of three hoped to convince the warring Lebanese communities they should accept.

It certainly did not, however, resemble in any way the solution that General Aoun and his supporters wished to see. They had never for a moment agreed with the notion that the Lebanese crisis ought to be arabized. Rather had they always sought for the Lebanese crisis to be internationalized, for the dominant majority of arbitrators would then be Christian and any solution proposed would go in the Maronites' favour and be accepted and guaranteed by the Superpowers and all the industrialized countries of the West and East.

General Aoun looked to France and the Vatican for help, and the French responded quickly. Early in August 1989, they set in motion a campaign to solicit international pressure for a cease-fire to the fighting in Lebanon. There was an immediate response from the United Nations Security Council, the United States, Great Britain, Saudi Arabia, Jordan and many other states, which gave great encouragement to General Aoun, who, as the *Guardian* put it, 'cannot but see in the new French initiative signs of the internationalization of the Lebanese struggle which he has always sought with his "war of liberation". To quicken that process, General Aoun may well, as the Syrians claim, have deliberately brought the war to its new intensity.' In fact, on 14 August, General Aoun appeared on British television to announce that there would be no cease-fire from him until he had chased the Syrian army from Lebanon by force.

As General Aoun's plan to enlist the help of the Vatican and the West to save the Christians and internationalize the Lebanese crisis took shape, the Western media, and especially the French, reported the killings and destruction in Christian East Beirut. Few reports, if any, told of the wholesale killings and destruction of Moslem West Beirut and the Druze villages. Several 'sources of information' went so far as to use photos and videos of the destruction in West Beirut with the claim that they showed what was happening in Christian East Beirut. This orchestrated propaganda was presented to his Holiness the Pope, who repeatedly cried, 'Genocide' – a cry that the French, with their claim to a historic mandate to protect the Maronite Christians in Lebanon, took up with vigour.

At this point, Europe, the United States and the United Nations joined in the outcry to save the Christians from the Moslem Syrians. They requested the Syrians and their allies to cease operations forthwith, though there was still no acknowledgement of the shelling by General Aoun and the Lebanese Forces. The French, taking the plot a stage further, sent eight warships, including an aircraft carrier, to patrol in Lebanese waters. Rumours quickly spread that the French intended, as they had in 1860, to intervene militarily to aid the Maronite Christians. The United States announced approval for the French move, but the Soviet Union declared, in no uncertain terms, that it would oppose any military solution to the Lebanese crisis; and so did Israel. The French promptly backtracked and declared that their military presence in Lebanese waters was for humanitarian reasons as well as to evacuate, if necessary, their nationals living in Lebanon.

It was an explanation that none of the warring parties believed. The Syrians and their allies issued the strongest warnings; General Aoun welcomed the military assistance of the French. A barrage of fierce opposition forced the French to pull back their naval forces and solemnly declare they were there to offer assistance to *all* Lebanese communities and had never intended to help any one community exclusively. Rumours persisted, however, that the French *tour de force* had been intended to alarm and intimidate Syria and its allies. If this was indeed the intention, then the French made a grave miscalculation. They should have known from experience that the Syrians and their allies, the Druzes and the Shi'ites, are not easily browbeaten and it would take more than eight warships to intimidate them.

General Aoun and his supporters were profoundly disappointed when the French pulled back. They were also angered by what emerged as the even-handed attitude of the United States. They were looking for a lot more than sympathy. In the mind of the general, those not with him were most certainly against him. Aoun embarked on daily attacks in the media, accusing the United States of treachery in failing to come actively to his aid for fear of sacrificing the lives of the eight American hostages still held by the Iranian sponsored Hizbollah. His blistering attacks culminated at the start of September in a wild demonstration by thousands of his supporters. They besieged the United States Embassy – which had early in the Lebanese war moved from Moslem West Beirut to the Christian East of the city – and carried banners insulting America while shouting angry threats and slogans. General Aoun threatened to cut off water and electricity to the Embassy and take twenty American hostages.

Fearing a repetition of the siege of the American Embassy in Teheran, the American Ambassador with all his embassy staff hastily left East Beirut in helicopters on 5 September, bound for the British military base on Cyprus. It seemed that General Aoun and his supporters had all too easily forgotten the former help obtained from the Americans in military training, provision of American weaponry and, most important, by the drawing of red lines around the Christian districts and positions, with guarantees to prevent the Syrians and their allies from ever overstepping those lines in any ground or air attacks. It had, moreover, mainly been the United States who set in motion the Arab League summit to try and resolve the Lebanese problems in a way to give the Christians a fair deal.

American efforts to support the Arab committee of three continued, despite General Aoun's hostile attitude, and helped prevent the committee growing disheartened while encouraging it to restart negotiations it believed to be at a dead end. It took tireless, determined efforts, but the

Arab committee finally succeeded in convening sixty-two members of the Lebanese Parliament – thirty-one Moslem Deputies and thirty-one Christian Deputies – for a meeting in October at al-Taif, Saudi Arabia, to discuss and hopefully agree on an Arab-sponsored solution possibly acceptable not only to the Lebanese but to all the parties involved in the Lebanese war.

The sixty-two Deputies settled down to weeks of discussion, argument and bargaining, guided and encouraged by the Arab committee of three. Lines of communication were open to them for keeping the war-lords of Lebanon, including General Aoun and all other interested parties, advised of the discussions, and to take advice on what should be accepted, what rejected. Ultimately they agreed by an overwhelming majority, with only three abstentions, to accept a detailed solution they and the Arab committee hoped would see an end to the sixteen years of war and restore sovereignty and integrity to Lebanon. The solution, better known as the Al-Taif Agreement, was hailed as a major breakthrough and a landmark by the Western Powers, the USSR, the Vatican, all the Arab countries and Patriarch Nasrallah Sfeir, the highest Maronite religious authority in Lebanon.

The Shi'ites, as the largest single community in Lebanon, had not initially been happy with the solution. It totally ignored their majority rights and gave them little in terms of power-sharing. Nevertheless they agreed to accept if all interested parties did likewise. The Druzes similarly did not like the agreement, their objection being that it contained no aim to abolish sectarianism in Lebanese national politics or government administration. They also objected on the grounds that it failed to specify clearly that the national armed forces should be reconstructed as an army for all the Lebanese, to defend the sovereignty and integrity of Lebanon, with its boundaries as a whole. The army would therefore be left to flourish as a sectarian force serving not the interests of Lebanon but those of certain of its communities.

Despite these misgivings, they also finally declared acceptance, provided all parties concerned accepted, too.

This left but one voice of dissension: that of General Aoun, who rejected the solution out of hand. Regrettably, he was much encouraged in his stand by the cynical machinations of certain voices – Western and Arab – who, having openly declared their support for the Al-Taif Agreement, now secretly urged the general to reject it. It was his opinion, the general declared, that the agreement did not oblige the Syrians to undertake an instant and total withdrawal. He would, he threatened, be prepared to use force to prevent the Christian Deputies from electing a president of Lebanon, as agreed in the al-Taif solution, and would go even further to bring about the dissolution of Parliament should the Deputies dare to defy him.

In the event, those Deputies who had discussed, negotiated and approved the Al-Taif Agreement, did indeed defy General Aoun. They met in the north of Lebanon to elect René Moawwad, a Maronite, as President of Lebanon and formally approve the reforms stipulated in the agreement. The general and his supporters were enraged. Their anger erupted in large-scale demonstrations to denounce the agreement, brand as traitors all those Christian Deputies who had approved it and claim it represented a sell-out of Christian Lebanon to the Syrians.

Even the patriarch himself became a target for their rage when a Maronite mob, together with members of the Lebanese army, attacked the patriarchal residence and forced their way in, breaking and burning furniture. Despite pleas and entreaties from the resident clergy, they dragged the patriarch from his bedroom in his nightgown, insulted and humiliated him and forced him to his knees to kiss a poster that carried General Aoun's portrait. In the patriarchate, they tore down the pictures of saints and previous patriarchs and replaced them with pictures of General Aoun; even going so far as to tear down a picture of His Holiness the Pope to be similarly replaced. The patriarch, lucky to have his life spared, hurriedly left for his summer residence in the north of Lebanon. The incident prompted a front-page headline in the *International Herald Tribune* of 7 November 1989: 'Lebanese Patriarch is Forced to Flee to Syrian-Held Region'. The caption to a photograph read: 'Clerics trying to calm Lebanese soldiers who stormed the home of the Maronite Patriarch, Nasrallah Sfeir, and forced him to flee.'

The outrage provided a character reference for the kind of soldiers General Aoun proposed using to maintain law and order among the Sunni, Shi'ite and Druze communities, once he had rid Lebanon of the Syrian army. The other religious communities of Lebanon united to denounce this brutal threat against the Maronite patriarch, and thus declared their sympathy and respect for a spiritual leader who had won immense general respect as a moderating influence in warring Lebanon. The Maronites were the one exception. The Lebanese Forces, the other splinter-group Maronite militias, the students and many others in the Christian community began belligerently declaring their support for the general and his clear objective to partition Lebanon and establish a pure Maronite state within the Christian enclave. The Christian Deputies who had negotiated and approved the Al-Taif Agreement, and certain other moderates, were in this the exception. But, like the patriarch, they had to flee the Christian enclave to preserve their lives.

From the time of their early migration to north Lebanon, early in the eighteenth century, and starting with their patriarch saint, John Maron, the Maronites had always tacitly accepted their patriarch not only as a religious leader but also as a political mentor. Their history demonstrated an acceptance of the patriarch's double leadership, without exception or deviation, until the end of the 1980s, when, it seems, they decided to reject their patriarch's leadership in favour of one that was purely militaristic and political.

The worst aspect of the Al-Taif Agreement was, in the eyes of General Aoun, that it clearly defined Lebanon as an Arab country, a member of the Arab League. For centuries the Maronites had refused to be considered as Arabs, despite the fact that they were Arabic-speaking in everyday life, and that the world in general saw them as Christian Arabs. The biggest concession they ever made in this respect was when, in the unwritten Covenant of 1943, they accepted that Lebanon should have an 'Arab face'. In any event, the general now moved swiftly to carry out his threats. He used a power, assumed but not legally possessed, to dissolve Parliament, declare the election of President René Moawwad null and void and announce new elections in Lebanon for January 1990.

16. Choice and Destiny in the Middle East

President René Moawwad was assassinated on 22 November 1989, seventeen days after his election and before he could make any attempt to form a government to help him with implementing the Al-Taif Agreement. Accusations as to who was responsible flew at every tangent. Denials and counter-accusations became prolific in equal measure. There was, however, a consensus of opinion over the fact that the assassination was carried out by professionals.

The finger of suspicion pointed first at General Aoun and his Deuxième Bureau (the army's military Intelligence unit, named after its notorious equivalent in the French army). Aoun and his supporters retaliated by accusing Syria. Iraq accused Syria and Iran of masterminding the outrage, and Iraq and the Palestinians were similarly accused. And as has become usual in the Arab world in cases of this sort, the finger of suspicion was also shortly pointed at Israel. Israel, it seems, is not averse to having fingers of suspicion pointed at her on such occasions. The Israeli Chief of Staff, Major-General Dan Shomron, was quick to declare that 'Moawwad's assassination underlined Lebanon's inability to establish a strong central government that could prevent terror incursions along Israel's northern border and that underlines the need for Israel's security zone in south Lebanon'.

President Moawwad's assassination was the latest in a long string of deplorable political murders and unlikely to be the last. None of the leading Lebanese communities has escaped its share of political murders. The Druzes lost Kamal Jumblatt, their charismatic leader, and Halim Takieddine, their supreme legal judge. The Maronites lost two presidents of Lebanon, Bashir Gemayel and René Moawwad, and two political leaders, Tony Franjieh and Dany Chamoun. The Sunni Moslems lost a prime minister, Rashid Karami, the Grand Mufti of Lebanon, Hassan Khalid, two parliamentary Deputies, Marouf Sa'd and Nazim Qadri, the president of the Islamic Council, Sheikh Soubhi Saleh, and its director-general, Sheikh Ahmed Assaf. The Shi'ites lost their religious and political leader, Imam Musa As-Sadr, who disappeared in 1978 and was never heard of subsequently.

To this extensive roll-call of the victims of political crime must be added the names of the Moslem journalists, Salim Lawzi and Riad Taha, and many others. Nor should anyone forget the collective murders of the CIA regional officers in the American Embassy car-bomb explosion, the American marines slaughtered in their Beirut International Airport headquarters and the French soldiers and officers who similarly died in theirs.

Nearly all these assassinations and political murders have one aspect in common: nobody can say who did them, and anyone who knows is never likely to tell. President Moawwad's assassination, like all those preceding it, has never been explained, and we need not expect it ever will be. The political and financial underworlds behind these crimes are too powerful for anyone to dare to expose them.

After Moawwad's assassination, it was believed that no one would have the courage to stand for election as President of Lebanon, 'the most dangerous post in the world', as it was accurately described on British television. But then, contrary to all pessimistic expectations, and in defiance of General Aoun's threats, the members of the Lebanese Parliament quickly met and elected a Maronite Christian, Elias Hrawi, to be President of Lebanon within barely forty-eight hours

249

of Moawwad's death. Eight hours after his election, President Hrawi announced his Lebanese Cabinet and assumed control of all of Lebanon, except for Israel's security zone in the south and the Christian enclave where General Aoun ruled supreme. The first act of the new government was to dismiss General Aoun as the officer commanding the Lebanese army and appoint another Maronite officer in his place. The general was then requested to move out of the presidential palace, which he had occupied when first appointed to head a transitional military government pending the presidential election. He was told that if he declined to hand over the army to his replacement and vacate the palace, he would leave the newly appointed government no alternative but to oust him by force.

General Aoun responded by calling the election of President Hrawi a farce and dismissing the formation of Hrawi's government as null and void. He declared himself and his government as representing the legitimate rulers of free Lebanon, and that he would fight to the finish before acceding to what he called the illegitimate government's outrageous demands. He was quickly backed not only by his supporters, who consisted mainly of the younger generation, but by a majority of Maronites, especially those of the militias. There were, of course, exceptions, but these remained in a small minority. A human wall was formed about the palace, ready and willing to sacrifice itself to protect the general and identify itself with his stand. An unexpected boost to his position came with the clandestine visit to Lebanon of thirty-three Deputies of the French Parliament, who arrived to express their solidarity with the general and became part of the human protective shield.

While this situation was developing, the United States, the Soviet Union, Saudi Arabia and the Arab League committee of three were appealing for restraint and indicating that no military force was to be used against the general. Lebanon hung on the brink of partition as the Maronite community stood firm behind General Aoun. All the international powers, super and not so super, who had wholeheartedly applauded the Al-Taif Agreement and the subsequent election of a new president for Lebanon, suddenly became reluctant to see the agreement enforced. France went a step further, renewing threats of military intervention and promising aid to the general if force were used to eject him. Thus, since the general declared he would fight to the death before he agreed to relinquish power, France in effect declared it would fight at his side if he came under attack. It was crystal-clear that the Maronite community preferred partition and the establishment of their own state to accepting the very modest modification of its power implied by the terms of the Al-Taif Agreement.

Even as all this was going on, Israel seized a ship laden with missiles for General Aoun, sent by Iraq. This escalation of weaponry profoundly worried both Israel and the United States. They took immediate steps to put an end to General Aoun's megalomaniac campaign to grasp power in Lebanon and sent envoys to discuss the situation with Israel's reliable allies, the Maronite Lebanese Forces. It was agreed with one accord that the Lebanese Forces should deprive the general of any exercise of power over Maronite Christian East Beirut. In Israeli eyes, Syria's presence in Lebanon was infinitely to be preferred to that of Saddam Hussein's Iraq.

General Aoun retaliated in his usual fashion by opening up an indiscriminate bombardment of East Beirut, destroying property and killing the innocent. For the first time, Christian East Beirut experienced the horrors of indiscriminate shelling which Moslem West Beirut had suffered incessantly for years. With the Maronites effectively split down the middle, Christian was fighting and killing Christian, but a far greater shadow hung over the scene: that of the imminent Gulf War, with its atrocities, horrors and secrets that may one day be exposed, its costs and the profits it generated for those who planned it. The United States, keen to see

251

Syria join the coalition against Iraq, gave Syria the green light to oust General Aoun. Within less than twenty-four hours, the general, accompanied by two of his aides, had fled his bunker in the presidential palace for the safe haven of the French Embassy, where he and his companions were granted political asylum.

To secure his financial future, the general had already had the foresight to transfer over $20 million from money levied while in power to his and his wife's joint account in a bank in France. Every effort by President Hrawi to persuade the French to hand over the general to the Lebanese government, together with the money he had misappropriated, fell on deaf ears. Eventually the general was given safe French transport to France, where he set himself up in a life of luxury, security and freedom.

Much has been written about the Gulf War, and much will be written in the years to come. Consideration of it has little place in the present book, except in so far as it marked the last faltering attempt by the Soviet Union as one of the Superpowers to influence events on the world stage. Subsequently, as the former Soviet bloc abandoned its Marxist ideology in favour of an improved and free market economy desperate for Western aid, especially from the United States, it seemed as though the Soviet Union, as it broke down into its national components, was virtually handing over to the Americans responsibility for finding solutions to the regional confrontations that the Russians had encouraged and sponsored for more than fifty years. So far as a solution to the Arab-Israeli conflict and related matters in the Middle East is concerned, the United States has left it to Israel to dictate policy, backed by unconditional American approval. The sooner the Arabs realize this reality, the sooner may such a solution be arrived at; and the Arabs will be fortunate if it falls short of the Zionist dream of Greater Israel.

The Lebanese problem remains of prime importance to

Israel, a major player in its origin and development. The Al-Taif Agreement, if approved by Israel, and even if enforced and approved by the Maronite community, holds out no prospect of solving all the Lebanese problems, though the general hope has been that it will at least mark an end to the killing and destruction. In fact, this is what has happened. The main foreign powers, who planned and executed the conspiracy against Lebanon, who financed and operated the sixteen-year war, issued their covert orders for the fighting to cease, and within less than twenty-four hours all the militias and the sectarian factions had stopped fighting and shooting and were willingly surrendering their arms. (It was, however, reported that the Maronite Christian militia, the Lebanese Forces, sold their weapons to Yugoslavia.)

There was one exception to the general disarmament: Hizbollah, with its Iranian national guards, was allowed to remain fully operational in south Lebanon against Israel. No question therefore existed of Israel being deprived of its *raison d'être* for remaining in its self-proclaimed security zone and carrying out daily air and ground attacks against Lebanese villages suspected of harbouring units of Hizbollah.

The effect of this tangled skein of motivations has been to place Lebanon's problems on a slow back-burner, producing a cease-fire and a truce; though it is highly doubtful whether it will achieve anything more permanent unless a solution can be found for the conflicts of the Middle East as a whole. The Lebanese problem has long been an integral and inseparable part of the festering, unmanageable quagmire of regional political intrigue and the ravenously insatiable fight for the profits of oil, arms sales and drugs trafficking. None of the foreign parties involved in the Middle East conflict want a permanent peace, whether these are industrialized countries competing for the profits of war or the powers who use the Middle East as a battlefield to settle their conflicts. Neither do the fundamentalist Zionists, with their powerful voice in

Israel, want to end hostilities, for it has come to seem that Israel's survival depends more and more on continuing its war with its Arab neighbours rather than on making peace. Certainly the expansionist Zionist plans for a Greater Israel, taking in Lebanon, are still far from being realized. Perhaps there is a clue in this to the recent rise of universal support for an Arab solution to the problems of Lebanon, for no such Arab solution will ever be acceptable to Israel. The Israelis may thus continue to justify their occupation of south Lebanon, pending a definitive solution to the Israeli-Arab conflict, and that may take a very long time to find, if it ever is.

Yet should the impossible happen and the peace talks between the Arabs and Israelis succeed, wholly or in part, there is one solution for Lebanon and its problems that seems to be under serious consideration by the Maronite Christians, the Vatican, Israel, France, the United States and some of its Western allies: to make Lebanon, the old Mount Lebanon with Beirut and Sidon annexed, a Christian state for the Maronites and the Druzes, with boundaries guaranteed by the international powers. It is a solution intended to safeguard Christian Lebanon against any Moslem aggression from surrounding Arab states. To remedy the Grand Liban fiasco, Tripoli and part of north Lebanon and the eastern Beqaa will be returned to Syria. South Lebanon will become an independent canton and given to the Shi'ites and to those Palestinians who left Palestine and who will never be allowed by Israel to return to their homeland.

In 1990, the United States emerged as the undoubted victor of the Gulf War and the world's one omnipotent Supreme Power. The Soviet Union failed to retain even a semblance of dignity, and grossly humiliated, soon ceased to exist, becoming partially replaced by a Commonwealth of Independent States begging for charity in the West and facing a legacy of economic and environmental problems of unimaginable complexity. The formidable army of the Soviet

Union, struck with shame and humiliation, was rendered confused and headless and subject to rival loyalties. At this point, the United States declared its intention to create a new world order to settle local wars, conflicts and confrontations and create peace and stability. And, no sooner was this declaration made, than the arms manufacturers went to work to exert pressures in every direction, producing arms to order and promoting weapons sales in ways that seemed a complete negation of the United States' good intentions in its stated ambitions to create a new world order of harmony. Proposals for the new order have subsequently been allowed to sink quickly to the bottom of the political agenda. At a time when the whole world looks to the United States to use its supreme power to promote a new world order to achieve peace and stability, it will be a profound tragedy if such a historic opportunity is totally lost.

Nevertheless the United States, with Russia in modest tow, has urged the Arabs and Israelis to pursue peace talks, apparently determined to bring about peace between the Arabs and Israel. This is not because they sympathize with the Arabs, or because there has been a change of policy in their boundless and blindfolded support for Israel, but because they need to stop the drain the annual subventions to Israel have been taking on the US Treasury. There are serious economic troubles for Americans on their own doorstep: the recession, the poverty of important sections of their population, to name only the most important factors. The 1992 riots and demonstrations in Los Angeles, San Francisco, New York and other cities across the country clearly indicated an urgent need for the United States to turn to financing economic and social development at home. Governor Bill Clinton's promise to make these issues a primary focus of attention contributed in large measure to his victory over George Bush in the 1992 US presidential elections.

In the wake of his landslide victory, however, Clinton lost no time in announcing that US foreign policy was to continue unchanged under his administration. He went even further to give an assurance that the Israeli-Arab peace talks should continue. The Arabs, for their part, felt wary, and wondered whether Clinton could be relied on, as much as Bush, to maintain pressure on Israel to agree to reasonable terms in the talks. During the election campaign, the United States' Jewish lobby and media had swung its support firmly behind Clinton, whose promises included unlimited aid to Israel; it is a debt of which Clinton must remain keenly aware.

But most Jews in the United States and Israel are today genuinely anxious to achieve peace. The Arabs therefore remain hopeful of seeing the peace process continue under US sponsorship. A peace between Israel and the Arabs is clearly in America's long-term interests. It would both stem the financial haemorrhage on the US Treasury and enable Israel to exploit the Arab wealth in natural resources and to profit from trade with the vastly populated Arab markets. Time only will tell what peace terms may eventually be exacted by the Clinton administration, and to what extent these favour Israel. But should the Arabs be pushed into a self-destructive rejection of the Israeli-dictated peace talks, then we may expect the war to continue for ever.

At the outset, the Arabs quickly and readily agreed to the peace talks, having taken the resolution in Casablanca to do so. The Israelis, by contrast, advanced many objections and initiated provocations that they hoped might drive the Arabs to boycott the talks. Arresting four members of the Palestinian delegation to the peace talks provided a glaring example of their tactics, but the United States remained adamant and the talks went on, despite the lack of any evidence of success beyond the fact that Arabs and Israelis were at last meeting round a peace table.

Contrary to what is universally believed, this was not the first time the Arabs had wished to negotiate peace with Israel.

The Times, in its issue of 24 January 1985, published an article headed: 'Arabs Wanted Treaties with Israel: "Britain Blocked 1949 Peace"'. In the light of all that has happened, the following extract from that article becomes of extreme interest:

> Secret diplomatic documents discovered recently
> show several Arab states were willing to conclude
> peace agreements with Israel more than 30 years
> ago, but were partly dissuaded from doing so by
> Britain, then the preeminent Western power in the
> Middle East. The classified British documents, each
> bearing the stamps Secret, Top Secret, Restricted and
> Confidential, show that Britain, which had military
> treaties with several Arab states, worked incessantly
> to prevent the establishment of peaceful relations
> between the new state of Israel and its Arab neighbours,
> especially Transjordan. British diplomats were apparently
> afraid that an Arab-Israeli peace might lead the Arabs
> to be less pro-Western, and they therefore urged
> Arab leaders not to make peace. King Abdullah
> (grandfather of present King Hussein) was anxious to
> come to an agreement with Israel but was restrained
> by Britain. The disclosures were made in highly
> secret minutes of a gathering of British Foreign Office
> representatives and ambassadors to the Middle East
> held on July 21, 1949, at the time the first Arab-Israeli
> war ended.

The minutes of the 1949 meeting were among several documents that apparently slipped through the net of official secrecy surrounding British diplomacy. From the documents, it appears that even the Arab régimes in Syria and Iraq were at times willing – according to British estimates – to reach some kind of accord with Israel, even as early as 1949. But British policy-makers played on Arab-Israeli rivalry to advance British military and economic interests from Suez to the Gulf. The British Minister in Beirut stated that Lebanon would doubtless follow the other Arab states, and was unlikely to conclude any agreement independently. Britain's fears of Israel stemmed from the fact that Israel, in the days soon after its independence, formally committed itself to a policy harnessed less to the West than to the policies of Arab states. The Arabs were tied in a variety of treaty relationships with Britain; Israel was not so tied.

The peace efforts of 1949 were never allowed to see the light of day. The Arabs have never subsequently been allowed to unite or to co-operate in any project that the West has considered harmful to the West's interests. These and other reasons place a formidable barrier in the way of hoping that the most recent round of peace talks, sponsored by the United States, will ultimately succeed. The Zionists do not desire peace, for their survival and ambitious plans depend increasingly on Israel's continued wars with its Arab neighbours, and peace would mean the abandonment of ambitions. The Zionists are also shrewdly aware that Israel has, as a result of the collapse of the Soviet Union and the ending of the Cold War, lost the strategic importance it formerly had for the United States. It is therefore strongly in their interests to promote and amplify the image of Islamic fundamentalism as a growing threat to Western interests and world peace.

The Arabs do not hate the Jews, and never persecuted them at the period in history when the Arabs ruled from Spain to China. Instead they co-operated with them and made good use of their expertise, especially in finance; it was the Christians of Europe who persecuted the Jews and treated them badly. The Arabs do, however, hate and fear the Zionists, with their ambitious plans for a Greater Israel stretching from the Taurus mountains in Turkey in the north to Sinai in the south. Their intention is to achieve this by chasing the Arabs from their land or by dominating them to force them into becoming the subject, underprivileged work-force of Greater Israel.

When Israel was created as a state, it was as a result of the British government's Balfour Declaration. This clearly specified that: 'It being clearly understood that nothing shall be done which may prejudice the civil and religious rights of the existing non-Jewish communities in Palestine.' In addition, Israel's Proclamation of Independence of 14 May 1948 declared: 'The State of Israel will devote itself to developing the land for the good of its inhabitants.' It also promised that, 'Israel will maintain complete equality of social and political rights for all its citizens, without distinction of creed, race or sect.'

The Zionists never for a moment honoured the pledges given in the Balfour Declaration, nor those contained in Israel's Proclamation of Independence. The Palestinian Arabs were not to be classified as citizens of the state of Israel, and therefore either had to leave or be ejected. There was no such people as the Palestinians, claimed the Zionists, and proceeded to precipitate the most scandalous and long-lasting refugee problem in modern history.

But powerful forces continue to oppose the realization of the wishes of the majority of Arabs and Israelis, who, despite everything, want peace and hate war. Among these forces stand the power-seeking politicians and the various fanatic religious and political groups of the modern world, but constantly looming above them all are the arms manufacturers, who will use every aggressive tactic to preserve their highly lucrative Middle East weapons market.

There has, since the Gulf War, been a steady accumulation of evidence to show the extent to which the dominant world powers, including Britain, originally helped Saddam Hussein to arm and to develop Iraq's weapons technology and war capability. At the end of the war, world leaders paid ardent lip-service to the need for strict arms-control policies to ensure future stability for the Middle East. They also anticipated that there would be more general arms and troop reductions in response to the ending of the Cold War.

Yet, soon after the Gulf War, Kuwait had signed a contract for $2,000 million of military defence equipment; Saudi Arabia had announced the purchase of seventy-two American advanced military aircraft for $55,000 million and reconfirmed a stupendous contract with the United Kingdom for £150,000 million of military hardware. Within two years, it seemed, all the good intentions were being overturned and the victory going once again to the arms dealers. President Clinton may have surprised everyone when he announced his plans to cut the US defence budget, but there was no indication of the countries of Europe, the Middle East and the Far East slowing down in the rate at which they armed or rearmed. Far from it. The United Kingdom had just signed contracts for missiles worth close to £600 million, ordered a fourth Trident nuclear submarine and back-tracked on plans to run down the numbers of personnel in the armed forces – anticipating a rising tide in the number of conflicts around the world that will need 'policing'. The United States and France had meanwhile been supplying Taiwan with military aircraft, to the annoyance of China; and the countries of East Asia are all, in the words of a headline in the *International Herald Tribune* of 19 March 1993, engaged in a 'colossal shopping spree' for up-to-date armaments. At the end of January, Russia had reached an accord with India to service and augment the country's air and ground weapons systems, more than 60 per cent of which were supplied by the former Soviet Union.

In the Middle East, at the same time as President Yeltsin secured his *coup* in India, the British prime minister, John Major, announced the consolidation of a deal with Saudi

Arabia for an order for forty-eight Tornado aircraft worth
over £4,000 million, and an agreement with Oman to supply
thirty-six Challenger 2 tanks at a price of £150 million. In
Britain itself, beleaguered by recession and unemployment,
the news was greeted with enthusiasm: several thousand jobs
could be guaranteed as a result. But as Adrian Hamilton
concluded in an article in the *Observer* on 31 January
1993, the policy more probably represented a policy of
'jobs today for disaster tomorrow'. Far from seeking to
damp down the universal threat posed by the arms trade,
the industrial nations see their arms manufactures as a main
hope in leading their economies out of recession.

Syria is buying arms; so is Iran. Egypt is receiving large
quantities of military equipment; so is Israel. 'There is
little doubt,' commented Hella Pick in the *Guardian* on
30 January 1993, 'that President Clinton will back Israeli
requests for new military equipment to maintain the arms
balance against the continuing build-up in Saudi, the other
Gulf countries and Iran.' By mid February, at IDEX 93,
a mammoth defence show in the Gulf, held in what the
International Herald Tribune of 15 February 1993 said
'has quickly developed into the world's most important
arms market' – featuring 350 weapons manufacturers from
thirty-four countries – France was triumphantly able to
announce a $3,000 million contract with the United Arab
Emirates for nearly 400 battle tanks, with future sales
of Mirage 2000 fighter planes also anticipated. The tank
deal brought the total value of high-technology military
hardware purchases by the Gulf states since the Gulf War to
$40,000 million, and the Arabic press meanwhile announced
that Saudi Arabia, Kuwait and the United Arab Emirates
had signed billion-dollar contracts with Italy for military
equipment, though the exact sums remained undisclosed.

The success of IDEX 93 represented, said the *International
Herald Tribune*, the 'biggest acquisition of armour since
1945' and went on to comment:

The all-out drive to sell weapons to the Middle East, which has witnessed more than a score of conflicts since World War II, flies in the face of the major powers' declarations that weapons deliveries to the volatile region should be severely limited. But the West wants to protect its oil supplies, and arming its Gulf allies is one way to do it.

America, Britain and France have been in open, sometimes cut-throat competition to lay hands on the 'rewards' – that is to say, the arms contracts – which they see as their due for having engaged in the Gulf War to protect the oil-rich Gulf states. The UN Arms Register, which came into force at the start of 1993, is unlikely to have much impact on reality: notification is voluntary. As Christophe Carle wrote in the *International Herald Tribune* of 19 March 1993:

> If a fully operational UN global arms trade register existed, it could scarcely do better than to register the fact that the Gulf War has done the arms trade no harm.
> With jobs and recovery at stake in the West, and Russia in dire economic straits, sales will continue until markets are saturated. This will happen in the Middle East before it does in Asia. But in the end, the export bonanza will only be a reprieve for arms industries now heading for a post-Cold War crash diet – unless one of today's favourite clients turns against the hands that furbished it with weaponry, becomes a new 'rogue state', and starts the cycle anew.

Meanwhile, in the opinion of some observers, the international arms trade is again already beyond hope of control. And this is the back-drop against which the Arabs and Israelis supposedly meet to negotiate peace.

The question therefore urgently arises: is not the time here for intelligent Arabs and intelligent Israelis to acknowledge how they have, for all of forty years, been manipulated into killing one another so these monstrous forces may achieve their ruthless objectives? The Arabs have been foolishly naïve in allowing themselves to be persuaded that they are fighting Israel alone. They should have realized that the dark forces of greed and power have always joined hands to ensure that the mighty United States and its allies were fighting for Israel. They should have known, too, that they would never be allowed to unite into a strong force opposed to Israel. Quarrels and squabbles were encouraged and promoted among them to keep them disunited and highly ineffective as a fighting force.

They did, on the other hand, hold the power of oil and its lucrative trade to exert pressure on both West and East to get them to suspend the abundance of assistance to Israel and join in efforts to bring about a reasonable and peaceful solution to the Arab-Israeli conflict. This was the course advocated by the late King Faisal of Saudi Arabia. He was assassinated before he could get his intentions in motion. His move died with him and was never permitted to be renewed. The Arabs should also have realized early in their fight with Israel that the help they received from the Soviet Union was vastly different in quality from that given by the United States to Israel. The Soviets sold them military equipment for defence purposes only, never for offence. They supplied them with verbal support, though even that was not consistent. They made low-tone noises of protest when necessary, but never did anything further. The United States and its allies, by contrast, poured in all the military and financial assistance Israel requested without limitation.

But the Soviet Union was never able to convince any of the Arab countries, not even the most radical of the socialist states among them, that they should embrace communism. Consequently, the terms of Russian support were restricted to Russia's own interests. On the other hand, the abundance of aid given to Israel by the United States and its allies was based not on any conviction that Israel represented

263

the one truly democratic country in the Middle East, but was intended to create a strong military bastion to guard and protect American and Western interests in the area. The Arabs, while recognizing the qualitative differences between the restricted support they received from the Soviet Union and the unlimited assistance Israel was given by the United States and its allies, nevertheless stubbornly embarked from the beginning on fighting a losing battle. The only good they achieved was to enable Israel to grow, with their indirect help, into the fourth strongest military power in the world, with, it is reported, an air force that is the third most powerful.

The disunited Arabs should have realized that Israel, with unlimited financial and military support at its disposal, and international Zionist sympathizers controlling the two most formidable forces in the world – the media and the banks – was impossible to defeat. It would have been in their interests to welcome the refugee Palestinians who in 1948 fled their homes in what had been Palestine, inviting them to settle and become integrated into the Arab countries in numbers proportionate to the size of each Arab country. Instead they decided, under the pretext that such a policy would keep alive and preserve the Palestinian cause, to leave them to live in humiliation, misery and destitution in refugee camps and tin shacks, existing for year after year on UN hand-outs amounting to a bare subsistence diet of 1,400 calories per day per person.

Forty years on, the Arab summit in Casablanca unanimously approved the PLO's proposal to admit the right of Israel to exist, and request Israel's approval for a Palestinian state to live in peace alongside Israel on land at present under Israeli occupation – the West Bank and the Gaza Strip. But it may be too late to persuade the younger generations of Israelis and Palestinians they could ever live together in harmony and friendship. And even if they accept the possibility, was it for such a solution that the Palestinians and the Arabs together struggled during forty long years of desperate fighting and violent resistance, involving the loss of thousands of Arab, Palestinian and Israeli lives? Was it for this that, for forty years, the Palestinians have lived in refugee camps and tin shacks, feeling rootless and abandoned? And finally, what hope has the new PLO proposal, as unanimously accepted and supported by all the Arab heads of state, of returning to the Palestinians the homes and lands taken from them by Israel?

As the Arabs know full well, if Israel ever were to agree to the PLO project, citizenship of the new Palestine state would be restricted to those Palestinians who have remained in Israeli-occupied Palestine. The land available to them is unlikely to consist of all the so-called occupied territories, for Israel may never let go of the West Bank and the Gaza Strip. Those Palestinians who left in 1948 and were confined to the refugee camps, along with the fighting commandos born out of these camps, will in the end have to be integrated within Arab countries. Intense pressure will be brought to bear on the Arab countries, from both West and East, to force them to accept the very solution they rejected over forty years before. The plans to integrate a number of Palestinians within Lebanon can only be seen as the start of this process.

How different much of the history of the post-Second World War world could have been, how much of the misery, suffering, destruction of property, degeneration of values and humiliation of the Arabs and Palestinians might have been spared, if only the Arabs had been realists. They would then, with compassion, have taken the unfortunate, dispossessed Palestinians into their countries and realized at the outset that it was futile to go to war with Israel, the United States and its allies, or to expect that any other great power would be willing to come effectively to their aid, not even the Soviet Union.

As for the Israelis, how much better situated they could have been if they had concluded a peace with the Arabs. They might never have grown into the formidable military power they are today, but they would certainly have developed into a formidable economic and financial power through utilizing their expertise to join with the Arabs in developing oil and other rich resources and benefiting in partnership from all the profits these could produce. Additionally, there would have been the benefits to trade of rich Arab markets 150 million strong.

And as for the Palestinians themselves: how much better off they might have been both outside Palestine and inside what is left of it if the hundreds of billions of dollars spent, first, by the United Nations on refugee camps, secondly, by the Arabs, the PLO and other resistance groups on the long, futile war with Israel (augmented by the billions more which could have been levied on Israel for the values of appropriated homes and lands), had all been spent on their resettlement in Arab countries and benefiting the Palestinian communities remaining in Israel. To this hypothetical largesse might also be added the generous contributions which could gladly have been given by the oil-rich Arab countries in thankfulness for avoiding wars and arms purchases. None of this would have been impossible had a peace agreement been concluded soon after the creation of the state of Israel. The Palestinians, both exiled and remaining, could have lived in comfort, peace and dignity and have avoided the prospect they now face of having to accept the same solution, but on terms to be resented by all the parties involved and in an impoverished and humiliating version of what could have been achieved forty years before.

It is still possible for the Arabs to preserve their countries from the evils of further wars and give the necessary boost and support to the solution proposed for the Palestinian-Israeli problem. But to do this this they must also, besides approving the PLO's suggested approach, become realists for once and unite in offering to make peace with Israel in the wake of their acceptance of the Camp David Agreement and the PLO proposal. It is by no means certain that the Zionists, whether of moderate or extreme views (Israeli 'hawks' have a way of turning into 'doves' and vice versa), will accept an accord offered by the Arabs, but at least the rest of the world will then witness that the Arabs held out the hand of peace to Israel.

Israel itself can never complain that it lacks intelligent citizens. At times it seems, indeed, to be overpopulated with them. It was a group of Israeli intellectuals, way back in 1968, who saw the potential benefit of Israeli-Arab co-operation. Acting voluntarily and privately, they formed in Jerusalem the Association for Peace-AFP. Its objective was the encouragement of discussion on the resolution of the Arab-Israeli conflict. AFP assumed that this conflict would be resolved by the year 2000. It advocated the setting-up by then of the Middle East Common Market – MECM – and proposed the distribution of its functions and activities as follows:

(a) In the year 2000 a Middle East Common Market will be in operation, based on principles similar to those of the European Common Market and in association with it. The headquarters of the Middle East Common Market will be in Beirut.

(b) Some of the major efforts of national economies in the year 2000 would be allocated as follows: UAR (Egypt): Engineering industries, steel, cars, motors. Israel: Electronics, computers, medicine. Syria: Food industries and textiles. Iraq and the Gulf: Petrochemical industries. Lebanon: Banking, trading, transport and communication services.

(c) The civilization of the Middle East in the year 2000 shares the universal heritage of Moslem-Christian-Jewish civilization into which has been integrated 21st century modern technology.

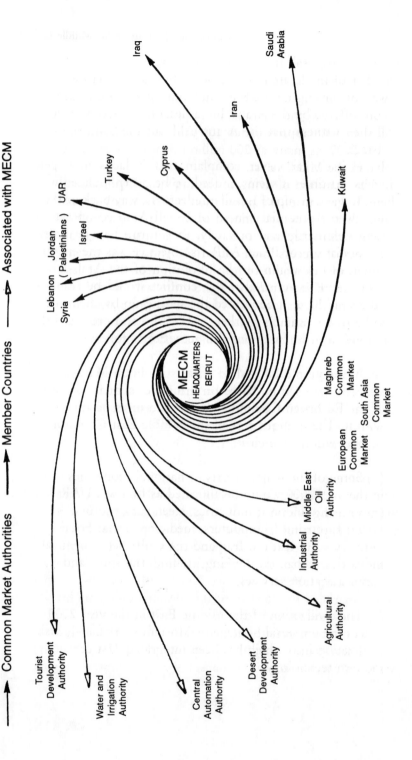

Legend (top): ──▷ Common Market Authorities   ──▶ Member Countries   ──▶ Associated with MECM

Member Countries: Lebanon, Syria, Jordan (Palestinians), Israel, UAR, Turkey, Cyprus, Iraq, Iran, Saudi Arabia, Kuwait

Centre: MECM HEADQUARTERS BEIRUT

Common Market Authorities: Tourist Development Authority, Water and Irrigation Authority, Central Automation Authority, Desert Development Authority, Agricultural Authority, Industrial Authority, Middle East Oil Authority

Associated: European Common Market, South Asia Common Market, Maghreb Common Market

Diagram to illustrate the Association for Peace – AFP's 1968 proposal for a Middle East Common Market

Within this common heritage a diversity of nations would evolve, each with its own unique contribution to human life in the region. The population of the Middle East in 1968 approximated 100 million people. In the year 2000, as many as 200 million people, or more, will live in the Middle East.
The standard of living of the individual will depend on the growth of the population or how many people will share the rising national income. It is assumed that birth-control techniques have been adopted, with varying degrees of success in all countries. And on the extent of national expenditure for military purposes, the less spent for military purposes, the more will be available to raising the standard of living of the population. More will also be available for constructive investment which in turn contributes to the rising standard of living.

If the Arabs should be pushed into a suicidal rejection of the peace plan imposed on them by the Israelis, then a scheme such as the MECM proposal will, of course, cease to be viable. But it also needs to be kept in mind that the younger Arab generations, fundamentalists or otherwise, are better educated than their parents and have a wider knowledge and awareness of world affairs. There will be nothing to stop them thinking in terms of an Arab common market and producing within it most of the goods and services they need; or importing from the East those goods and services which they cannot produce locally. A common market is a viable possibility for the Arabs because all the Arab countries have common frontiers, whereas Israel could never establish a similar market while it continued to be surrounded by hostile boundaries and lacked any frontier with a friendly country with whom to negotiate the necessary terms and conditions. This is not to say that the West would readily allow the Arabs to form a common market that ran contrary to its own interests. The West would certainly try to spoil such an idea. Nevertheless the prospects for success of an Arab common market are not something to be ignored by the younger Arab generations.

It is true that the revenue from the sale of oil to the Arab OPEC members was, between 1973 and 1985, many billions of dollars, but while this represented enormous wealth, it was still less than a third of the sales revenue of the seven largest oil companies, known as the 'Seven Sisters', and less than a quarter of the annual gross revenues of the five largest multinational Western corporations. Nevertheless it was considered far too large a sum to be left in the hands of the Arabs to manage, especially if this were done jointly with the Israelis in a proposed Middle East Common Market with its headquarters in Beirut and a philosophy of raising the respective populations' standard of living through decreased military expenditure.

The West's plan was to recoup the money spent on the purchase of oil by the sales of arms to the Middle East. To this end, huge increases in military expenditure were stimulated by provocation and encouragement of wars in the area. Hence both the Arabs and the Israelis allowed themselves to be manipulated into a long war for that very purpose. The Arabs were the losers, the Israelis the apparent winners, but how might the Israeli gains compare, in the long run, with what their real gains could have been by managing the Arabs' investment and trade under a Middle East common market? And what value does one set on the thousands of lost human lives in the Arab-Israeli wars? David Levy, then Israel's foreign minister, disclosed in Moscow in January 1991 that Israel had lost 17,000 dead in its six wars, while the Arabs had lost more than 80,000. How is one to compare the value of the quality of a life lived in comfort, prosperity and peace compared with one lived amid conditions of instability, terror, hatred and fear and the ever-present threat of violent death?

The Lebanese and the Israelis are alike in possessing creative, aggressive, profit-toned business minds. They could together have created a formidable finance and trade force with which the developed nations would have found it extremely difficult to compete. Consequently, Lebanon and Israel were never to be allowed to combine to manage the Arab oil wealth or have a say in its investment; and what better way could there have been to manipulate Israel and the Arabs into perpetuating their hostilities than to promote the destruction of Lebanon. The project for a Middle East Common Market was smothered, and possibly its creators were smothered as well, and Lebanon's banking and trade, its economic, financial and social structures, were sentenced to death and scheduled for destruction.

The time is here for all intelligent Israelis, and the Jewish residents of every country in the world, to question the Zionist political leaders as to why Greater Israel? Israel was created to provide a haven for the persecuted Jews, but there are no more officially sanctioned persecutions of the Jews in our present world. To provide a national home for fanatic religious Jews to return to, and die and be buried in, hardly seems to require a militarily powerful Greater Israel. And how much will it cost Israel and the Israelis in terms of revenue and human life to maintain such a powerful military force? Why not, instead, have peace with the Arabs rather than aim to dominate them by military superiority? And how could a negotiated peace fail to produce infinitely greater rewards in co-operation and benefits than one obtained by coercion?

The time is also ripe to seek to revive the project of the Association for Peace-AFP and for Israel to create with the Arabs a Middle East common market, thus generating, properly and legally, all the funds needed by Israel and the Israelis so they no longer have to beg continually for charity and contributions from an increasingly reluctant US Congress. But it is evident that the Zionists do not wish to see the peace talks sponsored by the Americans succeed. It is

271

also evident that the Americans are wary of exerting pressure on the Zionists to accept peace. Instead, they are applying all the pressure they can on the Arabs, and they may in the end succeed in persuading the Arabs to accept a peace dictated by Israel.

This assumes, of course, that the Americans will be able to force the arms manufacturers to abandon the lucrative Middle East arms market. It also assumes that the Arabs will not be over-pressurized to the point where, in the face of Israel's imposition of terms and conditions for a peace treaty which they find uncompromising, unacceptable and humiliating, they make a suicidal rejection of it. The cost of such a rejection will, in terms of human life and money, be horrific for the Arabs and Israelis alike.

As for the Druzes, whatever solution is imposed on them, they, who are fatalists, will resign themselves to God's will, in prosperity or adversity, and accept with dignity and fortitude whatever is decreed as the ultimate solution to the Arab-Israeli conflict. Moreover, they continue strongly to believe that what is written is written and have a solemn faith in all that the Druze *Uqqals* have been predicting according to their religious teachings: that the end of the world is at hand, the Day of Judgement will soon be with us. Armageddon is to be in the Middle East. The *Uqqals'* predictions have, say the Druzes, always been right. The great powers of the world, as they seek to control and exploit its resources, fail to realize that they are no more than implements in the hands of destiny, and that in the end their stratagems and ambitions will be nothing but vanity and delusion.

BEDFORDSHIRE LEISURE SERVICES COUNTY COUNCIL

List of Selected Sources

Abu-Izzedine, Najla M., *The Druzes*, E. J. Brill, Leiden, 1984.

Andréa, Général Charles Joseph Édouard, *La Révolte Druze et l'insurrection de Damas, 1925–1926*, Payot, Paris, 1937.

Ball, George, with a Preface by Professor Stanley Hoffmann, *Error and Betrayal in Lebanon: an Analysis of Israel's Invasion of Lebanon and the Implications for US-Israeli Relations*, Foundation for Middle East Peace, Washington, DC, 1984.

Ben-Dor, Gabriel, *The Druzes in Israel*, Magnes Press, Jerusalem, 1979.

Burckhart, John Lewis, *Travels in Syria and the Holy Land*, John Murray, London, 1822.

Carnarvon, Earl of, *Recollections of the Druzes of the Lebanon, And Notes on Their Religion*, John Murray, London, 1860.

Churchill, Charles Henry Spencer, *Mount Lebanon; a Ten Years Residence, from 1842 to 1852*, 3 vols., Bernard Quaritch, London, 1853.

Churchill, Charles Henry Spencer, *The Druzes and the Maronites under the Turkish Rule from 1840 to 1860*, Bernard Quaritch, London, 1862.

Copeland, Miles, *The Game of Nations*, Weidenfeld & Nicolson, London, 1969.

Ewing, William, *Arab and Druze at Home*, T. C. & E. C. Jack, London, 1907.

Hitti, Philip K., *The Origin of the Druze History and Religion: With Extracts from Their Sacred Writings* [sic], Columbia University Press, New York, 1928.

Hitti, Philip K., *Lebanon in History: from the Earliest Times to the Present*, Macmillan, London, 1957.

Jumblatt, Kamal, *I Speak for Lebanon*, Zed Press, London, 1982.

Makarem, Sami Nassib, *The Druze Faith*, Caravan Books, New York, 1974.

Maundrell, Henry, *A Journey from Aleppo to Jerusalem at Easter AD 1697*, Oxford, 1703.

Oliphant, Lawrence, *The Land of Gilead*, Blackwood, London, 1880.

Parfit, Canon Joseph T., *Among the Druzes of Lebanon and Beshan (Hauran)*, Hunter & Longhurst, London, 1917.

Puget de Saint Pierre, *Histoire des Druzes, peuple du Liban, formé par une Colonie de Français*, Cailleau, Paris, 1762.

Randal, Jonathan C., *The Tragedy of Lebanon: Christian Warlords, Israeli Adventurers and American Bunglers*, Chatto & Windus, London, 1983.

Salibi, Kamal S., *A House of Many Mansions: the History of Lebanon Reconsidered*, I. B. Tauris, London, 1988.

Salibi, Kamal S., *The Modern History of Lebanon*, Weidenfeld & Nicolson, London, 1965; reprinted Caravan Books, New York, 1977.

Sandys, George, *A Relation of a Journey begun An. Dom. 1610*, London, 1615.

Seabroke, W. B., *Adventures in Arabia*, Harrap, London, 1928.

Silvestre de Sacy, A.I., *Exposé de la religion des Druzes*, 2 vols., Paris, 1838; reprinted Librarie Orient, Paris, 1964.

Springett, Bernard H., *Secret Sects of Syria and Lebanon*, Allen & Unwin, London, 1922.

Timmermann, Jacobo, *The Longest War*, Chatto & Windus, London, 1982.

Volney, Constantin-François de Chasseboeuf, Comte de, *Travels through Syria and Egypt in 1783, 1784 and 1785*, London, 1787.

Index

United Arab Republic (UAR),
156, 267
United Kingdom: role in
Middle East, 139, 174, 221,
241, 259; blocking of peace
talks (1949), 256–7, 258;
arms supplies to Middle
East, 216, 218–19, 259–62;
see also British
United Nations, 182, 217,
221, 238, 239, 242, 264, 266;
Security Council, 187, 217,
241; Arms Register, 262
United Nations Forces (Unifil),
182, 199
United States of America, 12,
13, 22, 159, 172, 173, 174,
176, 177, 179, 182, 185,
186, 187, 198, 199, 200, 214,
216, 220, 252, 260; hostile
attitude to Druzes, 15–17;
manipulation of elections
in Lebanon, 155–6, 157–8;
support for Israel, 206, 215;
and role played in Lebanon,
14, 230, 232, 241, 242, 243,
250, 251, 254, 256, 258,
265; and 'new world order',
255–6; arms supplies to
Middle East, 216, 219–20,
223, 262–3, 264
Upper Yemen, 43
Uqqals, Druze initiates, 7, 8,
15, 27, 28, 29, 30, 33, 34,
39, 40, 57, 64, 65–6, 67, 70,
73, 193, 271; murder of the
600, 80, 81, 82
Urqub, 131
US Congress, 271

US Navy, 16
US Sixth Fleet, 228
US State Department, 158, 214,
219; Treasury, 255, 256
USSR, 16, 17, 173, 187, 220,
242, 244, 250, 252, 254–5,
258, 260, 265; arms supplies
to Middle East, 216, 219–20,
263–4; *see also* Russia

Vatican, 85, 91, 174, 176,
228, 233, 241, 244, 254;
Library, 30
Vichy French, 11, 148, 149
Vienna Library, 30
Vietnam War, 160
Volney, Constantin-François
de Chasseboeuf, Comte
de, 3, 68, 104

Wadi et-Taym, 63
Wadi Sirhan, 144
Warsaw ghetto, 184
Washington DC, 186, 214, 219
Wazzan, Chafic, 172
West Bank, 183, 232, 264
West Beirut, 166, 171, 185, 186,
191, 199, 225, 226, 227, 239,
241, 243, 251
World Priorities, 219
World's Religions, The, 6
Worsley, Mrs, 2

Yamanis, *see* Yamanites
Yamanites, Druze clan, 101,
102, 103, 111, 204
Yazbak, Abdal-Salam, 105
Yazbakis, Druze clan, 104, 105,
151, 157, 180, 192